# The East End Plays: Part 1

# The East End Plays
# Part 1

*Three plays by*

George F. Walker

Talonbooks
1999

Talonbooks
P.O. Box 2076, Vancouver, British Columbia, Canada V6B 3S3
www.talonbooks.com

Typeset in New Baskerville and printed and bound in Canada by Hignell
Printing.

Second Printing: September 2005

The publisher gratefully acknowledges the financial support of the
Canada Council for the Arts; the Government of Canada through the
Book Publishing Industry Development Program; and the Province of
British Columbia through the British Columbia Arts Council for our pub-
lishing activities.

The Canada Council | Le Conseil des Arts    Canadä
FOR THE ARTS | DU CANADA
SINCE 1957 | DEPUIS 1957

**Canadian Cataloguing in Publication Data**

Walker, George F., 1947-

The East End plays, part 1
ISBN 0-88922-413-7

I. Title.
PS8595.A557E3 1999      C812'.54      C99-910804-2
PR9199.3.W342E3 1999

# CONTENTS

# Introduction

Set in "the working-class east end of a big city," *The East End Plays* mark George F. Walker's return to his home turf. In the near-mythic tale of Walker's artistic origins, the working-class kid from east end Toronto was driving cab in 1970 when he saw a flyer on a lamp post soliciting plays for the new Factory Theatre Lab. He submitted a script, had it accepted for production, and in short order became the Factory's playwright-in-residence and a central figure in Toronto's dynamic alternate theatre movement. Walker made his reputation in the seventies and early eighties with far-flung excursions into exotic B-movie theatrescapes in plays like *Beyond Mozambique* and *Zastrozzi*, and with the stylish political intrigue and film noir baroque of *The Power Plays* and *Theatre of the Film Noir*. Beginning with *Criminals in Love* in 1983, the family plays that comprise this volume reside in more familiar, more domestic territory.

The working-class family play already had a pretty solid pedigree in modern English-Canadian drama before Walker took a crack at it. Ann Henry's *Lulu Street*, David French's *Leaving Home*, and David Fennario's *Balconville* among others present characters struggling to find dignity and community under challenging economic conditions complicated by the internal strains of family life. Typically realist in style, their drama leavened with comedy, these plays go back through Miller and Odets to O'Casey and Ibsen. But Walker's *East End* family trilogy, like everything else he has written, looks and feels different. He privileges philosophy over sociology and comedy over drama. Melding irony, absurdism and dark wit with utopian yearning and a strangely old-fashioned humanism, he evokes not Ibsen and Miller but the imposing genius of Chekhov. Well, maybe three parts Chekhov plus one part Joe Orton and the surprising potential of a happy ending.

Walker positions the three sisters Gail, Mary Ann and Elizabeth at the centre of the action. Together with their mother Nora and Gail's boyfriend (and later husband) Junior, they wrestle with the scary idea that their destiny is inevitably rooted in the family, an extraordinarily toxic environment as embodied in the warped patriarchy of Junior's father Henry and the sisters' father Tom. As it becomes clear that family can't be escaped, Nora and her daughters begin instead in their own eccentric ways to re-imagine how to make it healthy and nurturing for *their* daughters. As poignant and at first unlikely as the dream of getting to Moscow, the genuine possibility of better living for these three sisters becomes more evident with each successive play.

Of the recurring characters only Gail and Junior appear in *Criminals in Love*, where the young lovers' modest fantasies of happiness prove impotent against the powerful megalomania of Junior's extended family of felons. Junior's frenzied infantile orality under the shelter of Gail's sweater provokes her to suggest that "it's time to move on." But overwhelmed, they can't move. Forced to fall back on the unlikely leadership of the philosopher-bum William K., they never find a way even to understand, much less a strategy to avoid, the apparent inevitability of the hanging shadow, the abyss.

With *Better Living* the momentum begins to shift (and economics to fade in importance). Paralyzed by the survivalist fascism of the nightmare father Tom, the sisters rely heavily on Nora's brother Jack, the lapsed priest, to mediate for them. (Fascinating essays could be written on the figure of the failed priest in Walker's plays and on the remarkable actor Peter Blais, a Walker regular, who premiered the roles of both Jack and William K.) But Gail contributes, too. And Nora—in her stunned, idiot savante fashion—begins to delineate an intuitive strategy of resistance and transformation: digging out the basement to get down to the foundations, understanding that "the future is something you make," and working tentatively towards a Chekhovian vision of imminent happiness.

By the end of *Escape from Happiness*, the funniest and most accomplished of these plays, the women are fully in control of the situation, if not of their own still shaky egos. Illicit power, they discover, whether of cops, criminals or terrorist fathers, can be neutralized. A healthy redefinition of family is well underway along with the rehabilitation of the play's mostly hapless men. Right from the brilliant opening scene, where Nora compels the battered Junior to get up and save himself, Walker offers a rich theatrical vision of east end resilience, a complex comic dance of life. "We're not alone." Believe it. "Life goes on ... "

**Jerry Wasserman**
*Vancouver, 1999*

# Criminals in Love

*Criminals in Love* was first produced at Toronto's Factory Theatre on November 7, 1984 with the following cast:

JUNIOR   Ted Dykstra
GAIL   Gina Wilkinson
WILLIAM   Peter Blais
HENRY   Dean Hawes
SANDY   Lesleh Donaldson
WINEVA   Barbara Gordon,

Director:  George F. Walker
Set Designer:  Reginald Bronskill
Lighting Designer:  Sholem Dolgoy
Music composed by:  John Roby

*Persons*

**JUNIOR DAWSON**, nineteen, Gail's boyfriend

**GAIL QUINN**, eighteen, Junior's girlfriend

**WILLIAM**, forty-five to sixty-five, a bum with a slight Eastern European accent

**HENRY "SENIOR" DAWSON**, early forties, a cheap crook

**SANDY MILES**, nineteen, lean, alert

**WINEVA DAWSON**, late thirties, former earth-mother, going to seed

*Place*

Various locations in the working-class east end of a big city. The set should be simple, suggestive, allowing spaces for inventive lighting.

*Time*

Almost summer.

*When you believe in things you don't understand, you suffer.*
—Stevie Wonder

## SCENE ONE

*Dusk.*

*A schoolyard. A small grassy slope. GAIL and JUNIOR are entwined. She is on her back with her hands behind her head. He has one leg over her thighs and his head under her sweater. He is making many varied and muffled sounds of pleasure. Her mild enjoyment turns gradually to restlessness and eventually impatience.*

*Behind them, some distance away, a bum is curled up against a wall.*

**GAIL:** Junior? ... Junior.

**JUNIOR:** (*something muffled*)

**GAIL:** God, Junior, it's time to move on ... try some other part of my body. Sex does not begin and end at my chest. Do you realize how much time you spend under my sweater.

**JUNIOR:** (*something muffled*)

**GAIL:** I'm beginning to think there's something wrong with you.

**JUNIOR:** (*pulls his head out*) I love them. I ... I can't think of anything else to say.

**GAIL:** But what can I do to you when your head is under there. I'm tired of running my fingers through your hair.

**JUNIOR:** That's all I need. My hair is sensitive. It's exciting, really.

**GAIL:** Let's stop. Let's talk.

**JUNIOR:** Five more minutes.

*He goes under the sweater again.*

**GAIL:** No, now.

**JUNIOR:** (*something muffled*)

**GAIL:** Junior. Get out of there!

*She grabs a fistful of hair. Twists. He yells. Sits up suddenly. Pause. She grabs her jacket from the grass beside her. Puts it on. Zips it up.*

JUNIOR:  Will you marry me.

GAIL:  You just had a vision didn't you. The two of us married and always together. Twenty-five or thirty years with your head under my sweater.

JUNIOR:  I dream about you. You're my salvation.

GAIL:  I hate it when you say shit like that. I don't think you even know what it means.

JUNIOR:  You save me.

GAIL:  From what.

JUNIOR:  My true destiny.

GAIL:  Which is.

JUNIOR:  Fuck all.

GAIL:  Pathetic. I hate it when you talk like this.

JUNIOR:  Fuck all is what I came from. Fuck all is where I'm going without you.

GAIL:  Just knock it off, okay.

JUNIOR:  Why do you like me.

GAIL:  What.

JUNIOR:  I just want to know why you like me.

GAIL:  I love you, honey.

JUNIOR:  Because I love you probably.

GAIL:  Probably, yeah. You give me your full attention. The first time we kissed even. You threw your arms around me. Closed your eyes and just held on. It wasn't the world's greatest kiss, but I said to myself here's a guy who can concentrate on what he's doing …

JUNIOR:  Will you marry me.

GAIL:  When I get a job.

JUNIOR:  I've got a job.

GAIL:  I know you've got a job. I didn't forget. The answer to your question was when I get a job.

**JUNIOR:** Why.

**GAIL:** You know why. Why.

**JUNIOR:** So you won't have to be afraid I'll fuck up.

**GAIL:** No. Jesus. Pathetic. Not that you won't fuck up. Just so I'll know there's something I can do to control things. Keep things moving. Whatever happens.

**JUNIOR:** Well, whatever happens just has to be me fucking up. I've been thinking about it and there just isn't anything else that can go wrong.

**GAIL:** There are things in this world beyond your control. Your plant could close. You could be laid off. You should have voted to unionize that place, you know.

**JUNIOR:** You should go to university, Gail. You're smart enough to be anything.

**GAIL:** Thanks. (*stands*) I need your advice really badly.

**JUNIOR:** Why are you getting pissed off.

**GAIL:** Don't tell me what I should do.

**JUNIOR:** It wasn't an order or anything.

**GAIL:** Look. Let's not get into the habit of talking about what we should do. What we could do. It's a dumb way to live so let's just kill that way of thinking right away. Let's just talk about what we want to do. I want to get a reasonably good job. Period.

**JUNIOR:** I want to get married.

**GAIL:** Great. Now we've got a plan. Something to aim for.

*He stands too. Puts his arms around her.*

**JUNIOR:** You look great. When you stood up I like that your body looked amazing. When you talked ... you talked like a lawyer. You're perfect.

**GAIL:** So are you.

*They kiss.*

**JUNIOR:** I need some advice.

**GAIL:** (*suspiciously*) Yeah?

**JUNIOR:** I'm supposed to visit my dad tomorrow.

**GAIL:** Yeah.

**JUNIOR:** In jail. He's in jail.

**GAIL:** Yeah, I know that, Junior.

**JUNIOR:** Well, should I.

**GAIL:** Don't you want to.

**JUNIOR:** He's ridiculous you know. He's the most ridiculous man in the whole world. He's a crook. That's bad enough. But he's a ridiculous crook. He can't even steal hub caps.

**GAIL:** Where's this leading.

**JUNIOR:** He's my legacy.

**GAIL:** What.

**JUNIOR:** I mean he's my destiny. I mean he's my family. I mean … he scares me. He's so ridiculous he's terrifying.

**GAIL:** Why don't you just take him a present. Something he can use in prison. A mission of mercy.

**JUNIOR:** He gets sentenced tomorrow. After my visit. That's why they brought him into the city jail … So?

**GAIL:** What.

**JUNIOR:** Well, I could estimate, I guess. Five years anyway. I mean I'd have to buy him something that would last.

**GAIL:** I know you want to talk about this, really talk about it … but it's hard, eh. We do this all the time, Junior. Talk about your dad. You use me to figure out what he means to you. Maybe you should just figure it out for yourself once and for all.

**JUNIOR:** Without you?

**GAIL:** Tonight. Before the visit.

**JUNIOR:** But without you.

**GAIL:** I'll go home.

**JUNIOR:** What'll I do.

**GAIL:** You can stay here. It's quiet here. You can think here.

**JUNIOR:** Sure. I guess. Are you leaving now. (*she kisses him*)

GAIL:  It's okay, honey. It's not a big deal. You've made him a big deal in your life. Think of some way to make him just what he is.

JUNIOR:  That sounds good.

*She starts off.*

GAIL:  Call me later.

JUNIOR:  Be careful. Walk quickly. Walk on the side where the streetlights are. Don't talk to anyone. (*she is gone*) Walk real fast. No, run instead. You can run beautifully. Go ahead. I'm watching! No one is following you. Run!

*He sits. GAIL comes back on. Firm look in her eyes.*

GAIL:  Look. Just relax. I can make it home just fine. I was brought up in this neighbourhood. I got along fine in it before I met you. I'm leaving now. I'm not going to run. I'm going to walk. And I'll be all right! So relax!

*She leaves. Pause. JUNIOR leans back on his elbows. WILLIAM, the bum against the wall, sits up suddenly.*

WILLIAM:  What ... What's all the ... Please don't kill me. Please. I don't eat garbage. Don't make me eat it. There's dead flies ... Please. What ... Where.

*He looks around. JUNIOR is staring at him. Long pause.*

JUNIOR:  Bad dream?

WILLIAM:  Another garbage-eating dream. It's recurring. Terrifying in its detail ... Where's your girlfriend.

JUNIOR:  Gone.

WILLIAM:  Argument?

JUNIOR:  Nah. You all right?

WILLIAM:  I'll have to check. (*checks his body*) Okay, so far. Just let me examine the essentials. (*puts his hand in his pants*) Dry as a bone, as the saying goes. I recognize you. You're one of the local kids. I've been seeing you around since you were this high. Ten, twelve years. You've certainly changed with time.

JUNIOR:  You haven't. You're even wearing the same coat.

**WILLIAM:** Passing ships in the night. That's what we are in a way. Urban freighters. I'm not carrying though. Absolutely without contents.

**JUNIOR:** What.

**WILLIAM:** I'm saying we've known of each other's existence all these years and we've never talked.

**JUNIOR:** My mom wouldn't let me talk to bums.

**WILLIAM:** She's had a change of heart, dear woman.

**JUNIOR:** She's dead.

**WILLIAM:** Ah. So what's the impediment. Can I join you.

**JUNIOR:** Sure.

**WILLIAM:** Or you could join me. Your preference, entirely.

**JUNIOR:** It's more comfortable on the grass.

**WILLIAM:** If you say so. (*stands with difficulty*) Actually I've found that grass is fine during the day but concrete is better for evening restings. No dew, you see. Doesn't get wet. I hate getting wet. It's the worst thing about my way of life. Involuntary bladder activity. Absolutely the worst thing there is.

*He sits next to JUNIOR. Puts out his hand.*

**WILLIAM:** William.

**JUNIOR:** Junior.

*They shake.*

**WILLIAM:** William … William.

**JUNIOR:** Yeah, I got it the first time.

**WILLIAM:** No. It's just that there used to be a last name that went along with it and I'm trying to remember what it is.

**JUNIOR:** Seriously?

**WILLIAM:** Please, no pity. I think it began with a K. William K … K … Well, I won't push it. Don't want to hemorrhage. (*groans, falls over*) Jesus. That was a pain. Probably the spleen.

**JUNIOR:** Listen, the liquor store's still open. I could go get you a bottle.

*JUNIOR is picking WILLIAM up.*

**WILLIAM:** Oh God, you think I'm an alcoholic. How quick they are to judge, Lord. We the meek of the earth. Absolutely without defence.

**JUNIOR:** I'm sorry. I thought …

**WILLIAM:** Oh. I drink. I drink much. Often. Almost non-stop. But I know, and here I use a relative term, when I've had enough. Therefore, honestly, and without smiling, I can say I am not an alcoholic. A bum, yes. There's a tricky distinction here. But enough of me. Why aren't you out with your peers. Pushing buttons in the electric amusement places. Fucking the dog. And the puppies too if the worst of us have our way.

**JUNIOR:** I've got some thinking to do.

**WILLIAM:** About your girlfriend?

**JUNIOR:** She's part of it.

**WILLIAM:** A fine girl. Very sturdy. I've observed her over the years as well.

**JUNIOR:** Yeah?

**WILLIAM:** From a discreet distance. No hands. Honestly. No touching ever. Of course I can't be responsible for my private thoughts and they are truly disgusting.

**JUNIOR:** You're kind of weird.

**WILLIAM:** But I function as a gentleman. When I function. What's the problem. The obstacle … The overall … the absolute thing you're wrestling with.

**JUNIOR:** Nothing easy to describe. Just how to get by. Hang on.

**WILLIAM:** Hanging on is the true problem of the age. I wrestle with it daily myself. So often I think of just giving up and letting myself plummet into the depths of degradation. Into the absolute pit. I'm so tired of this bourgeois existence.

**JUNIOR:** Mister, I kinda know what that word means, and it ain't you.

**WILLIAM:** Once again I call upon the rules of relativity. From my perspective, I see a great distance yet to fall. I feel positively middle-class in comparison.

**JUNIOR:** You're a bum.

**WILLIAM:**  Truth is, I'm just pretending. Yes, I have a bank account! I can withdraw money at any time. Check into a hotel. Order up a steak. Have an all-night bath with bubbles. Drink cognac. Live splendidly.

**JUNIOR:**  Why don't you!

**WILLIAM:**  Why should I!

**JUNIOR:**  Why shouldn't you. Or why don't you.

**WILLIAM:**  You have a truly devastating aptitude for logical debate. I think I'll answer the first question. I don't do these things because I am not destined to live like that.

**JUNIOR:**  What.

**WILLIAM:**  I was about to tell you about the "call of the pit." Its great echoing voice. "Come down, William," it says. "We know you want to."

**JUNIOR:**  You said destined. You know about destiny?

**WILLIAM:**  I am the inventor of the modern connotation.

**JUNIOR:**  I've got a thing about destiny.

**WILLIAM:**  Then we should talk more.

**JUNIOR:**  No. It's a bad thing. I should go.

> *JUNIOR stands. WILLIAM pulls him down.*

**WILLIAM:**  Sit down. Destiny as a concept of the mind and soul is what you're afraid of. I'm talking pure economics, politics, social patterns. I'll have to tell you my entire story for you to understand.

**JUNIOR:**  That'd be great. Sometime soon.

**WILLIAM:**  What's wrong with now.

**JUNIOR:**  I thought I'd go for a walk. I think better walking.

**WILLIAM:**  I talk well sitting or walking. I'll come along. You don't have to listen. But seriously do you mind. I would love some company.

> *They look at each other. Pause.*

**JUNIOR:**  Sure. Okay.

> *He helps him up.*

**WILLIAM:**  Where to.

**JUNIOR:** We'll just walk.

*They start off.*

**WILLIAM:** It's always hard to leave a place you're fond of. Goodbye, wall. Goodbye, concrete. Goodbye, grass. Now where were we. Ah, yes. My life. My absolute history ...

*They are leaving.*

*Blackout.*

## SCENE TWO

*Visiting room in the city jail. A table. Two chairs. JUNIOR in one. His father HENRY in the other*

**HENRY:** So didya hear what happened to Joe Meecher. Someone knifed him in the laundry room. He's in the infirmary. They can't get his blood to clot. (*shivers*) He's gonna die. (*pause*) You don't seem concerned.

**JUNIOR:** I'm not. Joe Meecher's a turd.

**HENRY:** He's your godfather.

**JUNIOR:** Like hell.

**HENRY:** Didn't your mother ever tell you. Joe held you at your christening. He's your goddamn godfather.

**JUNIOR:** I'll pray for him, all right?

**HENRY:** You don't pray. Don't give me that. Just show a little concern.

> *Pause.*

**JUNIOR:** I was talking to your lawyer.

**HENRY:** Stay away from my lawyer. If you talk to my lawyer that's technically a consultation. He could add a hundred bucks to my bill.

**JUNIOR:** You're on legal aid, you don't pay.

**HENRY:** You dumb fuck. Sure I pay. When I get out they garnishee my wages.

**JUNIOR:** If you get a job.

**HENRY:** That goes without saying.

**JUNIOR:** If you get out.

**HENRY:** That goes without ... Whatya mean if I get out.

**JUNIOR:** Your lawyer says that technically you're a chronic offender.

**HENRY:** My lawyer has no regard for me as a human being! I could tell by the way he picked his teeth during my trial. I wanted to put my fist in his mouth and yank all those teeth right out of there.

**JUNIOR:** It has nothing to do with him. It's up to the judge.

**HENRY:** Now I'm worried. You've got me worried. I hope you're happy. They could put me away for twenty years.

**JUNIOR:** I just thought you should be prepared.

**HENRY:** You're all heart.

**JUNIOR:** Listen. Maybe the judge will feel sorry for you. I mean what's the farthest you ever got from the scene of a crime. Fifty yards?

**HENRY:** You still seeing that girl. Grace.

**JUNIOR:** Gail.

**HENRY:** She's good looking isn't she. Healthy. Right? I'm just making small talk.

**JUNIOR:** Yeah. Listen, I brought you something.

*JUNIOR puts a small packet on the table.*

**HENRY:** What's that.

**JUNIOR:** A pen.

**HENRY:** A pen?! Is it a Parker T-Ball Jotter. Ooh, I always wanted one of them.

**JUNIOR:** I don't think they make them anymore. This is a Scriptomatic. It glides across the paper. And it's got a clock in it. I thought you could use it.

**HENRY:** You were wrong. (*picks up the box*) But thanks anyway.

**JUNIOR:** It's guaranteed. You can get refills. It's a good pen.

**HENRY:** Cost a lot? (*JUNIOR shrugs*) How's the job.

**JUNIOR:** Good.

**HENRY:** Shipper, right?

**JUNIOR:** Assistant.

**HENRY:** Little things? Big things?

**JUNIOR:** A graphics company. Little things. We use couriers mostly. Lots of stuff to the airport. Deadlines. That kind of thing.

**HENRY:** Don't let the pressure get to you.

**JUNIOR:** I won't.

HENRY:  The pressure got to me. It was just the pressure. Before the pressure I didn't do crime.

JUNIOR:  The pressure got to you early in life, eh?

HENRY:  What's that mean.

JUNIOR:  You botched your first break-in when you were seventeen. Who knows how many there were before then.

HENRY:  That was the first. I got caught first time out. (*laughs*)

JUNIOR:  Yeah. That's what I figured. Dammit, Dad, couldn't you have just got the message.

HENRY:  What message.

JUNIOR:  That you weren't very good at it.

HENRY:  I was young. I had my whole life stretching out in front of me. You have to expect some early failures. That's my advice to you. Expect some early failures.

JUNIOR:  It's great advice.

HENRY:  Look. We haven't got much time. I want to tell you about your Uncle Ritchie.

JUNIOR:  Did he get knifed.

HENRY:  No. He's out. He's made connections. The thing is, he'll be contacting you.

JUNIOR:  Why.

HENRY:  He needs a little help on some of his projects.

JUNIOR:  No way.

HENRY:  He needs to use the house to store some things on an on-and-off-and-on-again basis.

JUNIOR:  No fucking way.

HENRY:  He'll be calling you.

  *Pause.*

JUNIOR:  Listen. I've been thinking about us. You and me. I think we should end our relationship.

HENRY:  What are you talking about, you dumb fuck. We're father and son. That's not a relationship. It's destiny.

JUNIOR:  What.

**HENRY:** You know … destiny.

*JUNIOR stands.*

**JUNIOR:** You don't even know what that word means!

**HENRY:** Calm down. Sit down. Sit down!

**JUNIOR:** I gotta go. I'm late for work.

**HENRY:** You help your Uncle Ritchie. He's my brother. You owe me.

**JUNIOR:** For what.

**HENRY:** Okay. You don't owe me. But there'll be money in it for you. You need all you can get. Your future isn't secure. You're not equipped. You should have stayed in school. No one quits school at sixteen anymore.

**JUNIOR:** I'm nineteen now. I'm doing all right.

**HENRY:** Your future sucks. I'm sorry. But the odds say that you'll be doing crime in a few years.

**JUNIOR:** Never.

**HENRY:** I've been thinking about it. It's in the blood.

**JUNIOR:** What are you doing. Are you insane. Saying things like that to me.

**HENRY:** There comes a time to be honest. This is it I guess. If you didn't want to face your true destiny you should have stayed in school.

*JUNIOR stands.*

**JUNIOR:** There's that word again. You haven't got a lousy clue what that word means and you keep throwing it in my face. Listen. Let's remember something. I quit school because one day while I was sitting in English class, you decided to rob the bank across the street. You failed miserably like usual and me and my friends and my teacher got to watch you from the classroom window being handcuffed and thrown into the paddy wagon. Embarrassment. Embarrassment made me quit school. No fucking destiny!

**HENRY:** I don't want to talk about the goddamn past. Sit down! (*JUNIOR sits*) Now listen, this is the truth. I owe your Uncle Ritchie this favour. If I welch he'll have me knifed. He's got friends inside. You gotta talk to him when he calls.

**JUNIOR:** I can't.

**HENRY:** I just told you the truth, you dumb fuck. We're talking about my life here.

**JUNIOR:** I can't.

**HENRY:** You'll do it.

**JUNIOR:** No.

**HENRY:** I'm telling you to do it. Don't say no.

**JUNIOR:** No.

> *Suddenly HENRY grabs JUNIOR's hair. Pulls his head hard on to the table. JUNIOR groans. HENRY lifts JUNIOR's head.*

**HENRY:** Don't say no.

**JUNIOR:** No.

> *HENRY pulls JUNIOR's head down on the table. JUNIOR groans. HENRY lifts JUNIOR's head.*

**HENRY:** Don't say no.

**JUNIOR:** No.

> *HENRY pulls JUNIOR head down and up three times fast. JUNIOR falls off his chair. Holding his forehead, HENRY stands. Looks at JUNIOR. Shakes his head.*

**HENRY:** Guard! (*looks at JUNIOR. Snaps his fingers*) Hey, get up. Stand up. Quick get up. Sit in the chair. You want to get me in trouble. Get up. (*JUNIOR struggles into his chair*) Good boy ... Guard!

> *Blackout.*

## SCENE THREE

*A booth in a corner of one of those burger places. GAIL and SANDY. SANDY is drinking a Coke. Eating fries. Smoking. Wearing a burger worker uniform. GAIL is writing.*

**GAIL:** What happened then.

**SANDY:** They flipped a coin. The tall one lost. The short one and me caught an elevator and went to his room.

**GAIL:** Were you scared.

**SANDY:** On the outside, no. But on the inside, yes.

**GAIL:** No one gets scared on the outside, Sandy. The outside is hair, skin, nails ... You mean you didn't let it show.

**SANDY:** Is that what you're writing.

**GAIL:** Yeah.

**SANDY:** Then I guess that's what I meant.

**GAIL:** So you're inside his room.

**SANDY:** First we're outside his room. At the door. He thinks the maid is in there. We wait. We whisper. He listens at the door. Stupid little jokes.

**GAIL:** Is this going anywhere important. Was the maid inside.

**SANDY:** No.

**GAIL:** Okay. You're in the room. The door's locked. Get to it.

**SANDY:** We did it.

**GAIL:** Go back just a bit.

**SANDY:** He said let's have a drink. I said no. He said let's talk. I said no. He said let's have a shower. I said no. I said let's get undressed. We got undressed. Then ... we did it. He did it.

**GAIL:** How.

**SANDY:** Badly.

**GAIL:** But how.

**SANDY:** What do you mean. Was he on top.

**GAIL:** Not exactly. I'm looking for a feeling. Describe the feeling.

**SANDY:** Nothing.

**GAIL:** Not the sex. The feeling in the room.

**SANDY:** Nothing. I don't know what you're getting at. I did it for the money.

**GAIL:** Was it sad. I want to know if you felt sad.

**SANDY:** You said we wouldn't talk like that. You know it's not sad. It's money. I don't know. Jesus, this was my first time.

**GAIL:** This is a lousy idea. No newspaper's going to buy this.

**SANDY:** Diary of a Teenage Hooker. I think they'll all buy it. Some of them will want pictures.

**GAIL:** Let's stop. Don't do it anymore.

**SANDY:** I'll do it for the money, if I need it. I've made up my mind.

**GAIL:** It'll make you sad.

**SANDY:** Don't say that!

> *JUNIOR and WILLIAM come on. WILLIAM has JUNIOR by the arm. JUNIOR's head is bandaged. GAIL jumps up on the table to grab JUNIOR's face.*

**GAIL:** What happened to you. Look at you. Look at him.

**JUNIOR:** Let me sit down.

> *JUNIOR slides in next to GAIL. WILLIAM stands at his side.*

**SANDY:** Gail, get off the table. They're all looking at us.

> *GAIL sits.*

**GAIL:** What happened.

**JUNIOR:** I'm a little dizzy. But I'm all right.

**GAIL:** Your dad did this, didn't he.

**JUNIOR:** I didn't handle him very well.

**SANDY:** Your head is swelling up like a melon.

**WILLIAM:** Okay. Everyone should relax. This is not a serious injury. Totally superficial, without doubt. I have the doctor's word on this.

**GAIL:** Who's he.

**JUNIOR:** William.

**GAIL:** (*whispering*) He looks like a bum.

**SANDY:** (*whispering*) He smells really bad.

**JUNIOR:** You get used to it.

**WILLIAM:** It takes time. But I can assure you it's worth the effort. I have much to offer.

**JUNIOR:** He took me to the hospital. He was waiting for me outside the jail and he took me straight to the hospital. He's had an incredible life. Well, not for the last ten years. For the last ten years he hasn't done a thing. But before that, wow.

**WILLIAM:** Excuse me. I'm being overcome by nostalgia.

*He slides down on to the floor.*

**SANDY:** Hey. Get up. This is a public place. You wanna get me fired?

**WILLIAM:** A pain. Somewhere near the heart. I rule out indigestion absolutely. Because I haven't eaten in a week.

*JUNIOR grabs SANDY's box of fries.*

**JUNIOR:** Here. Eat these.

**SANDY:** Those are mine, Junior.

**JUNIOR:** I'll buy you more. If he doesn't eat he won't have the strength to get up. (*to WILLIAM*) Take it.

*WILLIAM takes the box.*

**WILLIAM:** French fries. One of my all-time absolute favourite foods. Good even cold. I've had many a vicious battle in the garbage with the neighbourhood cats over these beauties.

*He takes one. Sucks on it.*

**SANDY:** He's making me sick. I'm going back on duty. (*stands*) I'll try to keep the manager in the kitchen till you get him out, of here. They're fanatics about cleanliness in this place.

**WILLIAM:** You have wonderful legs.

**SANDY:** Who asked you to say anything about my legs.

**WILLIAM:** Perhaps if you could imagine the way I looked before I looked like this, before the mighty fall, you could treat it like a compliment.

**SANDY:** But who the hell asked you!

*She leaves.*

**JUNIOR:**  She seems edgy.

**GAIL:**  She turned her first trick.

**JUNIOR:**  You can't be her friend anymore, Gail.

**GAIL:**  I'll forget you said that.

**JUNIOR:**  But if she's going to be a hooker, I don't think you'll …

**GAIL:**  Listen. She tried it out to see if she could do it. So she'd know in an emergency.

**JUNIOR:**  What kind of emergency.

**GAIL:**  Financial.

**WILLIAM:**  That makes sense. Always be prepared.

**GAIL:**  Look! Either he gets up and sits down like a human being or he leaves!

**JUNIOR:**  Can you make it into the seat, William.

**WILLIAM:**  I'm willing to try. I have deep respect for this young woman's tone of voice. (*gets to his knees*) Just a little help if it's no bother.

> *JUNIOR helps him into the booth. WILLIAM slides off the chair onto the floor. JUNIOR picks him up. Puts the fries in front of him. WILLIAM sucks on some more fries.*

**JUNIOR:**  William. Would you like a coffee.

**WILLIAM:**  No.

**GAIL:**  What's wrong, Junior, what are you trying to avoid telling me.

**JUNIOR:**  Nothing.

**GAIL:**  Why aren't you looking at me.

**WILLIAM:**  It's a sad story.

**GAIL:**  What is.

**WILLIAM:**  I weep. Look, a tear on my cheek. I have been reached personally and sincerely by this tragedy.

**GAIL:**  What tragedy.

**WILLIAM:**  He'll tell you. In his time.

**GAIL:**  Junior, what the hell is it.

**JUNIOR:**  Nothing really. Just dumb bad luck. My head hurts.

*JUNIOR lays his head on GAIL's shoulder.*

**WILLIAM:** A little comfort. There, there. Shush. Sleep. Dream.

**GAIL:** Please be quiet. (*to JUNIOR*) Tell me, honey.

**JUNIOR:** Tell her, William.

**GAIL:** How can he tell me. What's he got to do with it.

**JUNIOR:** He's good with words. Really. He'll tell it good. You'll probably enjoy the telling even if the story itself depresses you.

*Pause.*

**WILLIAM:** I have your permission?

**GAIL:** Go ahead, William.

**WILLIAM:** First a summary. It has been a bad day for your loved one, my friend here. His father refused to end their relationship. Then beat him up. Later in the afternoon he got fired from his job.

**GAIL:** Oh Jesus.

**WILLIAM:** But that's not the worst. This is the worst. He has been coerced into an involvement in criminal activity.

**GAIL:** Oh no. Oh Jesus.

*She is petting JUNIOR's head.*

**WILLIAM:** That was the summary. Let me rinse my mouth and give you the poetic details.

*He picks up what's left of SANDY's Coke.*

**GAIL:** Jesus. Shit.

**JUNIOR:** (*to WILLIAM*) Excuse me.

*JUNIOR lays his head in GAIL's lap. WILLIAM wipes away a tear. Touches JUNIOR's arm affectionately, then GAIL's. GAIL looks up towards the ceiling.*

**WILLIAM:** I speak now from the heart of experience. I use words like destiny and fate and despair. I talk of the great abyss which beckons us all. I speak of the great underclass of our society, the doomed, the forgotten, the outcasts. I describe the fine line which separates the lands of function and dysfunction. I put it in terms which cover the spectrum. The political. The philosophical. The poetic. Occasionally I use the vernacular. I talk of the great fuck up. Of getting shafted, getting screwed up the ass. Without even a kiss. I describe the human condition. I tell you Junior's story. Your story. And if I may be so bold, our story ... Because aren't we all in this together. Aren't we all friends here. Can't you feel the bond. Isn't this the absolute truth.

*And WILLIAM continues ... gesticulating, wiping away tears.*

*Fadeout.*

## SCENE FOUR

*The living room of JUNIOR's sad little house. A sofa and a lamp.*

*WINEVA DAWSON is standing in the middle of the room. A cigarette in her mouth. Holding a cardboard box. Looking around. She mutters something, puts the box down behind the couch. Looks around again. Leaves.*

*JUNIOR Comes on from another direction with a glass of water and a bottle of aspirin. Takes a few. Washes them down. Takes the cushions from the sofa and opens it up into a bed. Blankets and sheets already in place. Strips to his underwear. Lies down under the covers.*

*GAIL comes on.*

**GAIL:** Take the aspirin.

**JUNIOR:** I did.

**GAIL:** Feel better?

**JUNIOR:** Not yet. Did you call your mom.

**GAIL:** Yeah.

**JUNIOR:** Is it okay for you to stay over.

**GAIL:** Come on, you know I don't ask her permission for things like that. I'm eighteen. I just let her know I'm all right.

**JUNIOR:** Did you send her my love.

**GAIL:** Sure.

**JUNIOR:** You didn't, did you.

**GAIL:** It would make her nervous if I sent her your love, Junior. I'm not sure she'd know how to take it.

**JUNIOR:** I like your mother.

**GAIL:** She likes you.

**JUNIOR:** That's not really true, is it.

**GAIL:** She thinks you're … interesting. She thinks we're an interesting match. She's not totally against it. Not totally.

**JUNIOR:** Well, maybe if you'd start sending her my love like I ask you, for chrissake!

GAIL:  Don't worry about my mother. How she feels about you isn't an issue. How'd you lose your job.

JUNIOR:  William explained it. Weren't you listening.

GAIL:  I must have phased out after he got to the part about your Uncle Ritchie.

JUNIOR:  Yeah. Terrifying wasn't it. He made it sound terrifying. William seemed to know all about my Uncle Ritchie. Maybe he's met him.

GAIL:  Where is William.

JUNIOR:  Sleeping on the pantry floor. I told him he could sleep inside but he said he couldn't re-enter civilization too quickly. He had to do it in stages.

GAIL:  Why's he doing it at all. Really, why's he doing it around you.

JUNIOR:  We've got a bond. He thinks I need a teacher.

GAIL:  A what? Never mind. We'll talk about William later. Tell me about your job.

JUNIOR:  Let's not talk about it. It's pathetic.

GAIL:  I want to know.

JUNIOR:  They received an anonymous call.

GAIL:  They?

JUNIOR:  Whoever owns the company. Well, maybe not the owners. Someone. I don't know. I don't know much.

GAIL:  Do you know what the call was about.

JUNIOR:  That car I stole when I was a kid? I've been trying to think if there's anything else.

GAIL:  You mean they didn't tell you.

JUNIOR:  The plant manager said he was under orders to let me go. Couldn't say why. Said he'd give me a hint though. Anonymous call. (*pause*) So?

GAIL:  I'm thinking … This wouldn't have happened if that place was unionized.

JUNIOR:  What should I do. Do you have a plan.

GAIL:  Give me a while, I'm thinking.

**JUNIOR:** Well while you're at it, what do we do about my Uncle Ritchie.

**GAIL:** Would he really have your dad killed.

**JUNIOR:** For sure. He's a real scuzz. The true criminal pig my dad could never be.

**GAIL:** If he's so good at it, why does he need you. Why does he need this place.

**JUNIOR:** Well listen, he's no fucking mastermind. I mean, he's good at it in comparison to my dad. He doesn't get caught every single time or anything.

**GAIL:** Well, we can't go along with it.

**JUNIOR:** We can't?

**GAIL:** You know we can't. You know that.

**JUNIOR:** Sure. Because it's my true destiny and we have to avoid it at any cost.

**GAIL:** Listen! Don't let this get to you. Keep it small. It's still small. Nothing's happened yet.

*She is rubbing his head.*

**JUNIOR:** Yeah. And anyway he'd just be using my house if worse came to worst.

**GAIL:** It can't happen! Not because it's your true destiny. We can't do it, that's all. We can't start.

**JUNIOR:** I could let him kill my dad.

*Pause.*

**GAIL:** Could you.

**JUNIOR:** I wish.

*WILLIAM comes on.*

**WILLIAM:** Hello. Apologies for the interruption.

**JUNIOR:** Is it too cold out there.

**WILLIAM:** No. Absolutely fine. I was just wondering … well, it's been almost twenty-four hours.

**GAIL:** He needs a drink.

**WILLIAM:** Nothing fancy. Some wine? Domestic will do.

**JUNIOR:** Sorry. Don't have any.

**WILLIAM:** Perhaps I aim too high. Almost anything works. Aftershave. Hair tonic. Vanilla extract ... just a sip. For the shaking.

**GAIL:** Are you suffering withdrawal.

**WILLIAM:** This is a possibility. I just had a lengthy argument with a large mongoose. It was speaking Japanese. (*starts to cry*) I tried. I tried so hard to understand. But it's such a difficult language.

**GAIL:** (*to JUNIOR*) D.T.s. (*jumps up*) Come with me, William.

   *She grabs his hand.*

**WILLIAM:** With you I will go anywhere. You are the child I never had.

**GAIL:** Yeah. You remind me a little of my father too.

**JUNIOR:** Where are you taking him.

**GAIL:** The bathroom.

**WILLIAM:** Yes. Good. Aftershave was honestly my first choice.

**GAIL:** (*to JUNIOR*) A shower. Cold water.

   *They leave. JUNIOR takes a couple more aspirin. WINEVA comes on. Stands there. Holding another box.*

**WINEVA:** Are they gone. Those voices. Are they gone.

**JUNIOR:** Who are you.

**WINEVA:** Are you Junior.

**JUNIOR:** Yeah.

**WINEVA:** I'm Wineva.

   *JUNIOR gets up.*

**JUNIOR:** Do I know you.

**WINEVA:** I'm Wineva. I'm your Aunt Wineva. Your Uncle Ritchie's wife.

**JUNIOR:** He's married? Since when.

**WINEVA:** Two years. Well, common law. It's the same thing. We're family. Aren't you going to give me a kiss.

**JUNIOR:** Maybe later.

**WINEVA:** Give me a kiss. Come on over here and give me a kiss. I'm your aunt. (*JUNIOR goes over. Kisses her cheek*) Was that so bad. Try to be a little friendlier from now on. We're family. Here. (*she hands him the box*) Put this behind the couch with the other one.

> *JUNIOR looks behind the couch. Looks at WINEVA.*

**JUNIOR:** Where'd that come from.

**WINEVA:** They're heavy aren't they.

**JUNIOR:** What.

**WINEVA:** That box. It's heavy.

**JUNIOR:** Yeah.

**WINEVA:** So why don't you put it down.

**JUNIOR:** Sure.

> *He does.*

**WINEVA:** So … Give me another kiss … I'm trying to establish contact here. (*he kisses her on the cheek*) That wasn't so bad. We're family. It's good for a family to have warm feelings for each other. I'm getting warm feelings for you. How are your feelings for me.

**JUNIOR:** What's in the boxes.

**WINEVA:** Why do you ask.

**JUNIOR:** I shouldn't ask?

**WINEVA:** I didn't ask. Why should you.

**JUNIOR:** So you don't know what's in them.

**WINEVA:** Why should I.

**JUNIOR:** How many more in your car.

**WINEVA:** It's a van.

**JUNIOR:** So there's a lot?

**WINEVA:** There's more. What's a lot.

**JUNIOR:** How many more!

**WINEVA:** A lot more!

> *Pause.*

**JUNIOR:** And you're bringing them all in here?

**WINEVA:** So are you. We're doing it together. Like a family. It's a family business.

**JUNIOR:** Yeah. What kind of business is it that the family's in.

**WINEVA:** Maybe you should get dressed before you go out to the van.

**JUNIOR:** Sure. (*he starts to get dressed*) So what kind of business is it. You didn't say.

**WINEVA:** A family business. You work out, or what? In a gym, or what? You're in fair shape. Your body is in fairly good shape. I'm not getting excited or anything but it's decent to look at.

**JUNIOR:** Yeah. Great. Thanks. You go ahead. I'll catch up. You shouldn't leave the van unguarded. Those boxes are valuable.

**WINEVA:** Is that what you think.

**JUNIOR:** You don't?

**WINEVA:** Did I say that.

**JUNIOR:** Are they valuable.

**WINEVA:** It depends what's in them, doesn't it.

**JUNIOR:** You go ahead. I'll catch up.

**WINEVA:** Sure. Give me a kiss. (*he walks over. Kisses her cheek*) That's real nice. You see, a warm feeling is developing. That's the important thing, right.

**JUNIOR:** Sure.

**WINEVA:** No matter what's in the boxes, no matter what the consequences, it's the warm feeling that'll see us through, keep us together, keep us loyal. Protect us from the shit. Once more for good measure.

> *She grabs his cheek. Hard. Kisses his lips hard. Taps his face. And leaves.*

**JUNIOR:** Holy fuck! (*turns in a few, circles*) Shit.

> *He runs off after GAIL. WINEVA comes on with another box. Looks around. Frowns. Puts down the box. Goes out. GAIL, JUNIOR and WILLIAM appear bending down in a tight grouping in a far corner of the room. WILLIAM is wearing an old bathrobe.*

**GAIL:** Where is she.

**JUNIOR:** Outside I guess. Look. A box. That makes three.

**GAIL:** We have to stop her.

**JUNIOR:** You can do it. I know you can.

**WILLIAM:** And as a last resort, there is always me, of course.

**JUNIOR:** No offence, William. Gail has a way with people like this.

**GAIL:** She's coming back.

**JUNIOR:** Do you have a plan.

**GAIL:** No.

**WILLIAM:** It might be a good idea to begin by standing up. That way for sure we don't look so foolish.

**JUNIOR:** Yeah.

*They straighten. WINEVA comes in. Another box. Another cigarette.*

**WILLIAM:** You. Madame. Put that box down.

**JUNIOR:** No.

**WILLIAM:** No? No. I mean do not put that box down. We do not want that box.

*WINEVA puts the box down.*

**WINEVA:** All of you. Over here. Come on. (*they move closer to her*) Over here. (*they move closer*) You must be Grace.

**GAIL:** (*to JUNIOR*) Who's Grace.

**JUNIOR:** (*to WINEVA*) Her name's Gail.

**WINEVA:** I've been told all about you. By the family. Give me a kiss … Come on. I'm Junior's aunt. It's the custom. Give me a kiss. (*GAIL goes and gives her a kiss on the cheek*) There. That was innocent enough. This must be your father.

**GAIL:** My … uncle.

**WINEVA:** Good enough … Give me a kiss, old-timer.

**WILLIAM:** First the matter of the boxes.

**WINEVA:** First the kiss. We have to be on terms before we go any further. Put it here. (*she points to her cheek. WILLIAM kisses her cheek*) Oh. Whew. Jesus. What's that smell on your breath. You been drinking Old Spice? (*laughs*)

**WILLIAM:** Yes. As a matter of fact I have.

**WINEVA:** Now all of you. Remember the bond. The warm feeling. You, Grace, especially. It will be a pleasure to be your aunt. You I like. You've got a very nice body. Ah, come on, relax. You can always stop me if I go too far.

**WILLIAM:** You have been sent by the notorious Ritchie, I assume.

**WINEVA:** Junior knows why I'm here. All we need from you is the loyalty of a loved one.

**WILLIAM:** But I …

**WINEVA:** Butt out. (*to JUNIOR*) Come on now, we've got a lot more out there.

> *She goes.*

**JUNIOR:** What should I do.

**GAIL:** Go ahead.

**JUNIOR:** Have you got a plan yet.

**GAIL:** No.

**JUNIOR:** I'll play along. Buy you some more time.

> *JUNIOR goes out.*

**GAIL:** Why does he think I can stop this. He thinks I can do anything. He has this picture of me in his head about twenty times the size of life. (*sits on the bed*)

**WILLIAM:** Don't give up.

**GAIL:** These things have their own momentum, you know.

**WILLIAM:** I think we should ask for a meeting with the uncle himself.

**GAIL:** Wouldn't help. I met him once. He's a real swine. He drools. You should see it. And it's not from drink. He's sober when he drools. He just stands there, gets some really evil thought in his head, and the saliva pours. Man, just thinking about him is making me sick.

> *WINEVA and JUNIOR come on. Put down their boxes. WINEVA starts off.*

**WILLIAM:** After you leave we will dispose of these boxes. They will be taken away. Lost in the vastness of the dark city. (*she stops*) This is a definite truth. I am not bluffing. (*she turns*)

**WINEVA:** Maybe you didn't kiss me hard enough. Maybe there wasn't enough feeling in it. Come here. Now! (*WILLIAM walks over. WINEVA grabs him by the collar*) This is big business. Ritchie has plans. This is just the beginning. There's more to come. We'll all do very well if we don't let each other down. If the bond holds. But if the bond breaks, people will get seriously hurt. Junior's father will be the first. It might not stop there. You could get hurt too. (*WILLIAM begins to cry*) What's wrong. Did I scare you.

**WILLIAM:** No. It's pain ... Pain deep inside. All my organs are rotting away, you see. This feels like the liver.

**WINEVA:** This will make you feel better. (*she kisses him. Hard. With tongue. Starts off*) Come on, Junior.

> *They both leave. WILLIAM sits down next to GAIL.*

**WILLIAM:** She is a truly terrifying kisser.

**GAIL:** I can feel a dark shadow hanging over our heads. Descending slowly. Junior and I are doomed. It's young love gone wrong. Deadman's curve. Teenage wasteland. In a couple of years we could have made it to the suburbs ... no, the suburbs are fucked up too. The country's the only answer. If we'd just had more time, the country ... an unlisted phone. Two good jobs.

**WILLIAM:** In times similar to these over the years, always, I have found it helpful to put things in historical perspective. We are dealing here with an absolute definite class. The criminal element.

**GAIL:** You guessed that much, eh.

**WILLIAM:** The point is, threats don't work. Neither will reason, nor compassion, obviously. No normal social dialogue. The logic is not there. The mind bent from years of repression.

**GAIL:** You think the problem with these people is that they're repressed.

**WILLIAM:** The class is repressed. When the class is repressed, it produces a certain percentage of moronic immoral slimy offspring.

**GAIL:** Is this taking us anyplace useful.

**WILLIAM:** It's a process. It takes time. We begin in the abstract. Eventually we move on. Settling finally in the area of logic. A problem exists. A solution also. It is necessary to the laws of the universe.

**GAIL:** And meanwhile the shadow hangs.

*WINEVA comes on with a box. JUNIOR follows with two.*

**WINEVA:** Finished.

**WILLIAM:** So soon?

**WINEVA:** How's your liver.

**WILLIAM:** Better. Thank you.

**WINEVA:** Great. (*to JUNIOR*) When I leave you have to put these boxes in the basement. Those are the instructions. Any problem with that. (*they all shake their heads*) No looking in the boxes. We'll know if you've looked. So no looking. Any problem with that. (*they all shake their heads*) Good. No hard feelings. I'm just doing a job. Doing my part. I'm married to the main man. (*to GAIL*) It's just a marriage of convenience. But it's still family. There's no sex but there's a bond. By the way, do you all understand what I really mean by 'family.' (*they all nod*) This is just the beginning. There's more to come.

**JUNIOR:** More boxes?

**WINEVA:** Just more. When you're needed you'll be contacted. Any problems with that. (*JUNIOR shakes his head*) The old-timer and the girl too. They're family now. They're informed. They're in. Right in the centre. Understand? (*they all nod*) Good. Great. Now kisses goodbye. Hard ones. With feeling. Come on. (*WILLIAM goes to her. Kisses her cheek. GAIL goes to her Kisses her cheek. WINEVA runs her hand through GAIL's hair*) Nice. Very nice. (*to JUNIOR*) Your turn. (*JUNIOR just stares at her*) Come on. (*pause*) Your kiss. It's mine. And I want it. Now! (*JUNIOR kisses her cheek*) Thanks.

*She leaves. Long pause. They all wander around the room in a daze.*

**JUNIOR:** When I was little I always wanted an aunt. (*he sits between GAIL and WILLIAM on the edge of the bed*) I'm sorry. (*he kisses her*) I'm sorry you're involved in this.

**\IL:** It's not your fault.

**JUNIOR:** I'm sorry anyway. (*he kisses her once, twice*)

**GAIL:** Wait. Why is it you always get affectionate at times like these. The worse things get, the more you kiss.

**JUNIOR:** Kissing you makes me forget. That's all I can say about it really. If I couldn't live my life under your sweater, I'd like to live it attached to your mouth.

**GAIL:** (*to WILLIAM*) Sad guy, eh. I think he probably means it too. (*to JUNIOR*) Don't you.

**JUNIOR:** Sure.

**GAIL:** Sure.

> *They hug. A long sustained kiss.*

**WILLIAM:** This love is a precious commodity. The two of you. I love this love you have. It should be nourished and protected. I will rise to the occasion. I will surround your love with an iron will! (*groans*) Ooh. Go away pain. Recede. Liver, spleen, bladder. Head. Heal. Ooh. Please. Jesus. Oh. (*sliding off the bed*) Oh God. Not the pancreas. The kidneys. (*he is on the floor, writhing. JUNIOR and GAIL stop kissing. Look at him*) Don't worry. I'll protect you. This is a promise. Ohhhh! Arrgh! Geeezz!

> *Blackout.*

## SCENE FIVE

*Late night.*

*Lights up on a section of street. SANDY is pacing. Dressed in high heels, tight jeans and sweater. Smoking. Looking around. After a moment she walks off. Lights out on this area.*

*Lights up on an alley off the street. JUNIOR, GAIL and WILLIAM are each sitting against a garbage can. WILLIAM is wearing a baseball jacket, sneakers. Ill–fitting but reasonably clean.*

WILLIAM: This I stress. I absolutely stress the following point. To understand the possibility of progress you must first identify the force which keeps you static. Is it external. Does it lie within. To find the answer you require self-awareness. Self-awareness is the thing. Junior, seriously, this is important stuff.

JUNIOR: William, excuse me for a minute. You know, Gail, I'd feel a lot better if you were home.

GAIL: I'd feel better if you were home too. Too bad for both of us.

*WILLIAM is staring at his hand.*

WILLIAM: I look at my hand. I picture it lying on the sidewalk, on the end of my arm. Limp. I picture someone stepping on it. Crushing my bones. Truly. I ask myself, could this have been avoided. Did this person step on my hand intentionally. On the other hand, what was my hand doing there in the first place.

GAIL: You'd passed out.

WILLIAM: I was speaking in the abstract, but yes, in fact, I had passed out.

JUNIOR: What time is it.

GAIL: Ten past midnight.

JUNIOR: They're late. We could leave. If they ask we could say … you were late.

GAIL: So they'll call us again tomorrow night. The night after. We've got to get involved a bit before we can take a stand. Get some information.

**WILLIAM:** There is of course a moral in the story of the crushed hand.

**JUNIOR:** Look, William, people will step on your hand every chance they get.

**GAIL:** Yeah, William, I mean listen, maybe you bring all this pain on yourself, did you ever consider that.

**WILLIAM:** Exactly my point. Good for you both. So we go on. We move slowly through the abstract darkness. Point by point we nail things down. But first I must take a piss.

*He wanders into the darkness.*

**JUNIOR:** I could have bought a gun. And when they showed up just shot them dead.

**GAIL:** Now you're thinking.

**JUNIOR:** Ah, this is a sad situation we've got here. They've got us on a leash. They're going to lead us around for the rest of our lives. We'll be slaves. Low-life criminal slaves. Until we're caught. God I can't stand the idea of you in jail. I've been thinking about it for hours. It's driving me crazy. Please go home.

**GAIL:** No.

**JUNIOR:** Please.

**GAIL:** Shush. What's that noise.

**JUNIOR:** Is it a pissing sound.

**GAIL:** Voices ... Listen.

*There are voices in the distance. Down the alley. Getting closer. Voices. Arguing voices. One man. One woman. Getting closer. Suddenly WINEVA appears out of the darkness.*

**WINEVA:** Good. You're here.

**GAIL:** Are you alone.

**WINEVA:** You have a problem with that?

**GAIL:** I heard two voices. A man and a woman.

**WINEVA:** Wrong. Just me.

*GAIL and JUNIOR look at each other.*

Where's the old-timer. I told you. I wanted all three of you.
What have we got here, a crack in the wall?

**JUNIOR:** What.

**WINEVA:** The bond. Is it breaking.

*WILLIAM is wandering back.*

**WILLIAM:** You know something, this alley looks familiar. This
building. I know this building. (*sees WINEVA*) Oh, hello.

**WINEVA:** Come here. Quickly. (*WILLIAM rushes to her. Kisses her
cheek. She breaks away*) There's no time for that shit. Now
listen, this runs like clockwork. Everyone does their part. The
girl keeps watch. On the street. Go.

**JUNIOR:** She stays with me.

**WINEVA:** Did someone die and leave you in charge. Do you know
something I don't.

**JUNIOR:** Look, lady ...

**WINEVA:** The clock is running. Remember your father.

**GAIL:** I'll be all right.

*GAIL starts off. JUNIOR grabs her.*

**JUNIOR:** If anything happens. Run. Get away. Promise.

**GAIL:** Yeah.

**JUNIOR:** No, promise. Jesus, promise. I'll go crazy.

**GAIL:** I promise. (*starts off*)

**JUNIOR:** Anything at all, and you run. No. Take a cab. It's late.

*GAIL is gone.*

**WINEVA:** Finished?

**JUNIOR:** You've got no right involving her in this. You and Uncle
Ritchie are shit. Insane shit too.

**WINEVA:** Finished now?

**WILLIAM:** You want us to do something. Please, why don't you tell
us what it is.

**WINEVA:** Well, I'm trying, aren't I. Now it's simple. That's the
door of the loading dock. We break it open.

**JUNIOR:** How.

**WINEVA:** The usual way.

**JUNIOR:** Yeah, what's that.

**WINEVA:** They told me you were a dumb fuck. They didn't tell me you were the dumbest fuck. Look, haven't I tried to be nice to you. Didn't I go out of my way to establish contact. Why the aggravation.

**JUNIOR:** I just wanted to make sure you know what you're doing.

**WINEVA:** Watch me. Now the door is my job. Don't worry about it. When I break it, you head in. A few feet inside along the left wall is a pile of about fifty boxes.

**JUNIOR:** (*to WILLIAM*) More boxes.

**WILLIAM:** Fifty boxes. That's a lot of boxes.

**WINEVA:** It goes like this. The kid hands them to the old-timer, the old-timer lines them up. In the meantime I'm getting the van which is parked at the end of the alley. I bring it back. We load. It's simple.

**JUNIOR:** What happens then.

**WINEVA:** Jesus. We leave.

**JUNIOR:** What happens to the boxes.

**WINEVA:** Guess.

**JUNIOR:** You bring them to my house. That's my house, you know. It's not Ritchie's. It's not my dad's. My mom left me that house. I have a responsibility to that house. It was never intended for work like this. My mother wasn't like that. Jesus.

**WILLIAM:** Perhaps we could find another place to store them.

*WINEVA approaches WILLIAM making kissing noises.*

**WINEVA:** I've got instructions. The instructions say the house.

**WILLIAM:** (*to JUNIOR*) It's gotta be the house.

**JUNIOR:** Like a fucking slave. Jesus, William when are we going to do something about this. What's the historical lesson here. I mean, come on!

**WINEVA:** What's wrong with him.

**WILLIAM:** A touch of nervous energy. He'll be fine.

**WINEVA:** Here's hoping. Okay, on the count of three.

**JUNIOR:** Jesus.

**WINEVA:** One. Two. Three!

> *WINEVA yells. JUNIOR and WILLIAM yell, fall on the ground. WINEVA picks up one of the garbage cans. Puts it over her head and attacks the loading door. Blackout on this area. Lights up in the street. GAIL is waiting. Nervously. Someone is coming. She turns her back. SANDY comes on.*

**SANDY:** Hey, I know you.

> *GAIL turns.*

**GAIL:** What are you doing here.

**SANDY:** Well, I sure hope it's not the same thing you're doing here.

**GAIL:** Look how you're dressed. You look stupid.

> *SANDY looks at herself.*

**SANDY:** Hey, it's the going fashion. It's not my idea. What am I supposed to do, break new ground.

**GAIL:** You promised you wouldn't work the street.

**SANDY:** You followed me, didn't you.

**GAIL:** No ... Yes ... No. Never mind. What are you doing, Sandy. You said if things came to the worst, if there was no money, no job, no husband, no future, you'd turn a trick or two in the hotels. That was the plan, the hotels.

**SANDY:** Suppose I got bounced from the hotels. I had to know if I could do it on the street. The plan wasn't complete. I'm completing it.

**GAIL:** It's dangerous.

**SANDY:** It's worth it. It's for my peace of mind. Relax. I know what I'm doing. What are you doing.

**GAIL:** Nothing. I'm still looking for work. I had an interview yesterday with a bank.

**SANDY:** I was sort of talking about now, right. You followed me, didn't you.

**GAIL:** No. I'm ... I'm standing lookout.

**SANDY:** For what.

GAIL: I don't know … the cops, I guess. Listen, this is a secret. Junior's breaking into a building down the alley.

SANDY: Why don't you just admit you followed me. You've got a right. You're my best friend.

GAIL: He's not alone. He's with William.

SANDY: That bum?

GAIL: And his aunt.

SANDY: The bum's got an aunt?

GAIL: Junior's aunt. She's the brains, I think. I don't know. Maybe she's the brawn. I don't know. I'm scared shitless.

SANDY: So. This is the truth, right.

GAIL: Yeah.

SANDY: Really.

GAIL: Yeah.

    *Pause.*

SANDY: I'm going to tell your mother.

GAIL: Get real. Come on.

SANDY: No, I'm serious. She told me to. Any sign that Junior was corrupting you and I'm supposed to report to her directly. I swore an oath.

GAIL: It's not Junior's fault. He's being blackmailed.

SANDY: I don't give a flying fuck about Junior. I'm telling your mother!

GAIL: Go ahead. I'll tell yours.

SANDY: Okay okay, forget the mother-telling thing. Listen. This is crime, Gail. What you're doing is serious crime. We should stop them.

GAIL: It's not so easy. There are complications.

SANDY: Nothing's more complicated than this. This is the first step to disaster. We should stop them. Figure the rest out later.

GAIL: Maybe.

SANDY: For sure.

**GAIL:** Yeah, maybe.

**SANDY:** Let's do it.

**GAIL:** Yeah? ... Okay. Yeah.

> *Two gunshots. They take two or three steps and are frozen by the wailing sound of a burglar alarm.*

**SANDY:** Too late.

**GAIL:** What should we do.

**SANDY:** Run.

**GAIL:** No. Junior's back there.

**SANDY:** Junior would want you to run.

**GAIL:** No. Take a cab. He wanted me to take a cab.

**SANDY:** A real criminal genius for sure. Let's go. Come on. Come on!

**GAIL:** No, no I can't.

> *SANDY grabs GAIL's arm. And pulls.*

**SANDY:** Come on!

**GAIL:** Junior!

> *A spotlight catches GAIL on the street, while another catches JUNIOR grimacing in pain in the doorway of the loading platform.*
>
> *Blackout.*

## SCENE SIX

*The visitors' room at the city jail. HENRY DAWSON and WILLIAM.*
*Staring at each other across the table. Long pause*

**HENRY:** Do I know you ... There's something familiar about you.

**WILLIAM:** I am a psychiatrist.

**HENRY:** Oh. Well, that's good. I'm glad you're here. Because they want to put me away for keeps. But I can be saved. I want to turn myself around. Society never gave me nothing but dirt. But I don't want to hold a grudge no more. I want you to reach right inside my head, reach right inside and turn it around. I'm willing. I'm ready. I'm able.

**WILLIAM:** Bullshit.

**HENRY:** No. Honest.

**WILLIAM:** Bullshit.

**HENRY:** Ah, come on. Really. Honest. Give me a break. Don't be cruel. Try me out.

**WILLIAM:** You are a big stupid shit-spewing asshole. One of the world's truly pathetic empty spaces. An enormous nothingness on legs. A total waste of time. Vomit. If I had a gun I'd shoot you.

**HENRY:** I want another doctor.

**WILLIAM:** Shut up. I warn you. If you make me angry I'll kill you with my bare hands.

**HENRY:** You are a lousy psychiatrist. I've seen a few of them. And you are the worst.

**WILLIAM:** It's a lie, stupid. I told it so they would let me see you. Now shut up and listen. Your son was nearly killed two nights ago.

**HENRY:** How do you know my son?

**WILLIAM:** Shut up. To be coerced into crime is one thing, to be coerced by incompetent fools is another. I could live a criminal life. I've seen the abyss. I've felt the pull. Even philosophically, I could come to terms with certain actions.

Perhaps against large corrupt institutions. This is hypothetical. I don't expect you to understand what I'm saying.

HENRY: Thanks.

WILLIAM: But to attempt to steal food from the Salvation Army headquarters is beneath contempt. Unjustifiable.

HENRY: So Ritchie finally knocked over the Sally Ann. He's been planning that job for two years.

WILLIAM: Then he is, and this I find almost impossible to believe, more stupid than you are.

HENRY: (*smiles*) Really. You think so.

WILLIAM: Oh, yes. Because in those two years he wasn't even able to discover that the warehouse is guarded by two armed security men.

HENRY: So Ritchie screwed up bad.

WILLIAM: And your son was wounded.

HENRY: That's rough. I'm sorry. Tell him I'm sorry if you see him, will you. So Ritchie screwed up. So. So who's the dumb fuck, eh. Tell me who the first-place dumb fuck is in this family.

WILLIAM: It's a crowded field. Look for a photo finish.

HENRY: What. Yeah. So you know my kid. Hey. Wait a minute. Now I know what's familiar about you. It's your clothes. They're mine. You're wearing my clothes. Where'd you get my clothes.

WILLIAM: In your closet.

HENRY: Hey, wait a minute. You were in my closet? You know my kid and you're in my closet. What is this. Are you taking over my life. This is weird. That's my life. Get your own.

WILLIAM: You have no life. You have no son. Now shut up because you are starting to make me angry. I want you to get word to your brother. From now on we do things our way.

HENRY: Our way.

WILLIAM: My way! And Junior's. Truth is if I had just my way I'd let them cut you open. But for some reason your son can't let this happen. Maybe because unfortunately he cares for you. Maybe because he really believes he's supposed to turn bad. That it's predestined or some such nonsense.

**HENRY:** It's true. It's in the family. The bad turn. It takes place in the head. You can't fight it. You have to give in.

**WILLIAM:** Tell your brother we want to meet with him personally. To discuss a ... new approach. A meeting is essential. These are further instructions. (*he hands* HENRY *an envelope*) I've written them down because we don't expect you to be able to remember them.

**HENRY:** Thanks.

**WILLIAM:** Do this quickly. If not I will trick Junior somehow and make sure that we adopt an attitude that prompts your brother to hurt you.

**HENRY:** Suppose I don't believe you.

**WILLIAM:** Personally I hope you don't believe me. I honestly do. Coming in contact with your type is revitalizing me. I'm gaining strength by the minute. A hatred of the purest kind is making me powerful. This is true. It's amazing. I could kill you on the spot and feel terrific.

**HENRY:** Mister. I don't know where you come from. But you're hard. What'd I ever do to you. Look at me. My life's a disaster. You should be nicer.

**WILLIAM:** I have great sympathy for the truly sad cases of our world. The victims. I have felt so badly that I fell amongst them. This is the truth. This is not melodrama. Their misery made me useless. I fell. But for you, I feel nothing. You use your own boy. Ruin his life. And he's a good one potentially. Have you seen him with his girl. This is love. You wouldn't know it anyway. I have to leave now. I feel my temper rising. (*groans*) Also a slight twinge in the lower intestine. (*stands*) Just one more thing. Please lean over a bit. Yes. A bit more. (*HENRY obeys.* WILLIAM *leans on the table*) I have a question. I want you to tell me the truth. I'll know if you lie and I'll take steps to have you hurt. Understand?

*WILLIAM is pointing a finger at HENRY.*

**HENRY:** Yes.

*WILLIAM notices that HENRY seems mesmerized by the finger.*

**WILLIAM:** The anonymous call to Junior's employer. This was made by his Uncle Ritchie, to somehow make Junior vulnerable?

**HENRY:** Yes.

**WILLIAM:** But how did Ritchie find out who Junior's employer was.

**HENRY:** I don't know.

**WILLIAM:** That's a lie, isn't it.

**HENRY:** Yes.

**WILLIAM:** You gave him the name of the employer.

**HENRY:** I had to.

*Pause.*

**WILLIAM:** You had to. Yes. I know. It was … predestined.

*WILLIAM grabs HENRY's hair. Pulls his head down hard on the table. Starts off.*

Hurts. Doesn't it.

*Blackout.*

## SCENE SEVEN

*JUNIOR's living room. GAIL, JUNIOR and SANDY. GAIL is just finishing changing a bandage on JUNIOR's leg. SANDY is watching and grimacing.*

**JUNIOR:** Finished? (*GAIL nods*) Let me walk. I feel like walking.

*He gets up. GAIL just lowers her head. Sits there.*

It could be worse. My head doesn't hurt much anymore. I wish my mother was still here. We could have a little talk. I could get really scared and she'd understand. She's the only person I could let myself get totally scared in front of. I get close with you, Gail. But with her I could lie down on the floor and pretend I was Jello. I knew this was coming when I was nine. Nine years old. I saw a picture of some guy getting hanged in a book my dad gave me. And I knew right away I'd hang too someday.

**GAIL:** Please. Stop. You're not going to hang.

**JUNIOR:** I feel already hung. They just have to take my body down. Bag it. Send it off for burning. I'm scared.

*GAIL throws herself onto the floor. Her arms around JUNIOR's legs*

I should have stayed small. Tried to get smaller. Really, really small. This big. So no one would notice. I know I was never really big but I wasn't small enough. Someone noticed I was around. Why are you holding onto my legs.

**GAIL:** Just holding.

**JUNIOR:** Yeah. But it looks pathetic. You're not pathetic.

**GAIL:** Neither are you.

**JUNIOR:** I'm not? She thinks I'm pathetic. (*to SANDY*) Don't you.

**SANDY:** You don't look so good at the moment, but I wouldn't say you were pathetic. She likes you. You must have something. I've been asking her for months what it is, but she won't tell me.

**JUNIOR:** I want to thank you for buying the first-aid stuff. I want to thank you for helping Gail get away ... Thanks.

**SANDY:**  Yeah … Hey, maybe that's it. (*to GAIL*) Is it because he's polite.

**JUNIOR:**  Gail. Please get up.

**GAIL:**  I know what my problem is. I'm too emotional. I'm an emotional mess. I'm not thinking clearly. It's the downside of love. I've got to stand back a bit. I know I can solve this mess. I just know it.

**JUNIOR:**  I know you can too. (*sits on the couch*)

**GAIL:**  Nah. You're being nice. I've let you down. I've got to stand back.

**JUNIOR:**  Get up. Please.

**GAIL:**  I mean fuck them. (*stands*) Those insane bastards. We've just got to get those rotten insane bastards out of our life.

**JUNIOR:**  Did you call your mom.

**GAIL:**  She's fine. I sent her your love.

**JUNIOR:**  Yeah? How'd you do it.

**GAIL:**  Just slipped it in. Junior sends his love.

**JUNIOR:**  How'd she take it.

**GAIL:**  All right. Nice. She said that was nice.

> *She sits beside JUNIOR. They hug.*

**JUNIOR:**  Too late though. Junior sends his love. Oh, by the way, I won't be home for awhile. I'm going to prison. Junior? Oh yes, don't worry he's going too. Separate prisons though. Christ, that's right. Gail. Separate prisons. I'll go nuts.

**SANDY:**  No one's going to prison. There's a plan.

**GAIL:**  What is it.

**SANDY:**  I have to let the bum tell you. It's his plan.

**JUNIOR:**  His name's William. Don't call him the bum, please. He's my only friend. He's from Europe you know. He used to be something big. He's been around. He's been in four revolutions. He grows on you.

**GAIL:**  That's kind of true.

> *WILLIAM comes on.*

**WILLIAM:**  (*raises his arms*) Look at me. I'm different.

*He is. He is wearing a new suit, shirt, shoes. Carrying a new briefcase. Hair is neat. They are all staring at him.*

It's an impressive sight, isn't it. I wish I could be you. Looking at me.

*Long pause.*

Someone must say something to break the ice.

GAIL: There's a purpose to this? This is taking us somewhere constructive? I mean I've got a guy here with a bullet wound. The future looks grim.

JUNIOR: How'd you get all this stuff.

WILLIAM: With money. From my bank account.

*JUNIOR, GAIL and SANDY look at each other. Shake their heads.*

GAIL: Sandy says you've got a plan. What is it.

WILLIAM: This.

GAIL: A new suit?

WILLIAM: Exactly. The suit is the answer. It is the cruise missile of social conflict. It exerts power. We need power. We must go on the offensive. To the disgusting underclass of society the suit is like garlic to Dracula. It makes them grab their genitals. It's an inbred reflex action based on years of grovelling. Even though you know in your heart that grovelling won't stop you from taking it in the groin. Because the suit ... shows ... no ... mercy.

GAIL: This is a thin plan, William. This seems pretty fragile.

WILLIAM: I'm going to demand we escalate. Demand a higher quality crime. A world beyond their grasp. It will scare them shitless. They'll back off.

GAIL: Desperate.

WILLIAM: Exactly. But sometimes desperate works.

*WINEVA comes on. Carrying two boxes.*

WINEVA: All right. You're here. That's good. Who's this.

GAIL: Just a friend. She can go. Go ahead, Sandy.

SANDY: I'm staying.

WINEVA: If she stays now, she stays forever. She's in or she's out.

**GAIL:**  Get out, Sandy.

**SANDY:**  Suppose the hooking fails. Suppose I lose my job. I'll be broke. I should know if I can do crime. I should know, just in case.

**WINEVA:**  That makes sense.

**WILLIAM:**  Yes. She's just looking for security. Other people invest in bonds.

**WINEVA:**  Nice suit, old-timer. (*to SANDY*) I'm going to do something to you now. It's just a thing we do. Don't get excited.

*She hands the boxes to WILLIAM. She kisses SANDY on the cheek.*

**WILLIAM:**  Where do these boxes come from.

**WINEVA:**  My van. The only two you managed to get out before the kid here screwed up.

**JUNIOR:**  Come on. There were two guards. Twenty feet away. I almost got killed.

**WINEVA:**  You screwed up. That was a big job and you blew it. You are the one to blame. We're blaming you. Get it?

**WILLIAM:**  Stealing cartons of food is to you a big job?

**WINEVA:**  There's a problem with that? You think food isn't important? Food is food, you dumb ass. It's the one thing we all need. It moves fast. It keeps its value.

**GAIL:**  It's a cheap crime.

**WINEVA:**  It's the best kind of crime. We've got a right to food. It's like bread. Everyone has a right to bread. In court you can say you were hungry. Who's to say we aren't hungry. Who's to say it wasn't a crime of necessity.

**JUNIOR:**  Me.

**GAIL:**  And me.

**WINEVA:**  Be careful now. Watch the bond. Keep it tight.

**WILLIAM:**  I asked for a meeting with Ritchie.

**WINEVA:**  Yeah? Is that why you bought the suit.

**WILLIAM:**  We want him here. I've got plans. I'm a powerful man. Look at me clearly. I'm making demands here. Things are going to be different. Get Ritchie.

**WINEVA:** He's busy.

**JUNIOR:** With what.

**WINEVA:** Mugging pensioners. Stealing change from children. Stamping on cripples. All the usual stuff.

**WILLIAM:** He's the boss. We want to talk to him and only him.

**WINEVA:** He's the boss?

> *She starts to laugh. It's a moderately high-pitched laugh. She throws her head back. It gets deeper. She doubles up. And the voice plummets into a deep roaring sound. The rest of them back away a bit. She straightens suddenly.*

He's the boss when I need it that way. To push out front. To make introductions sometimes. Sometimes I let him plan something. The Salvation Army job was his. It had his stamp on it for sure. Pure fucking stupidity. He drools. He walks into walls. He reads five words an hour. I use him mostly when I want someone mauled. You annoy me anymore and you'll meet him all right. I'll have him come over here and set your clothes on fire. He likes shit like that. Maybe he'll just molest you all. You keep annoying me and you'll find out! Now old-timer, you said you've got plans.

**WILLIAM:** You wouldn't like them. I'm dealing here with a very large crime.

**WINEVA:** That's good. I'm up for that. That job the other night was just a test of your loyalty. I like suits. If suits is what you all want, we'll buy them. We'll do suit jobs. That's no problem. Let's talk. Oh, I forgot. We made the papers.

> *She takes a rolled-up section of a newspaper from her pocket. Hands it to GAIL.*

It's circled. Read it to them. Come on.

**GAIL:** "Police speculate that the break-in at the Salvation Army headquarters is the work of a new gang of thieves based in the east end of the city. In conjunction, the mayor and several aldermen are demanding a crackdown on street crime, prostitution—"

**WINEVA:** Etcetera, etcetera. We've made an impression. They're squirming. Their bond isn't strong like ours. It can be cracked. We're going to make history.

**WILLIAM:**  Criminals make no history. They just make news.

**WINEVA:**  You dumb ass. You don't get it, do you … Here it is. I'm going to give it to you fast. Right now. This isn't crime. It's politics. It's you know … destiny. I'm no criminal. I'm a fucking revolutionary!

*They all mutter and look at each other. Pause.*

You have a problem with that?

*Blackout.*

## SCENE EIGHT

*A long path of light. GAIL and SANDY are walking through it. Both wearing trenchcoats.*

**SANDY:** There's no future in revolution.

**GAIL:** Depends on the revolution.

**SANDY:** Well, there's no money in it for sure.

**GAIL:** Sometimes there's enough.

**SANDY:** Hey, are you for this.

**GAIL:** No. I was talking about revolutions. What I've read about them. This is something different. Suicide probably. We'll all die young.

**SANDY:** I could leave. I don't know why I'm going with you.

**GAIL:** You should leave.

**SANDY:** On the other hand it's an experience. I might learn something I can use later in life.

**GAIL:** Besides, she said if you didn't show up she'd track you down and slit your throat.

**SANDY:** There's that too. She's mentally ill, right. I mean she's not quite human.

*They are leaving.*

**GAIL:** At least now we've got a purpose. Before it looked like we were being dragged along by a bunch of sub-moronic creeps without a clue. Now at least I know what it is we're supposed to do. We're supposed to destroy the world.

*The path of light dims. Lights up in an alley. JUNIOR and WILLIAM are each sitting against a garbage can.*

**WILLIAM:** These alleys all look the same to me.

**JUNIOR:** The garbage cans are newer.

**WILLIAM:** My insides feel like one enormous throbbing ulcer. I'm bleeding to death internally. I'm almost certain of this.

**JUNIOR:** If we get out of this alive, I think you should see a doctor. Maybe a few doctors.

**WILLIAM:** Terrifying. Where would they begin. Once they got a
look at my insides they'd have to give me the bad news. I've
always been able to live with the possibility that these pains
might be imaginary. But once the doctors tell you you're sick
then for sure you're sick. Doctors can kill you with words ...
You know something, for a few brief hours this afternoon I
felt entirely well.

**JUNIOR:** You looked good too.

**WILLIAM:** The theory of the suit is an old one. People used to be
extremely afraid of them ... I've been out of touch.

**JUNIOR:** We're sinking, aren't we. I mean this is it. What you call
the deep pit. I can feel it for sure. We're inside, about halfway
down.

**WILLIAM:** I'll be honest with you. Yes.

**JUNIOR:** And no way to get back up?

**WILLIAM:** Some people would tell you just to think positively.
These are people, of course, who have been able to spend all
their summers outdoors. Probably their grandmothers had a
lot of money. Others would tell you to pick yourself up by the
bootstraps. These are people who have forgotten anything
they might have known about life. Still others would call for a
critical examination of many different factors. A searching
for alternatives. I used to be one of those. But I've taken this
trip before. At a certain point you just hold your breath till
you reach the destination. The bottom, so to speak.

**JUNIOR:** With a thud.

**WILLIAM:** Pretend you're a feather. Think about it. Try to float
down. Gently. At this point, this is my only advice.

**JUNIOR:** Thanks.

**WILLIAM:** But I have been known to make miraculous
comebacks. We'll see. Maybe I'm just in a mood.

*SANDY and GAIL come on.*

**JUNIOR:** You came.

**GAIL:** That's right. You thought I wouldn't?

**JUNIOR:** I prayed you'd meet someone on the way, and fall in
love.

**GAIL:** Just stop it, okay. You're not responsible for me in any way.

**JUNIOR:** You think you're responsible for me. Why can't I feel the same way.

**GAIL:** Because when you feel that way it just turns you to mush ... Where is she. Is she late again.

**JUNIOR & WILLIAM:** Yes!

**JUNIOR:** Let's leave. Let's just go somewhere.

**GAIL:** Where.

**JUNIOR:** Someplace warm. Where we can be naked. Lie down. Sleep.

**GAIL:** With what. You've got money?

**JUNIOR:** It doesn't matter. I can't go. They'll kill my dad.

**WILLIAM:** This is a true equation of the world. These four lives are made equal to the life of your father, that pile of vomit. I'm starting to get angry again.

**SANDY:** What's that noise.

*Two voices coming. One deep. One high.*

**GAIL:** It's Wineva.

**SANDY:** And someone else. Listen.

*The two voices have stopped their progress and are having a loud argument.*

**GAIL:** No, just Wineva. She has two voices.

**SANDY:** Yeah, well one of them is speaking Spanish.

**WILLIAM:** With this woman, I'm afraid we are dealing in extreme schizophrenia.

**GAIL:** Like a split personality.

**WILLIAM:** No ... Pretend my fist (*holds it up*) is the place we all know as reality. Things happen here. Shopping. Eating. Going to work. We all spend most of our time here. But the schizophrenic just visits this place occasionally. (*uses a finger from his other hand to demonstrate*) Usually this person spends most of the time out here. In the special place. The place of personal definition. The other reality. It has great detail, this other place. It takes a great imagination to invent it from scratch. An imagination that can be truly terrifying.

*SANDY has been nodding knowingly. WINEVA tumbles out of the darkness. Carrying a knapsack. Wearing a red beret.*

**WINEVA:** Whew! That was a rough one. He thought he had me. Tried to use his voice on me. But I won't wash his floors. I won't stay home and wash his fucking floors while he goes out and changes the world.

**WILLIAM:** He? You mean Ritchie?

**WINEVA:** No. This is some other guy. This is the guy who follows me around making demands. Wants me to be docile. Stay at home. Be his good little woman. He's kinda handsome. But he's very demanding. And he's starting to piss me off ... So you're all here. Good. When I call the army it comes. Wait a minute. Where are the hats.

*They all produce black berets.*

Come on. Put them on.

*They obey.*

Good. When it's all over we'll gather round for kisses. Why are you staring at me like that. You think you detect a weakness. Forget it. Don't ever make the mistake of thinking you know more about my disease than I do. Now gather round for the plan.

*They do.*

This is the back of a building owned by one of the largest banks in the country. They do business out of this building with some of the world's biggest creeps. Missile builders. Drug lords. Any life sucking asshole with a few billion to hide. Tonight we're sending them a message.

*She takes off her knapsack.*

**JUNIOR:** What's in there.

**WINEVA:** You like mechanical things? Who here likes mechanical things. Who appreciates a job well done.

*She takes out a gizmo.*

**WILLIAM:** That is a bomb.

**WINEVA:** "That is a bomb." I expect more from you, old-timer. Maybe some appreciation of the difficulty involved here. Or maybe you think it's easy.

**WILLIAM:** You're going to detonate it.

**WINEVA:** You have a problem with that?

**WILLIAM:** Why do you need us. The bang will speak for itself.

**WINEVA:** Any asshole can detonate a bomb.

**WILLIAM:** My point exactly.

**WINEVA:** Be careful ... What I'm saying is I have plans beyond the bomb. These plans involve you.

**JUNIOR:** You know, I thought we were going to steal something.

**GAIL:** Me too.

**WINEVA:** Really. What about you.

**SANDY:** Oh, I just came along. I thought I might learn something useful. Pick up a skill.

**WINEVA:** You're quite the little self-starter aren't you. (*to GAIL*) What the hell is it you thought we were going to steal.

**GAIL:** Documents.

**JUNIOR:** Yeah. Documents. You know, something important.

**GAIL:** Something vital.

**WINEVA:** All right. Sure. Okay. We'll steal something. I'll incorporate theft into the plan.

**JUNIOR:** Okay. But no bomb. People could get hurt.

**WINEVA:** People are supposed to get hurt, you dumb fuck. Try to picture the scenario where the world gets destroyed without anyone getting hurt ... Look, all right, I know the problem here. You don't really care if anyone gets hurt, not really. You just can't live with the responsibility. Revolutionaries have always had this problem. But I've solved it. I've solved the problem of responsibility. You wanna know how? None of your fucking business. Now here's the plan.

**JUNIOR:** No way.

**GAIL:** He's right.

**JUNIOR:** No way at all. No.

**WINEVA:** Watch it. Be careful. You've been warned.

**WILLIAM:** No bomb.

**WINEVA:** But the bomb's just for openers. Then we're going to kidnap the chairman. He's in there now, working late. It's all planned.

**GAIL:** No bomb.

**WINEVA:** I'm willing to throw in a theft. We can steal anything you want.

**JUNIOR:** No goddamn bomb. And that's it.

**WINEVA:** Really?

**GAIL:** We're all together on this.

**WILLIAM:** We stand firm. This is a certainty. There will be no explosion. No bomb.

**WINEVA:** You're sure about that.

    *She is holding it.*

**WILLIAM:** We are determined. We stand here together. United.

**WINEVA:** Well, if you stand here longer than twenty seconds you'll be dead. I just set it. It's going off.

**WILLIAM:** This is a bluff.

**WINEVA:** The hell with you. No one tells me I can't use my bomb. No one! I should have kissed you much much harder. I should have kissed you to death.

**WILLIAM:** (*to the others*) I truly believe this is a bluff. She is unstable. But not necessarily suicidal.

**WINEVA:** Suicidal, my ass. We'll all be martyrs. Ten seconds. Eight seconds.

    *They swarm her. Wrestle. WILLIAM gets the bomb from her. Holds it up proudly.*

**WILLIAM:** Got it!

**JUNIOR:** Jesus Christ! William!

**WILLIAM:** Oh.

    *WILLIAM throws the bomb. JUNIOR grabs GAIL. They all run.*

    *Blackout. Sound of an explosion.*

## SCENE NINE

*JUNIOR's living room. WINEVA is sitting on the floor in a corner wrapped in a blanket. Chewing an edge of it. WILLIAM is pacing. With a slight limp. GAIL is bandaging JUNIOR's arm. They are on the pullout bed.*

**GAIL:** You know Junior ... you didn't have to fall on top of me to protect me.

**JUNIOR:** Yeah. I did.

**GAIL:** I mean we could have just kept running.

**JUNIOR:** Stuff was flying all around. Better it hit me than you.

**GAIL:** Why. Never mind ... This hurts I guess.

**JUNIOR:** But the leg is better. And the head doesn't bother me at all anymore. You know I've been thinking. Maybe this will only stop when I've got a wound on every part of my body. Maybe that's the destiny.

**WILLIAM:** I absolutely forbid the use of that word from now on. Add to that fate. Also legacy ... Please forget those words. You will do this for me and I will not talk about the abyss ... This way we can begin to recover ... Even now I am thinking of ways to do this.

*WINEVA makes a loud prolonged hissing noise.*

**GAIL:** How long has she been sitting there. It seems like hours.

**JUNIOR:** She's the scariest person I ever met in my life. I mean no one else is even close.

**GAIL:** And the noises she makes. What are the noises all about. What was that honking noise she made an hour ago about. Do we have to spend the rest of our young tragic lives listening to her honk and whinny and whistle.

**WILLIAM:** (*points to WINEVA*) I want to kill her! Get me some wire! I want to put it around her neck! She's doing no good with her bomb! She's just ruining lives here. (*to JUNIOR*) Do you have any wire? No, seriously. She's badly damaged. We'll put her out of her misery.

**WINEVA:** I heard that. (*getting up slowly*) Harsh. It was harsh.

*She goes and sits on the bed next to GAIL and JUNIOR.*

I didn't mean to make a bad impression. I was just trying to provide leadership. I love you people. You're the people I do my work for. You're the working class. The peasant class. Everything I've ever done I've done for you.

*She puts her head on GAIL's shoulder.*

I've got some books for you to read. If you don't know how to read I'll teach you. Teach you how to rise up. Get free. Smash the barriers that keep you hopeless. But first I need some sleep. (*lies down*) It's so hard. Being the last person in the world who really gives a shit is just so hard.

*She closes her eyes. SANDY comes in. Carrying a newspaper and a bag of groceries.*

**SANDY:** We're famous. No, that's wrong. (*to WILLIAM*) What's the word when you're famous but it's not good.

**WILLIAM:** Infamous.

**SANDY:** That's it. I knew I was close. That's what we are. It's kind of scary. (*she hands GAIL the paper*) The front page. At the bottom. (*GAIL is reading to herself*)

**WILLIAM:** This could be important. I'm thinking here of public opinion, when we come to trial. What does it say.

**GAIL:** We're terrorists ... Or we're desperate criminals. Or we're trying to start a race war ... They can't seem to make up their minds. It was all a prank. Organized crime. No, no. Yes. Here ... They settled on one. We're definitely terrorists. But with a strong local criminal element.

**JUNIOR:** Barbados.

**GAIL:** What.

**JUNIOR:** Barbados. I've seen the ads. It looks great. We could just walk slow. Everyone walks slow. Everything is done slow. Maybe I could get a job fishing. Slow fishing. One hour to bait the hook. One hour to let out the line. Six hours sitting. Waiting. Keeping your eyes closed. Can you picture it.

**GAIL:** Yeah. (*her eyes are closed*) Yeah. I'm picturing it now.

*He puts his arms around her. They kiss. Lie down.*

**WILLIAM:** I like it when they do that.

SANDY: Yeah. Why are you looking at me like that. You're not getting any ideas are you.

WILLIAM: I'm too old for you probably.

SANDY: Yes. You are.

WILLIAM: It's been so long.

SANDY: I don't care.

WILLIAM: I'm sorry. Occasionally I regress. Circumstances force me into a dark corner. Turn me into a beast. I look at your legs. And my old self has the vilest thoughts.

SANDY: Thoughts are one thing. I can live with thoughts. Just don't get any ideas for action.

WILLIAM: But you don't mind if I visualize in my mind. That's okay?

SANDY: Sure. I guess.

*He is looking at her. She squirms a bit.*

All right. That's enough. I mean it! I'm going to make something for us to eat.

*She leaves.*

WILLIAM: That's all right. You don't have to be here. I've got the picture. It's in my mind. We're on a beach. You are the same. I am younger. (*closes his eyes*) All right. Yes! It's better there, so we'll go there. We'll leave! Children. Sit up. Please. (*JUNIOR and GAIL sit up*) There's no other choice. It's the only way I can protect you. I thought we had to stay and fight this through. I thought you had a stake in this world here. That running away would solve nothing for you. But running away is absolutely the best thing to do when the world tries to make you insane. Sure. Barbados. Wherever. Somewhere warm. We'll go.

JUNIOR: How.

WILLIAM: I have money. In a bank. I told you but you didn't believe me.

GAIL: We still don't believe you.

**WILLIAM:** You'd feel a lot better if you did. Part of your problem is an absence of positive options. This makes you think in circles. I mean you have to believe in something. You might as well believe in me.

**JUNIOR:** How'd you get this money.

**WILLIAM:** The usual way. I acquired it in my previous life. I put it away anticipating my fall. I heard the voice from the pit and I opened a daily interest savings account. For emergencies. This qualifies.

**GAIL:** Can we. Really.

**WILLIAM:** We must.

**GAIL:** How.

**WILLIAM:** We just go.

**GAIL:** But things ... My mom. Things.

**WILLIAM:** We'll solve all problems eventually. But first we become safe. We put distance between us and the negative force.

**JUNIOR:** My dad. If we leave ... Remember what they said they'd do to him.

**WILLIAM:** Your father doesn't deserve any consideration.

**JUNIOR:** But ... it's for me. How I'd feel.

*He lowers his head. Long pause. GAIL looks at WILLIAM. WILLIAM gestures GAIL towards JUNIOR.*

**GAIL:** Junior ... I'm going to ask you for something. You have to look at me. This is the last time I'll ever do this. I promise ... Do this for me. Let's go.

*Pause.*

**JUNIOR:** All right ... I'd have gone any time you asked.

**GAIL:** I know.

*Pause.*

**WILLIAM:** Wonderful. This is wonderful. This is a way to protect you. I have a purpose. The pain recedes.

*He hugs them. SANDY comes on.*

**SANDY:** What's going on.

**JUNIOR:** We're leaving.

**GAIL:** We're escaping.

**WILLIAM:** We're going somewhere better.

**SANDY:** Where.

**WILLIAM:** South. Do you want to come.

**SANDY:** I don't know. What's south. Are there opportunities there. How's the economy.

*Suddenly the room is flooded by two or three strong shafts of light. A voice booms through an electric megaphone.*

**VOICE:** Attention in there. This is the police. All occupants outside. Hands behind their heads. Repeat. This is the police. Come out. We have armed men all around you.

**JUNIOR:** Get down.

*They all get down on the floor.*

**WILLIAM:** This is more than bad luck, you know. There is something else at work here. I absolutely refuse to believe this had to happen.

**VOICE:** We're going to give you five minutes! I repeat. Five minutes!

*WINEVA sits up suddenly.*

**WINEVA:** What. Who's giving me five minutes. What's going on here.

**GAIL:** The police. The police are outside.

**WINEVA:** Yeah? Great. (*jumps out of bed*) You. Kid. Where'd you put that first bunch of boxes.

**JUNIOR:** In the basement.

**WINEVA:** And you didn't look inside?

**JUNIOR:** No.

**WINEVA:** Boy, are you in for a surprise.

*She runs off.*

**WILLIAM:** If I could just put my finger on why this is happening.

*A knock. HENRY DAWSON comes in.*

**HENRY:** Don't shoot, eh. It's me. Your dad.

**JUNIOR:** What are you doing here.

**HENRY:** They sent me in to talk some sense into you. To bring you out peacefully.

**WILLIAM:** Now it makes sense!

*WILLIAM screams. And attacks HENRY. Grabs him by the collar. Shakes him. Throws him on the bed. Sits on top of him.*

I'm going to ask you a question, moron. If you lie I'll bite your jugular vein in two. Understand?

**HENRY:** Yes!

**WILLIAM:** How did the police know we were here.

**HENRY:** They had an informer.

**WILLIAM:** This next question will be more difficult for you. But I urge you to answer properly. Who was the informer.

**HENRY:** It was …

**WILLIAM:** You. Say it, moron. Say "It was me."

**HENRY:** It was … me … I had no choice. A chronic offender. This gets me ten years off my sentence. I read about those two jobs you pulled in the paper. I put two and two together.

**WILLIAM:** And for the first time in your whole life you got the right fucking answer!

**HENRY:** I was due for a break …

*WILLIAM grabs HENRY's neck. Starts to squeeze.*

**WILLIAM:** This isn't working. I want to kill him. Junior get me some wire. No wire? A shoelace will do. Anything.

**JUNIOR:** It doesn't matter, William.

**WILLIAM:** It matters more than anything in the history of the entire world. It matters more than God. Take my word for it.

**JUNIOR:** William. I'd feel better if you didn't.

*Pause.*

William.

*WILLIAM looks at JUNIOR. Gets up. Sits on the bed. HENRY sits up. Rubs his neck.*

**HENRY:** Thanks, son.

*Pause.*

Hello, Grace. Long time no see, eh.

*WINEVA rushes on. Carrying a box. Ripping it open.*

**WINEVA:** All right. It's coming down, the total shit is coming down right here. They've been begging for this. And I'm the person who's going to give it to them. Everyone catch.

*She is tossing grenades to them from the box. They are juggling them. Yelling.*

Total Armageddon. Apocalypse Now, my ass. Apocalypse *now*. Right now. Get me the Wagner. I know what to do with that Wagner crap. I'll blow their assholes through their brains. No time for kisses. But I love you all. Where's the goddamn pin on this thing. Ah, here's the little bugger.

*WILLIAM tackles her. JUNIOR grabs her grenade. WINEVA is squirming. Yelling.*

Get off me! This is my war! I'm warning you, man. You're interrupting history. Get off. Get the fuck off.

**WILLIAM:** You better help me. She's strong.

*JUNIOR helps him pin her down. SANDY and GAIL jump on her too.*

**WINEVA:** That's nothing. Four to one. That's not enough. Jesus! Just let me throw one. Just one. Please. Goddammit you scuzzy know-nothing dumb fuckhead asshole pig-screwing losers!

*SANDY hauls off and knocks her out with her fist. Pause.*

**WILLIAM:** Thank you.

**SANDY:** Yeah ... You know something ... These grenades are real.

*SANDY walks off. Staring at grenades. WILLIAM and JUNIOR, out of breath, plop down next to GAIL. HENRY walks over to WINEVA. Looks down.*

**HENRY:** That's your Uncle Ritchie's girlfriend, eh. So. So, she's supposed to have all these brains. If you hear him tell it she's something special ... So what ... It still happens doesn't it. It still goes like this.

*They are all looking at him.*

This is the way it goes, Junior. This is the way it goes. You better come out (*starts off*) See ya later!

*He leaves. Pause.*

**GAIL:** You opened up that wound again.

**JUNIOR:** It's all right.

**GAIL:** Let me look at it.

**JUNIOR:** I just remembered something he said to me once when I was a kid. My dad. We were out in the park. I don't know why. And there were some kids playing baseball. We sat there quietly watching them for a while and then he looked at me and said, "What's the purpose of this game?" I thought he meant something important by it at first. That it was one of those meaning-of-life questions. Then you know what? I realized the dumb jerk just didn't understand the rules. I mean baseball. Where'd he spend his life. In a cave? I gotta believe he blackmailed my mother into marrying him. I gotta believe it was something like that or I'd go crazy.

*Light shafts flash. The voice comes on.*

**VOICE:** Come out. We want you to come out now.

**GAIL:** I guess we better go.

**WILLIAM:** I will of course be arranging for a first-class lawyer. Things will not be too bad. Unfortunately this is just speculation.

**GAIL:** It's … just so frustrating. (*she puts her head on JUNIOR's shoulder*) Where's Sandy.

**SANDY:** Right here.

*SANDY walks on.*

**GAIL:** Where were you.

**SANDY:** Down the hall. Looking out the window. You should see the crowd out there. Fifty cops. Two hundred people. Five TV cameras. It's kind of scary.

**GAIL:** Are you going out.

**SANDY:** Nah. I'm going upstairs. I need a hot bath.

**GAIL:** They'll just come in and get you.

**SANDY:** I can handle that. I need a bath. (*starts off, stops*) Ah, what's the use. I might as well go out there and get it over with. (*starts off in the opposite direction*) I'm just a bit confused here. If there was only something I could gain from this. Just about anything would do.

**WILLIAM:** Are you looking for anything in particular.

**SANDY:** Profit. Profit is the best thing. I understand that the best.

**WILLIAM:** Well, perhaps you could sell your story to the press. Diary of a Teenage Terrorist or something to that effect.

**SANDY:** Really?

**WILLIAM:** You'd have to jazz it up.

**SANDY:** I could do that.

**WILLIAM:** Tell a few colourful lies. Talk about your past. Truly exploit yourself and everyone you know.

**SANDY:** I could do that. If you guys don't mind.

**GAIL:** Okay with me.

**JUNIOR:** Sure. Go ahead.

**SANDY:** Yeah. I will. See you later.

    *She leaves. WILLIAM gets up.*

**WILLIAM:** I'll go out too. Tell them you'll be along. Take your time. I'll tell them a long story to keep their minds occupied. I'll use poetry. They'll be dazzled. You could have an hour or two alone, if I reach top form.

**JUNIOR:** What about her.

**WILLIAM:** I'm taking her with me. (*he goes over to WINEVA*) This is a person of terrifying logic here. I would very much like to attend her trial, just to hear her defend herself. And scare the jury out of their minds ... Listen ... I'm sincerely sorry. I thought for sure I could save you.

**JUNIOR:** You were wrong.

**GAIL:** Yeah, it's bigger than you, William. Whatever it is ... is enormous.

**WILLIAM:** Other people would want to talk in terms of social patterns. Real things, like economic reform. Re-education. They'd dismiss the theory of the hanging shadow with a sneer. These are people who are members of another class. The skiing class. The long outdoor-summer class. Historically, philosophically, they make me sick. The hanging shadow of course exists. I say fuck it, but it exists. Take your time coming out, please.

*He picks up* WINEVA. *Puts her over his shoulder.*

I love you both.

*He starts off.* WINEVA *raises her head.*

**WINEVA:**  Hey. Where are we going.

**WILLIAM:**  We're going out there to give them a piece of your mind.

**WINEVA:**  Great.

*They leave.* JUNIOR *and* GAIL *are sitting on the edge of the bed.* JUNIOR *puts his arms around* GAIL.

**JUNIOR:**  What happens now.

**GAIL:**  We go to jail.

**JUNIOR:**  No, seriously.

**GAIL:**  What do you mean. You still think I can solve this mess, don't you. You've got a picture of me in your head a million times bigger than everyone else. Standing there, with some magical tool, fixing the world like it's a car or something.

**JUNIOR:**  Well, if anyone could do that it'd be you.

**GAIL:**  We're going to jail. Young lovers doomed, taking the plunge. This is that cliff, Junior. That one I read about in a dozen books ... In the books it was a bit romantic.

**JUNIOR:**  You'll think of something.

**GAIL:**  Please. Stop saying that. You're going to drive me nuts.

**JUNIOR:**  Sure. What do you want me to say instead.

*He kisses her forehead.*

**GAIL:**  Just be ... realistic.

*JUNIOR puts his arms around GAIL.*

**JUNIOR:**  Sure. Okay ... Okay, we're going to jail. But it won't be too bad. There's no serious time inside involved here. You might even walk away. There's ... what's that called.

**GAIL:**  Extenuating circumstances.

**JUNIOR:** Yeah. That's right. There's that. Don't worry.

**GAIL:** I'm not. Not about that. Not really. Any separation would be kind of lousy.

**JUNIOR:** Really.

**GAIL:** But it's not that ... Tell me this isn't the start of something bad. Just the beginning of a bad life, you know.

**JUNIOR:** It's not ... Now you tell me.

**GAIL:** It's not.

**JUNIOR:** You're sure?

*Pause. GAIL shrugs.*

**GAIL:** No. And that's what really scares me.

*Pause.*

**JUNIOR:** You know what scares me? I could get mad. I could get really mad I could kill someone.

**GAIL:** Anyone could feel like that sometimes.

**JUNIOR:** Could you.

**GAIL:** Yeah, I think so.

**JUNIOR:** Could you kill someone.

**GAIL:** I think so.

**JUNIOR:** Who.

**GAIL:** Anyone. It would depend.

**JUNIOR:** Depend on who made you mad

**GAIL:** Yeah.

**JUNIOR:** Could be anyone. Scary.

**GAIL:** Yeah I don't want to go out there.

*He kisses her head.*

**JUNIOR:** Then let's see if they've got the stomach to come in and get us.

**GAIL:** Yeah. Let's. In the meantime

*She starts to pug his shirt off over his head.*

**JUNIOR:** Now?

**GAIL:** Now.

**JUNIOR:** What about them. Outside.

**GAIL:** The hell with them. I mean it. The hell with them.

*She kisses him. They wrap themselves around each other. Settle back. GAIL leans back. Smiles. Holds out the bottom of her sweater. JUNIOR smiles. Slowly puts his head inside.*

*Blackout.*

*End.*

# Better Living

*Better Living* was first produced by Toronto's CentreStage Company at the St. Lawrence Centre on May 15, 1986 with the following cast:

JACK  Peter Blais

JUNIOR  Doug Greenall

GAIL  Catherine Disher

NORA  Marion Gilsenan

MARY ANN  Nancy Palk

ELIZABETH  Dixie Seatle

TOM  Michael Hogan

Director: Bill Glassco
Set Designer: Douglas A. McLean
Lighting Designer: Lynne Hyde
Costume Designer: John Pennoyer

*Persons*

**NORA**, late forties

**JACK**, early fifties

**GAIL**, seventeen

**MARY ANN**, twenty-seven

**ELIZABETH**, thirty

**TOM**, early fifties

**JUNIOR**, late teens

*Note*

There is an intermission between Scenes Five and Six.

## SCENE ONE

*The kitchen of an old run-down house in the east end. A screen door leads to an overgrown backyard. There is a doorway into a hall. A door leading to the basement. In one corner a wicker rocker. Beside the rocker a pile of yellowing newspapers. The linoleum floor is warped and slopes badly. The walls are partly painted, partly papered. In the yard is an old '62 Mercury sedan, an old maple tree, and by the house, a small electric generator. The kitchen window is open. The cable from the generator runs through the window and into the basement.*

*NOTE: In the 1999 Toronto production (for which many of the revisions in this version were made) there was an attempt to show a little more of this world. An upstairs area was roughed in and some of the backyard, including the tree, was plainly visible.*

*As the lights come up the kettle is whistling on the stove. The radio on the fridge is blaring with rock and roll. JUNIOR and GAIL are upstairs having sex. They are both young and loud. Suddenly the sound of drilling. They stop. There is a priest at the screen door.*

*The priest hollers hello then comes in. Looks around. Sees the cable going to the basement. Frowns. Turns off the radio. Goes to the stove. Turns it off. Takes the kettle and starts to make himself a cup of tea. As he is doing this JUNIOR, in his underwear, walks in from the hall. Sees the priest. Turns. Runs off. The priest takes his tea to the table.*

*The drilling stops. GAIL, in her underwear, leans in from the hall.*

GAIL: Oh, hi. I thought it was you. Just checking.

*The priest smiles. Nods. GAIL turns back into the doorway. Yells.*

GAIL: It's okay, Junior! It's just my uncle! (*entering kitchen*) Uncle Jack, you gave my boyfriend a real scare. He thought they'd come to get him or something.

JACK: He's a fugitive from the Church?

GAIL:  Come on, you know what I mean.

JACK:  I hardly ever know what you mean, Gail. His name is Junior?

*GAIL gets something to drink from the fridge.*

GAIL:  Yeah. He rides a motorcycle.

JACK:  Is that why his name is Junior.

GAIL:  Maybe. Listen, you're not going to tell me it's a sin or something are you.

JACK:  I had a motorcycle once.

GAIL:  Not motorcycles. Sex. Sex outside the Church.

JACK:  You've been having sex outside the church?

GAIL:  Come on, outside the Church's domain. You know, the domain of marriage.

JACK:  The domain of marriage is highly overrated.

*Sound of drilling resumes. JACK shouts over the din.*

JACK:  You can screw your brains out and it won't make a bit of difference. As for the sin of it. Who cares!!

GAIL:  (*shouting as well*) Are you saying you don't care how I lead my life, Uncle Jack!

JACK:  You got it!

GAIL:  You used to!

JACK:  No. I just said I did! What the hell's going on! Where's your mother!

*Drilling stops.*

GAIL:  That's her. In the basement. She's building an addition to the house.

JACK:  Whatya mean an addition? Turning the basement into a rec-room? Panelling? That sort of thing?

GAIL:  No. Tunnelling. Digging. That sort of thing. She's putting the addition underground. Under the backyard. She's got this plan. A big square room under the backyard. Don't you think that's weird.

JACK:  A bit.

GAIL: Junior thinks it's weird. He says it won't work. You need beams. Big beams for support. Where's she going to get beams.

*GAIL's clothes, a sweater and jeans, are scattered around the kitchen and hallway. She starts getting dressed.*

JACK: She'll probably give up when she reaches the outer wall. It's concrete.

GAIL: It's gone. She's four feet out from the house now. You wouldn't believe the mess down there. Mud. Sludge. It's like a mine shaft or something. I think she's going crazy. You're her brother. You should talk to her.

JACK: What should I say.

GAIL: Say this. Say we don't need an extra room. Say Mary Ann and the baby can have my room. And I'll sleep in the attic.

JACK: Oh, I get it. Mary Ann is coming home.

GAIL: No surprise there, right. Not for me anyway. I knew that marriage wouldn't last. Mary Ann's just like Mom and Mom kills marriage. She killed her own, right.

JACK: Not exactly.

GAIL: Well where's my father. Gone. Dead? Insane? Some new life somewhere? He's not here though is he.

JACK: People have been telling you for years that wasn't your mother's fault.

GAIL: Yeah but you're all liars.

*GAIL starts putting on her boots.*

JACK: What.

GAIL: No offense. It's just that when it comes to talking about my Dad I think you're full of shit for some reason.

JACK: Really.

GAIL: Do you want something to eat.

JACK: No.

GAIL: You look like crap.

JACK: How's school?

**GAIL:**  Community college? Oh cool. Real cool. I'm gonna quit. Are you going to try and talk me out of it.

**JACK:**  No. Quit. Become a hairdresser. Who cares.

**GAIL:**  I'm not smart enough for anything else.

**JACK:**  Please. You're smart enough to do anything you want.

**GAIL:**  I knew you'd try and talk me out of it. I love you.

*She kisses his head.*

**GAIL:**  Okay. I'll stick it out for one more year. But that's it.

**JACK:**  Like I said. Who cares.

**GAIL:**  I love you. You wanna know why?

**JACK:**  Not really.

**GAIL:**  Because you love me. It's that simple.

*JUNIOR comes in. Dressed. Jacket over his shoulder.*

**JUNIOR:**  Let's go. It's time.

**JACK:**  Time for what.

**GAIL:**  Time to go. Junior, this is my Uncle Jack.

**JUNIOR:**  Pleasure to meet you, Your Honour.

**GAIL:**  Junior's a Protestant. "Your Honour" is just for judges, Junior.

**JACK:**  Force of habit, eh.

**JUNIOR:**  I guess. Well, it's time.

**JACK:**  Actually it's past time. Look … (*looks at his watch*) … You're late.

**JUNIOR:**  For what.

**GAIL:**  He's kidding.

**JUNIOR:**  Yeah? (*to JACK*) Kidding. Hey, that's great, man. Good for you. I mean that.

**JACK:**  I'm sure you do.

**GAIL:**  Get going. I'll catch up.

*JUNIOR leaves.*

**JACK:**  Charming young man. And a real way with words too.

**GAIL:** Don't judge him too harshly. It's his father who's the real criminal. A record this long.

*JUNIOR's voice from outside singing an Aerosmith song.*

**JUNIOR:** "I was crying when I met you ..."

*JACK goes to the kitchen window. He looks out at JUNIOR singing his guts out.*

**JUNIOR:** "Now I'm trying to forget you ..."

**GAIL:** I'm trying to ... suggest alternatives to a life of crime. I've told him he has singing talent ... (*notices JACK's look*) Yeah okay. But it'll keep him busy for awhile.

**JUNIOR:** (*still looking for that Aerosmith essence*) "Crying ... Cryy-yyy—innnggg ..."

**GAIL:** See you soon. Talk to my mother.

**JACK:** I will.

*GAIL leaves. JACK starts toward the basement door.*

*NORA sticks her head out from the basement door. She is wearing a floppy black rubber rain hat.*

**NORA:** Criminals. She brings criminals into my house.

*NORA comes into the room. She is also wearing a rainslicker, gloves and boots.*

**JACK:** Oh my God.

*NORA removes her work clothes. She hangs them carefully on a row of hooks as she speaks.*

**NORA:** He's a burglar. I've got friends on the police force who've told me how burglars work. He's casing this place for a break-in. And he's got someone working on the inside.

**JACK:** You mean Gail?

**NORA:** I think she's over-stimulated. Too much copulation. Generally I don't mind. I even encourage it up to a point. All my daughters have been encouraged to copulate for the good of their general health. But Gail's had too much. And now she's at this guy's mercy. He's probably just too damn good at it. A machine. A sex machine. And a break and enter artist. I was hoping she'd do better.

*NORA is down to her summer dress and rubber boots now.*

**NORA:** Have you noticed how much Gail looks like her father?

**JACK:** It's true.

**NORA:** You know what, Jack. I think it's a possible case of possession. It's possible her father has seized her soul. Do you think you could investigate.

**JACK:** Exorcism is frowned on, you know.

**NORA:** Generally speaking, a wise position. It tends to encourage hysteria. But in Gail's case it could be the genuine thing. Be discreet, dear. But the next time you see her, give her a whiff. You remember Tom's smell. Give her a whiff and see if the odour is familiar.

**JACK:** I'll try.

**NORA:** Tea?

**JACK:** I have some.

**NORA:** I'll join you. (*making herself a cup*) I don't care for the stuff much but it gives me something to do with my hands.

**JACK:** Nora, I think we should talk about this ... work you're doing in the basement. I mean it seems like a ... big project.

**NORA:** It is.

**JACK:** Well maybe you should get some professional—

**NORA:** Yeah I know. Gail thinks I'm crazy. And I know she has reasons for thinking that. But they're stupid reasons. She doesn't understand my initiative. Where would my family be now without my initiative. We need more room. I can't go up. It's expensive. I can't build on the left. Attached. I can't build on the right. Attached. I could have built on the back but then we wouldn't have a yard. The kids, the little ones will need a yard.

**JACK:** Digging a room under the ground is dangerous, Nora.

**NORA:** Beams, right? I know all about beams. Gail's criminal friend thinks he knows more about beams than me. But I've got friends who are architects and they told me about all that beam stuff. I'll put them in myself. I'm developing strength by the day. Sure there are dangers. I had a cave-in last week. But the little ones will need a backyard. So underground is the only choice.

JACK: What "little ones." You mean Mary Ann's baby?

NORA: It won't stop there. My daughters are coming home. The economy is not sympathetic to women with babies. So all my daughters will be coming home as soon as they have a baby. And once they're here they'll probably have more babies. In fact, I'll encourage it. Mary Ann will have more soon. Elizabeth will have some as soon as she's established in her profession.

JACK: Elizabeth has been practising law for five years now, Nora.

NORA: Elizabeth does not want to practise law as a profession, Jack. Law is just an inroad to her true destination.

JACK: Which is what.

NORA: Elizabeth will enter politics and be in charge of foreign affairs, so she can send huge amounts of aid to all the poor people in Third World countries. Our Elizabeth has a heart the size of a mountain. She's like you.

JACK: She's like you.

NORA: She's like us.

JACK: Nora. I have something to tell you.

NORA: You're ill.

JACK: No.

NORA: Please, be honest. If you're ill, tell me. I know you've lost your faith but you shouldn't let it kill you.

JACK: Nora, I haven't lost my faith. I've just lost my enthusiasm. And that won't kill me, it will just make me pathetic. Now sit down. This is going to be a shock.

NORA: (*sitting*) I can't be shocked. I won't let myself be shocked. (*standing*) Wait. Maybe I can't be shocked. But I can be upset destabilized ... devastated. (*sits*)

JACK: I received a phone call this morning. From Tom.

NORA: Tom who.

JACK: Your husband.

NORA: He's dead, thank God. I saw him die. In my dreams. Hundreds of dreams. Hundreds of deaths. Cruel, slow. Painful.

**JACK:**  He called. He's on his way home.

**NORA:**  (*stands*) Excuse me. I have work to do. For my daughters. And their daughters.

> *NORA grabs her work clothes and goes downstairs. JACK sighs. Then goes over to the basement door.*

**JACK:**  Nora! He said if you don't let him come home he'll go to the police. He'll go to the police with proof that we tried to kill him.

**NORA:**  (*from basement*) That's silly. A prank. Stupidity. The stupidest thing I've ever heard.

> *NORA lets the jackhammer rip. JACK shouts over the noise.*

**JACK:**  Nora! Listen. There could be proof. Think back a little. Remember. Please, just try to remember!

> *Sound of drilling stops suddenly.*

**JACK:**  We did try to kill him!!

> *JACK realizes too late he has shouted this last line unnecessarily. NORA appears at the top of the basement stairs.*

**JACK:**  Can you remember.

**NORA:**  I can if you want me to, dear.

**JACK:**  We tried our best to kill him.

**NORA:**  If you say so. It's hard to believe though.

**JACK:**  Yes it is.

**NORA:**  I mean it's just not like us to fail at something like that. Especially when we're trying our best … Well maybe we weren't trying our best at all.

> *NORA goes back down the stairs. JACK just lowers his head.*
>
> *Blackout.*

## SCENE TWO

*MARY ANN, thin, nervous-looking, is in the middle of the kitchen, turning in a slow circle.*

**MARY ANN:**  It's worse. Is it my imagination. No, it's definitely worse. How could she let it get worse.

*ELIZABETH comes in from the hall. Carrying several pieces of luggage. Wearing a business suit. Looking annoyed.*

**ELIZABETH:**  It costs money to make it better.

**MARY ANN:**  Couldn't you give it to her.

**ELIZABETH:**  She wouldn't take it. I'm supposed to be saving for my campaign fund.

**MARY ANN:**  I can't stay here.

**ELIZABETH:**  (*starting off*) Okay I'll take you back home.

**MARY ANN:**  I can't go home. I just left home. I can't go back.

**ELIZABETH:**  Well, you've got a problem then don't you.

**MARY ANN:**  It smells.

**ELIZABETH:**  I don't smell anything.

**MARY ANN:**  You're used to it.

**ELIZABETH:**  How. I don't live here.

**MARY ANN:**  Lucky you. Why can't I stay at your apartment.

**ELIZABETH:**  Because I don't want you there, Mary Ann.

**MARY ANN:**  You really like living alone?

**ELIZABETH:**  That's not what I said. I said I don't want *you* there.

**MARY ANN:**  Why not.

**ELIZABETH:**  Because I'd have to take care of you. Cook for you. Wash for you. Always be telling you cute little jokes to help you forget your troubles. Other than that, it'd be a blast.

**MARY ANN:**  I thought you loved me. You always said you loved me. Maybe you were lying. Were you lying.

**ELIZABETH:**  Yes. I was.

**MARY ANN:** You can put my luggage down, you know. You don't have to stand there holding it like a martyr. I know you think I'm weak.

**ELIZABETH:** You are weak.

**MARY ANN:** Please don't be cruel. You never used to be cruel. Being a lawyer has made you cruel.

**ELIZABETH:** Are you going to cry.

**MARY ANN:** No.

**ELIZABETH:** I know you want to.

**MARY ANN:** I don't cry anymore. I'm much stronger. Marriage has made me tough. Look at me. Take a fresh look at me and tell me if I'm not tough.

**ELIZABETH:** Go ahead. Cry if you want.

**MARY ANN:** Thank you!

*MARY ANN bursts into tears. Cries for awhile. Holds out her arms to ELIZABETH to come here for a hug. ELIZABETH just looks at her.*

*JACK comes up from the basement. Carrying a flask.*

**JACK:** Ah. Happy reunions. (*takes a drink*) The heart bursts. The stomach churns. Words fail. (*takes another drink*)

**MARY ANN:** Uncle Jack.

*MARY ANN runs to him. Throws her arms around him.*

**MARY ANN:** I'm home. My marriage failed. You knew it would.

**JACK:** I did?

**ELIZABETH:** You didn't?

**JACK:** We can discuss this in more detail with even less clarity a little later. Elizabeth, can I talk to you outside for a moment.

**ELIZABETH:** Absolutely.

*ELIZABETH drops the luggage. JACK and ELIZABETH go into the backyard. NORA is standing at the basement door.*

**NORA:** Don't feel left out. They were always close. They both have mountainous hearts. He just wants to confide in her. He's lost his faith. He'll fall a great distance if he doesn't get it back. He's a great man. He played hockey when he was young. And he had an interesting sexual life. He sacrificed a lot to become a priest.

MARY ANN: Hi, Mom.

NORA: I'm covered in mud or I'd give you a kiss. You know that don't you. I kissed you a lot when you were younger. I have nothing against kissing. I encourage it. Remember?

MARY ANN: Yes.

NORA: Where's the baby.

MARY ANN: I left her with Larry.

NORA: Who's he.

MARY ANN: My husband.

NORA: Does he like babies.

MARY ANN: He likes his own.

NORA: Well, what can I say. I was hoping you'd bring me a baby.

MARY ANN: She's coming … eventually. I needed some time on my own.

NORA: Why.

MARY ANN: To … you know. Think.

NORA: Think about what.

MARY ANN: Things.

NORA: What things.

MARY ANN: Things about me. How I feel. Why I feel the things I feel and why—

NORA: No no, take my advice. Get your baby back. Your husband could become fond of it. Stranger things have happened. I can't afford the legal costs if we have to go to court to get her back. And don't expect Elizabeth to work for nothing. She's saving for her political campaign. Take my advice. Call Barry.

MARY ANN: Larry.

NORA: Call him. The phone is in the living room.

*ELIZABETH comes in.*

NORA: Tell her to call Barry!

**ELIZABETH:** Call Barry!

**MARY ANN:** Larry!

**ELIZABETH:** Do it!

*MARY ANN groans. Leaves.*

**NORA:** She still does what you tell her. I like that. The oldest still has influence. The family structure is intact. She looks awful, doesn't she. Like a bird. A frightened ... bird. Isn't she. A bird.

**ELIZABETH:** Yeah yeah, she's a bird.

**NORA:** I hate birds. I'm sure Mary Ann knows that. Do you think she's behaving like a bird to get back at me for something awful I did to her when she was young. Did I do anything awful to her when she was young.

**ELIZABETH:** Mom, you have to be quiet for a minute. Okay?

**NORA:** Are you thinking. You have your thinking look on. It used to scare me when you were little. I thought you were having abdominal pains.

**ELIZABETH:** Uncle Jack told me. About Dad wanting to come back.

**NORA:** Your Uncle Jack is not well. Don't listen to him until he gets better. He drinks, you know. Not a lot. But enough to get him fantasizing.

**ELIZABETH:** Listen to me.

**NORA:** You're frightening when you talk like that. When you say "listen to me." It's the tone of voice. I know it's necessary for your career but it scares the ones who love you.

**ELIZABETH:** Listen. Dad's not coming back here. No way. If that son of a bitch sets one foot in this house I'll kill him.

*MARY ANN is standing in the doorway.*

**MARY ANN:** So will I.

**NORA:** Great. We could all kill him. That would be nice. If your father was alive he'd need killing, we all know that. But he's dead. He died in some remote jungle. Five years ago. A tree fell on him. Crushed both his legs. He lay in a primitive jungle clinic for five days. Without the benefit of morphine. Out of his mind with pain. Agonizing brutal pain. And then he died ... They buried him in a swamp.

**MARY ANN:** You never told us that. I never knew that. Did you, Elizabeth.

**ELIZABETH:** She just made it up.

**NORA:** You know I can't make things up, Elizabeth. I have no talent for that kind of thing at all. I've got a copy of the death certificate.

**ELIZABETH:** Get it.

**NORA:** It's in the vault. The bank vault. You know in the little box. I'll have to find the key.

**ELIZABETH:** What about his pension. He was on the police force for fifteen years. You must have some money coming to you.

**NORA:** I'll make inquiries. Now why don't you two make us all something to eat and I'll just finish up downstairs. Have to put the tools away. Always clean the tools. Put them away. Start fresh the next day.

*NORA goes downstairs.*

**MARY ANN:** She's worse. Isn't she. She's living in a fourth tense. She's taken past, present, future and combined them somehow. Look, she's still got Dad's old car in the backyard.

**ELIZABETH:** She says she'll sell it when she gets the right price.

**MARY ANN:** It's been there for eleven years. And listen to how she talks. Private. Obsessive. She's got private obsessive plans for that car. She's worse.

**ELIZABETH:** She's not ... worse. She's just more intense.

**MARY ANN:** Well, why. Why is she more intense? Menopause?

**ELIZABETH:** Give me a break. Menopause doesn't make women dig holes under the ground. Only intense, single-minded women ... dig holes under the ground.

**MARY ANN:** That's what she's doing down there? That's what all the mud is from?

**ELIZABETH:** You didn't ask?

**MARY ANN:** I was afraid to ask.

**ELIZABETH:** Yeah. Because you're a bird.

**MARY ANN:** What.

**ELIZABETH:** A bird! You're a fucking bird! Listen, what are you trying to pull with this bird stuff anyway. You know Mom hates them. What did she ever do to you?!

**MARY ANN:** What are you talking about?!

**ELIZABETH:** Wake up. Take responsibility for your own problems. You're twenty-seven years old. Act it!

**MARY ANN:** Okay!

**ELIZABETH:** Good!

**MARY ANN:** I mean I'll try. I'm not sure I'm ready to just all of a sudden—

**ELIZABETH:** I give up. Listen, just cook us all some supper. I've got to go get something. (*starts off*)

**MARY ANN:** What.

**ELIZABETH:** You don't want to know.

**MARY ANN:** I hate it when you do that. If I didn't want to know why would I —

**ELIZABETH:** (*turning back*) A gun. Yeah you heard me—a gun. Our Dad, Mister Wonderful, is coming home. And I'm going to blow his goddamn head off. Sorry you asked?

**MARY ANN:** No. I meant what I said before. I'll kill him too.

**ELIZABETH:** We both can't kill him. Cook supper. And call Larry.

**MARY ANN:** Barry! (*smiles*) Yeah, Larry.

**ELIZABETH:** And get your kid back. Mom wants the kid here.

**MARY ANN:** Okay.

**ELIZABETH:** By the way when are you going to give her a name.

**MARY ANN:** What's the hurry.

**ELIZABETH:** She's eight months old.

**MARY ANN:** I'm worried about making a mistake. Suppose I give her the wrong name and she's stuck with it her whole life.

**ELIZABETH:** Pitiful. (*starts off again*)

**MARY ANN:** Elizabeth.

**ELIZABETH:** (*stopping*) What!

**MARY ANN:** You were just kidding about the gun, weren't you. Kidding about killing him. I was. You were too, weren't you.

**ELIZABETH:** Oh, sure. What did he ever do to deserve being killed.

*She leaves.*

**MARY ANN:** It's worse. It's definitely worse.

*Blackout.*

## SCENE THREE

*Later.*

*It's dark outside. MARY ANN is stirring sauce on the stove. GAIL is sitting and reading at the table. NORA is busy putting a black tablecloth and candles on the table. And talking.*

**NORA:** I've been drilling and digging for days. Everything was going great. But yesterday I came across the roots of that old maple tree. They're huge. They gotta go. They'll be right in the middle of the new room. Don't worry. There are ways. Dynamite maybe.

*GAIL and MARY ANN look at each other.*

**NORA:** Don't worry. I'll buy a book that tells me how to do it right. There are books out now that tell you how to do everything. In theory there's nothing you can't do if you can find the book. Actually, finding the book is the only problem. Maybe I'll write a book that tells people how to find the book that tells them how to do what they need to do. Anyway it's great. I'll get rid of the big maple's roots and learn a little about dynamite at the same time. (*lights the candles*)

*JUNIOR comes in the back door.*

**JUNIOR:** Hey!

**GAIL:** Hey.

**JUNIOR:** Why didn't you come over to that place I said I'd be.

**GAIL:** I didn't want to.

**JUNIOR:** Whatcha doin'.

**GAIL:** What's it look like I'm doing.

**JUNIOR:** It looks like you're reading.

**GAIL:** Good for you.

**JUNIOR:** How come you're always reading. And stuff. How come you never want to hang out with my friends.

**GAIL:** Because your friends are assholes, Junior.

**JUNIOR:** All of them?

**GAIL:** Yeah. Every single one.

*She goes back to her book. JUNIOR sits down next to her.*

**NORA:** Okay. Finished. Gail. Get the lights.

**GAIL:** I'm busy … Mary Ann!

**MARY ANN:** (*stirring intently*) What.

**GAIL:** Turn off the lights.

**MARY ANN:** No.

**NORA:** It won't work if you don't turn off the lights.

**MARY ANN:** I really don't want to do this Mom.

**NORA:** You used to like it, dear.

**MARY ANN:** No I didn't.

**GAIL:** That's me, Mom. Mary Ann never liked seances.

**JUNIOR:** Seances? (*standing*) Hey. I've got stuff to do.

**NORA:** Tell him to stay put. We need a man.

**GAIL:** Why.

**NORA:** Because we're calling the spirit of a man. A man who only respects other men.

**JUNIOR:** It won't work. I don't believe in this stuff. I'm too real. I'll shatter the mood.

**NORA:** Gail. I need him. Tell him it's a way of repaying me for all the food he's eaten.

**JUNIOR:** Why doesn't she ever talk to me directly.

**NORA:** Gail. Tell him.

**GAIL:** She's got a point. You owe her.

**JUNIOR:** Hey. Didn't I give her advice about the beams.

**NORA:** Amateur advice. Tell him to do this or there will be no more uninhibited behaviour allowed in my house.

**GAIL:** She means we can't do it here anymore.

**JUNIOR:** She knows about that?

**GAIL:** Jesus, Junior. Is she deaf. Is she blind.

**JUNIOR:** I thought she was … you know … "naive."

*GAIL grabs JUNIOR. Sits him down. NORA turns off the lights.*

GAIL: Jesus. Look, just do it. It's no big deal. We call the dead once a month. All our dead relatives. Who are we calling tonight, Mom.

NORA: Your father.

GAIL: What.

MARY ANN: Count me out. I'm cooking.

*MARY ANN concentrates hard on the sauce.*

GAIL: Who says he's dead.

NORA: I do.

GAIL: Since when.

NORA: Today.

GAIL: He died today?

NORA: No, I'm *saying* he died today. He died five years ago.

GAIL: Mary Ann! Is she telling me the truth here! Is he dead. Did you know.

MARY ANN: Leave me alone. I'm stirring my sauce.

GAIL: I don't believe this. You're unbelievable, Mother. Don't you think we've got any feelings.

NORA: I can see this is a sore point with certain people. A dead father usually is. I'm just trying to help.

*GAIL turns the lights back on.*

GAIL: How is this helping. You're supposed to be comforting in situations like this. You know, put your arms around me. Break it to me gently. Oh no, not you. You call a seance.

NORA: You fail to understand what I'm doing.

GAIL: You fail to explain what you're doing.

NORA: I forget to explain, Gail. I have a lot on my mind. Mary Ann, you tell her.

MARY ANN: I'm not saying anything. I'm cooking. Then I'm going to sleep. I'm sorry I came.

GAIL: Then leave.

MARY ANN: I can't.

**GAIL:** Then talk, you gormless twit.

**NORA:** Be kind. She's nervous.

**JUNIOR:** Something sure smells good.

**MARY ANN:** Thank you. It's my sauce.

**GAIL:** Jesus Fucking Christ. What a bunch of dickheads. Look. Someone tell me what's going on or I'll go berserk. I'll scream. I'll break things. (*picks up a frying pan from the counter, bangs it down hard*) I'll kill!

*NORA stands. Advances on GAIL.*

**NORA:** Look. Her father's eyes. Her father's temper. Her father's dirty language. Gail, do you feel something inside you. Some alien presence. Some masculine force.

**GAIL:** Mary Ann! What's she talking about?

**MARY ANN:** She thinks you're being possessed by Father's ghost.

**JUNIOR:** I gotta leave. Really.

**GAIL:** (*in a deep violent voice*) Hey! You! Shut up! Stay put! Or you fuckin' die!!

*NORA suddenly grabs GAIL's head with both hands.*

**NORA:** Tom. You evil man. Leave this child. In the name of the Father and the Son and the Holy Spirit I command you to leave this poor innocent child. You evil murdering bastard!

*GAIL screams. Faints.*

**JUNIOR:** Holy fuck.

**NORA:** It's done. Tom's evil spirit is out of her. The seance isn't necessary. Do you believe me now, Mary Ann? Your father is dead.

*TOM suddenly appears at the screen door. His face dimly illuminated by the outside light.*

**TOM:** Bullshit.

*He is a solidly built man. Tough. Worn. Wearing a plaid shirt. Work-pants and boots. An old beaten fedora. They all look at him. Hard. TOM opens the door. Comes in. Looks around.*

**TOM:** Nothing changes. Things just fall apart. Be careful though. The worst is yet to come.

*Suddenly* ELIZABETH *appears from the hall. Wearing an evening dress. Holding a gun. She fires it five times in his direction.*

*Blackout.*

## SCENE FOUR

*One hour later.*

*TOM and JUNIOR at the table. A bottle of whiskey. Two glasses.*

**JUNIOR:** I can't believe she did that. That was ... unbelievable, man.

**TOM:** She was trying to scare me to death. But I can't be scared anymore. I've been scared to the limit.

**JUNIOR:** I was scared. I didn't know blanks sounded like ... you know ... real bullets.

**TOM:** The secret is in expecting the unexpected and expecting it to be bad. No use expecting anything good. It never comes. The secret is expecting the worst. But knowing when it's only sneaking around. When it's just teasing. And when it's actually coming right at you.

**JUNIOR:** I don't know what that means.

**TOM:** Who are you, anyway.

**JUNIOR:** Junior Dawson. I'm Gail's boyfriend.

**TOM:** Gail's the youngest.

**JUNIOR:** I know that.

**TOM:** She was only seven years old the last time I saw her. Which one of those women was Gail.

**JUNIOR:** The one lying unconscious on the floor.

**TOM:** Did she have a fit.

**JUNIOR:** I don't know. Maybe.

**TOM:** She had fits when she was a baby. Her mother was in labour thirty-six hours. Gail was born with brain damage. She took medication. It cost a fortune but I paid it gladly. The fits went away. When did they come back.

**JACK:** I don't know.

**TOM:** You should. If you're serious about her, get to know her liabilities and her strengths. What are her strengths.

**JUNIOR:** I'm not sure. She's funny.

**TOM:** Gets that from her mother's side. Wacko. The whole family.

**JUNIOR:** No . I meant she's got a good sense of humour.

**TOM:** She does? What's she find funny.

**JUNIOR:** Everything.

**TOM:** Everything? What's so funny about everything. I'd be suspicious. When she was young she'd laugh before she got her fits, you know. Maybe that's what brought them on. She'd laugh until she lost her breath and then her eyes would roll back in her head. We'll put a stop to it before it gets outta hand again. Don't do anything that encourages her to laugh. You might start by dressing differently.

**JUNIOR:** She says she likes the way I dress.

**TOM:** Maybe it's just good for a laugh. Take precautions. Buy some real clothes. Do you have a job.

**JUNIOR:** I'm a musician.

**TOM:** What do you play.

**JUNIOR:** I sing.

**TOM:** Sing something.

**JUNIOR:** Ah … Maybe later.

**TOM:** Definitely later. Where do you live.

**JUNIOR:** At home. With my dad.

**TOM:** What's he do.

**JUNIOR:** I don't wanna talk about it.

**TOM:** What's wrong, you ashamed.

**JUNIOR:** No. Well, yeah. I am.

**TOM:** Hey! Never be ashamed of your father. Unless of course he's a crook. Is he a crook.

**JUNIOR:** Yeah. He is.

**TOM:** That's rough. But let's not dwell on it.

**JUNIOR:** You were a cop. Weren't you.

**TOM:** That's right. Fifteen years. Seven in uniform. Eight as a detective. Holdup. Fraud. Missing persons. I did a bit of everything.

**JUNIOR:** You do homicide?

**TOM:** Sure. Who do you want killed. (*laughs*) Just kidding ... A little policemen's humour. Do you pay board at home.

**JUNIOR:** Sure.

**TOM:** How'd you like to live here for nothing.

**JUNIOR:** You want me to live here? Why?

**TOM:** I need a bodyguard. I need protection.

**JUNIOR:** From who?

**TOM:** Guess.

**JUNIOR:** Them? You need protection from your own family?

**TOM:** You said it. Not me. So it's a deal? You stay here until I say you don't.

**JUNIOR:** Sure.

*ELIZABETH comes on. Carrying an old duffel bag.*

**ELIZABETH:** (*to JUNIOR*) You. Out.

**JUNIOR:** But I'm supposed to be—

**ELIZABETH:** Out. Shitface. Before I pull you out by the hair.

**JUNIOR:** (*stands*) Okay. I'm leaving but it's not because I'm afraid. It's because I'm—

**ELIZABETH:** Out!!!

*ELIZABETH stamps her foot. JUNIOR leaves.*

**TOM:** That boy scares easy.

**ELIZABETH:** Do you recognize this.

**TOM:** Sure. It's my old duffel bag. The one I used to keep my uniform in.

**ELIZABETH:** Right. It's the only thing in this house that belongs to you. I want you to take it and get out!

*She heaves it at him violently. He catches it. Lays it down.*

**TOM:** Sit down, Elizabeth. Let's talk.

*TOM sits. ELIZABETH begins to move, in an agitated manner, around him.*

**ELIZABETH:** Let's not.

TOM:  I have a legal right to be here.

ELIZABETH:  That's not true. Do you know what I do for a living. I'm a lawyer.

TOM:  No kidding. How'd you manage that.

ELIZABETH:  Hard work. A fierce sense of competition.

TOM:  I meant the money.

ELIZABETH:  Prostitution.

TOM:  Student loans, or something?

ELIZABETH:  Prostitution. Look what are you doing here.

TOM:  I'm needed here.

ELIZABETH:  Yeah? You got a message, eh. Someone here sent you a message that they needed you.

TOM:  I've been everywhere. I have experience in the real world. The Third World. I've seen starving people everywhere. They can't take it much longer. They'll be coming here soon looking for relief. I'm here to protect my family.

ELIZABETH:  (*smiles*) Oh, I get it. You're nuts, right?

TOM:  Read the newspapers. Carefully. This idyllic existence won't last much longer. Those starving people are getting restless. They want what we've got. You'll need me. I'll teach you how to hide the food. Disguise your wealth.

ELIZABETH:  Look around. What wealth.

TOM:  This place is a palace compared to what they're used to ... How much do you give your mother.

ELIZABETH:  Nothing.

TOM:  Nothing?

ELIZABETH:  Yeah, nothing. She won't take it. Anyway I don't have any—

TOM:  I thought you said you were a lawyer.

ELIZABETH:  A legal aid lawy—

TOM:  How does she get by.

ELIZABETH:  She works.

TOM:  Where.

**ELIZABETH:** Here. She stuffs envelopes. And that's the last question I'm answering. What the fuck do you care how my mother gets by? You deserted this family. You left us in emotional and financial ruin, you rotten bastard. I remember what you did here before you left. You're lucky they didn't have you locked up.

**TOM:** They're lucky I didn't have them locked up.

**ELIZABETH:** I'm calling the police.

**TOM:** That would be a mistake. Talk to your mother first.

*GAIL comes in. A blanket wrapped around her.*

**GAIL:** Yeah. Talk to Mom, I dare you.

**ELIZABETH:** Get back to bed.

**GAIL:** Who are you talking to, your filing clerk.

**ELIZABETH:** I mean it, Gail.

**GAIL:** "I mean it, Gail." Give me a break. I'm not a kid anymore. You can't intimidate me.

**ELIZABETH:** Great. I don't want to intimidate you. I just want you to get the hell out of here!

*She grabs GAIL's hair and drags her into the hall.*

**GAIL:** Ouch. Stop it. I mean it.

**ELIZABETH:** Upstairs. Out of sight. And stay there until I say you can come down. (*comes back into the kitchen. To TOM*) Now it's your turn.

*Suddenly GAIL pounces from the hall. With the blanket. Throws the blanket over ELIZABETH's head. Turns her around. Forces her through the basement door amidst a lot of cursing and shouting. Closes the door. Locks it. Turns slowly to look at TOM.*

**GAIL:** You're my dad, eh.

**TOM:** Yeah. That's who I am, Precious.

**GAIL:** Precious. That's me, eh. I've missed you, you know. I don't even have a picture of you. They threw them all out. You really pissed them off.

**TOM:** A little misunderstanding.

**GAIL:** I know all about it.

**TOM:** You do?

**GAIL:** Well not really. I was pretty young. But I've drawn conclusions based on certain things and I've decided I'm on your side.

**TOM:** I'm glad, Precious.

**GAIL:** Look, you don't have to overdo the "Precious" thing. I mean it takes some getting used to. So are you hungry. We've got spaghetti sauce. It's good by itself. Just in a bowl. Mary Ann was cooking supper. She always leaves something out. This time she left out the spaghetti.

**TOM:** (*laughs*) How is Mary Ann.

**GAIL:** She's a nervous wreck. And since she saw you, she's a totally hysterical nervous wreck. She's in bed. Shaking. Really, you have a major negative effect on these people. (*laughs*) So do you want some sauce.

**TOM:** Yeah. With bread.

**GAIL:** Sure. (*sets about getting him something to eat*) So listen. I'm quitting school. I've decided to become a hair stylist.

**TOM:** Good for you.

**GAIL:** Yeah. So that's all right, eh. It's not stupid?

**TOM:** I don't know.

**GAIL:** I'm not smart enough to be anything else.

**TOM:** That's too bad.

> TOM eats.

**GAIL:** So … So here we are. I had a dream about this. It was a bit different really. We kissed and hugged. It's okay though. Maybe that's awkward. But … maybe, you know, it's not. Who knows.

**TOM:** I can kiss you. I can do that.

**GAIL:** Sure. I can do that too. Sure.

> *They both rise awkwardly. Lean over the table. TOM gives GAIL a quick peck on the cheek. They look at each other. GAIL throws her arms around his neck.*

**GAIL:** Look the truth is I'm smart enough to be anything I want. I'm smarter than Elizabeth and she's a lawyer. When you get to know me you'll see that. I just want to leave school because I've given up. I don't care. That's depressing, eh.

**TOM:** Is it.

**GAIL:** Sure it is. Someone as smart as me giving up is depressing as hell. The thing is I'm emotionally deprived. Deprived of love. I think it's Mom. She's been weird since you left. Not loving. Caring, if you know the difference, but not loving.

**TOM:** Your mother was always weird. It's in her blood. Her whole family's paranoid schizo. I'm surprised she's not in the mental hospital by now.

**GAIL:** That's kind of cruel. I don't want you talking about my mom like that.

**TOM:** Okay.

**GAIL:** Anyway, you're missing the point. We're talking about me. I need love. Attention. So if you're going to stay you've got to do your job right. You've got to be a real father. Generous. Affectionate. You know … nice. And then maybe I'll stick it out in school one more year. No promises. We'll see how you do. (*banging on the basement door*) They're trying to escape. Don't worry. I'll protect you. I mean I'll do my best. They're awesome when they're aroused. Especially Elizabeth.

> *The door crashes open. ELIZABETH is carrying a baseball bat. NORA is carrying a shovel. TOM lowers his head over the bowl. Pulls down his hat. Eats. GAIL grabs the whiskey bottle from the table.*

**GAIL:** Stay where you are. I won't let you hurt him.

**ELIZABETH:** What has he been telling you, Gail.

**GAIL:** Plenty. Getting nervous?

**ELIZABETH:** He can't be trusted. He lies.

**GAIL:** (*to TOM*) She's nervous. The truth makes her nervous.

**ELIZABETH:** Oh, fuck off.

**GAIL:** You fuck off. This guy's my dad. He's going to liberate me. You're liberated, why can't I get liberated.

**ELIZABETH:** From what.

**GAIL:** From her!

**ELIZABETH:** Shut up. Do you want to break her heart.

**GAIL:** She broke mine. She ignores me. She lives in her own world. Maybe it's in the basement. Maybe it's on another planet. Jesus, Elizabeth, I need a parent. Dad stays.

**ELIZABETH:** Sure. If he's alive when I'm finished with him, he can stay.

**NORA:** Why is she calling the stranger "Dad."

**ELIZABETH:** What.

**GAIL:** What are you talking about.

**NORA:** Who is this man. Do you know him.

**GAIL:** She's starting. The antennae are out. Airwaves from space. Alien images flowing through her brain. (*cups her hands*) Earth to Mom. Beam in, Mom. We've got news from home. This is your husband!

**NORA:** No. I'm sorry. I realize dead fathers are sore points with certain people but I don't think I should be expected to accept marriage to total strangers.

**ELIZABETH:** Are you saying this isn't Dad, Mom?

**GAIL:** That's right, encourage her.

**ELIZABETH:** Mom. This is Dad. Believe me.

**NORA:** Well, if it makes you happy, Elizabeth, this man can be your father. I didn't know you felt so strongly about it.

**GAIL:** I'm gonna start smashing things!

**NORA:** However, your real father is dead and now inhabits the body of your sister here. (*to GAIL*) Tom, I thought I told you to leave that child, in the name of the Father and—

**GAIL:** That's it. This piece of shit goes first.

   *She picks up the rocker.*

**NORA:** Oh, not the kitchen rocker. That belonged to my mother. He hated my mother. (*to GAIL*) Tom, put that down. I'll give you fifty bucks if you put it down.

**GAIL:** Don't call me Tom. (*to ELIZABETH*) Tell her to stop calling me Tom. Tell her that's Tom. Tell her she can't keep pulling this shit.

**ELIZABETH:** Mom. Stop. Please.

**NORA:** First tell him to put that rocker down. Give him fifty bucks. Fifty bucks was his usual price to cease destruction.

**ELIZABETH:** Put it down, Tom.

**GAIL:** You called me Tom.

**ELIZABETH:** I'll give you fifty bucks.

**GAIL:** Oh I get it. Humour her. Well fuck you. I want a hundred!

*NORA rushes GAIL. Grabs her.*

**NORA:** Out. Out you vicious bastard. Putrid love-killing madman. Leave this child alone. Out out! In the name of the Father the Son—

*GAIL screams. Faints. NORA has hold of the rocker. ELIZABETH leans her head against the refrigerator. JACK bursts through the screen door.*

**JACK:** Who screamed.

**ELIZABETH:** Gail.

**NORA:** Not exactly.

**JACK:** (*kneeling over GAIL*) What's wrong with her.

**NORA:** It's all right. I think it worked this time. I exorcised him, Jack. I smelled his evil spirit as it left her body. Don't be angry, Jack. I know it's not sanctioned.

*NORA looks over at TOM. Walks to him. She puts out her hand.*

**NORA:** We haven't been introduced.

*ELIZABETH turns. Wraps her arms around the refrigerator and groans loudly as she tries to lift it.*

*Blackout.*

## SCENE FIVE

*MARY ANN and JACK. JACK is sitting in the rocker. Drinking whiskey. MARY ANN is making an apple pie from scratch. At the moment she is working on the crust.*

**MARY ANN:** I'm worried. About my future. I'm worried that my past didn't prepare me for my future. I'm worried about my basic failure to understand how the world operates. I'm worried that I won't bring my baby up right. That I can't teach her how the world operates. I'm worried about the world she'll live in. That something is deeply wrong with it. That there's a general lack of faith and security in the world and in life in general. It's too much. Maybe it's all too much. I don't understand it but maybe that's because it's too much, too complicated. Yeah. Money. Love. Responsibility. Family. Work. Crime. Food. God. Children. Insanity. Friends. Sickness. Death. Shopping. Traffic. Teeth. Pollution. War. Poverty. Infidelity. Ignorance. Fear. Shoes. Hats. Nuclear power. Cats. Winter. Sex. I worry about all those things and more. All the time. It's awful, really.

**JACK:** Have you ever considered suicide.

*She looks at him.*

**JACK:** Don't look at me like that. Officially I'm totally against it, but in your case it might be a legitimate option.

**MARY ANN:** I had this dream once. I was outside somewhere with a whole bunch of people. It was a fantastic day. Everyone was happy. Birds were singing. There was an incredible rainbow on the horizon. All of a sudden the air was filled with beautiful music. And God appeared in the sky. Smiled down at everyone. Everyone smiled back. Then God beat me to death with a hammer.

*Pause.*

**JACK:** That's the saddest thing I ever heard.

**MARY ANN:** Nah, that's nothing. I've had way worse dreams than that.

**JACK:** Promise me you'll never tell me about them.

**MARY ANN:** I might have to.

*She puts the pie in the oven.*

**JACK:** You forgot to put the apples in that pie.

**MARY ANN:** You think I'm neurotic, don't you! Fussy and neurotic.

*TOM comes up from the basement.*

**TOM:** Hi. Is there a tape measure around.

**MARY ANN:** Are you asking me. I don't know. Look, if you're going to be staying here awhile you have to learn not to ask me questions.

**TOM:** Sure. Okay.

**JACK:** There's one in the bottom drawer, on the left.

**TOM:** Thanks. (*opens drawer*) Yeah. Here it is. Thanks. Now we can get precise. Precision is poetry, that's my motto.

**JACK:** It's a great motto.

**TOM:** I've got others.

**JACK:** I can hardly wait to hear them.

**TOM:** Great. See ya.

*TOM goes into the basement.*

**MARY ANN:** Why is he still here.

**JACK:** I've got a motto of my own that might answer that for you. Here it is. Ready? "Life. Is. Dumb."

**MARY ANN:** Are you drunk.

**JACK:** Getting there.

**MARY ANN:** So … do you think he's changed. Different? Better?

**JACK:** I don't know. Maybe.

**MARY ANN:** Okay … but … he's still my dad. And what does that word mean, really? To me Dad just means trouble … confusion … violence. You know what I think. I think everything that's wrong with me can be traced back to him.

**JACK:** You could be right.

**MARY ANN:** Why do you think he's back? What does he want. He must want something.

**JACK:** I don't know.

**MARY ANN:** Well, what are you going to do about it?

**JACK:** I don't know.

*NORA and TOM come up from the basement.*

**TOM:** It's a great project, Nora. Like I said. It has ambition. Flexibility.

**NORA:** (*to JACK*) He thinks it's ambitious and flexible. He saw the ambition of it right away. We had to discuss it awhile before he saw the flexibility.

**TOM:** All it needs now is precision.

**NORA:** Precision is poetry.

**TOM:** I'm gonna go measure that old car out there. By measuring, I can determine it's weight. We're selling it for scrap.

*He goes out.*

**NORA:** Ambition, flexibility and precision are things I've admired all my life. He knew that about me as soon as he saw it.

**JACK:** Saw what? That hole down there?

**NORA:** Jack, please. It's not a hole. It's a room. And it could be more. It could be anything. It could be a new way to live. An underground world. A place to keep vegetables. A safe place to hide.

**JACK:** Uh... Hide from what?

**MARY ANN:** An underground world. What do you mean by an underground world.

**NORA:** I'd better let the stranger tell you.

**JACK:** Nora, he's not a ...

**NORA:** What?

**JACK:** He can't stay.

**NORA:** In theory, you're right. It could be a disruption of the family unit. But he has a certain kind of knowledge of the world. He knows things that might help us live better.

**JACK:** He knows nothing you can't find out for yourself. Remember there are all those books you can buy.

**NORA:** In theory, you're right. I'm an independent person with strength and initiative, and I certainly don't need a strange man to help me get by. I think I've proven that point. But, Jack, this man reads the newspapers. Carefully. He's figured certain things out. And he has information about the future.

**JACK:** What kind of information.

**NORA:** He's got proof about the coming of bad times.

**MARY ANN:** Gee Mom, are these the good times.

**NORA:** Well, of course these things are all relative. But the bad times coming are very bad times and he's got proof.

**JACK:** What.

**NORA:** A letter. A highly official government letter. Written to someone in the government from someone else in the government. You see the future isn't really the thing we think it is. To people like us the future is an open space filling up with things we can't see until we get there. But for certain other people high up in the government the future is something you make. And these people have decided to make it bad.

**JACK:** Why.

**NORA:** They've got their reasons. Overpopulation. The impurity of the social system or something. And very big deficits. Also it's possible they're just mean. It's all in the letter.

**JACK:** You've seen the letter.

**NORA:** Yes, but I can't tell you its exact content. It's a secret.

**JACK:** And how did Tom get it.

**NORA:** Also a secret. And please don't call him Tom.

**JACK:** That's his name.

**NORA:** An unfortunate coincidence. But that doesn't mean we have to use it. It creates painful echoes.

*TOM comes in.*

**TOM:** Three hundred and fifty dollars! That's how much that car will be worth as scrap.

**JACK:** Precisely?

**TOM:** Just about. The point is, it's worth nothing at the moment. It's just taking up space.

**NORA:** Exactly.

**JACK:** Precisely.

**TOM:** This man's a sceptic. Too many years living in the shadow of God. It sucks the free will right out of a man. I've seen priests all over the world. They're in pain. Priests in the Third World are the worst off. Some of them want to help. Some of them even die to help. But it doesn't. Not much anyway. Priests who die for a cause, that's an overrated thing.

**JACK:** Nora, could you and Mary Ann leave me alone with Tom for a moment.

**MARY ANN:** I'll go. I'd love to go. Where should I go.

**NORA:** Where would you like to go.

**MARY ANN:** To my room.

**TOM:** Not much can be accomplished in your room. Why do you want to go there.

**MARY ANN:** (*to NORA*) Tell him to stop asking me questions.

**NORA:** (*to TOM*) Just until she gets used to you.

**TOM:** Sorry. I forgot.

**NORA:** By the way,Tom. Do you mind if we don't call you Tom. Do you mind if we call you...Tim?

**TOM:** Sure. Tim's okay with me. (*to JACK*) How about you.

**JACK:** Sure. Call me Tim too. Who cares.

**TOM:** Nora. Why don't you take Mary Ann somewhere and explain how we're going to expand the stuffing business.

**MARY ANN:** Expand the what?

**NORA:** My envelope-stuffing business. We've got plans to make it into a going concern. It could provide a solid base income. Come with me and I'll explain it to you.

**MARY ANN:** No I don't want to hear about it.

*NORA goes to MARY ANN.*

**NORA:** It's all right. I'll just give you an outline. No details. Promise.

*They're leaving.*

**NORA:** Details worry you more than anything, don't they, dear. .

**MARY ANN:** Yes. They do.

**NORA:** I thought so.

**MARY ANN:** Details can be really scary.

**NORA:** I know. I know.

*They are gone.*

**TOM:** Weird family.

**JACK:** You think so.

**TOM:** Sure do. Full of neurotic tendencies. Undirected energy.

**JACK:** I suppose you think it's because they've been living without a man.

**TOM:** Nah. I'm not simple-minded. I've seen the world. I've seen both sexes in the world. One does as well as the other. These people here are just not organized, that's all.

**JACK:** These people here were traumatized ten years ago by a vicious madman. Lesser people would have crumbled. These people here just became … disorganized.

*While they talk, TOM checks out the kitchen's problems. A mark on the window. A leaky tap. One of the burners on the stove. The refrigerator door. The warped floor, etc.*

**TOM:** Sure. Listen. I never said they didn't have strength. They just don't have a system.

**JACK:** You seem to be missing my point.

**TOM:** You seem to be having a hard time making your point.

**JACK:** Well … Couldn't you just leave them alone.

**TOM:** You're worried about their safety. You think I'm going to harm them again.

**JACK:** I'm a little worried about that, yeah.

**TOM:** As I remember it Jack, you tried to kill me on three separate occasions. That's right isn't it? Three? The disconnected brakes on the car. The loose step going down into the basement. And the big one. That guy. That goof you hired to shoot me. I mean really I think I'm the one who should be worried about his safety here. But why dwell in the past. I'm willing to let bygones be bygones.

**JACK:** Thanks.

**TOM:** I used to be messed up. I know that. It was my job. I saw a lot of anxious people when I was a cop. A lot of scum too. Not that I'm blaming my job. I'm not even blaming the scum. Anyway the point is that was then and this is now. And we're going to create something here. Something better. Something based on cooperation. And connected to the reality of the place. In this place it's a kind of consumer cooperation. In a way, we're going to be making our own government here. One that we can trust. Construction projects like the one in the basement, selling useless things like that car, even stuffing envelopes ... These projects will be the foundation of a new world. A world dedicated to survival through cooperation and self-protection. In bad times you work for two basic reasons. To get something done. And to keep people busy so they don't worry. History is going to play a dirty trick on this country. The sins of global imbalance are all coming home to roost. And we have to be prepared. Now if you'll excuse me I've got a schedule to follow down below. Five feet a day. (*starts off, stops at doorway*) By the way, all this worrying about what happened to this family ten years ago is garbage. What's going to happen in the future will make that seem like Christmas morning if we're not ready.

*He goes into the basement. JACK seems dazed.*

**JACK:** My God.

*He sits. Sound of a motorcycle in the backyard. GAIL and JUNIOR come in from the back. She goes to the fridge. JUNIOR is carrying a knapsack.*

**JUNIOR:** You sure it's okay? I mean Elizabeth ...

**GAIL:** Forget Elizabeth. She's not in charge anymore. Dad wants you here. He's got all these ideas.

**JUNIOR:** What ideas?

**GAIL:** I don't know. I don't really understand them. But the thing is, Junior. He's my dad. And he's back. And that makes us ... well kinda like a family. And we never were really before. And if you wanted to … cause I think of you kinda as my … Well if you wanna just stay and be part of that family that'd be great.

**JUNIOR:** I'd really be a part of the family?

**GAIL:** That's what my dad says. He says he needs your help with his … ideas.

*She starts off.*

**JUNIOR:** But what about my singing career.

**GAIL:** (*turns back*) Your singing stinks, Junior.

**JUNIOR:** Whatya mean it stinks.

**GAIL:** I mean you're no good. You suck.

**JUNIOR:** Come on. I took singing lessons for a whole year, Gail. Because you said I had … potential.

**GAIL:** I'll make it up to you.

**JUNIOR:** I don't think so. How you gonna do that.

**GAIL:** I'm gonna take a bath. Wanna get in with me?

**JUNIOR:** Definitely.

*JUNIOR follows GAIL up the stairs.*

*MARY ANN comes in.*

**MARY ANN:** (*to JACK*) What's wrong with you.

**JACK:** I'm worried.

*MARY ANN sits.*

**MARY ANN:** Well aren't you going to ask what's wrong with me.

**JACK:** (*sighs*) What's wrong with you.

**MARY ANN:** She lied. She told me all the details. And they were really frightening … What are we going to do.

*JACK smiles. Shrugs. They sit in silence.*

*ELIZABETH storms in.*

**ELIZABETH:** Okay I've only got five minutes. I've got a trial on dinner break. Did you talk to her.

**JACK:** We've got a dicey situation here. Your mother really wants him to stay.

**ELIZABETH:** Why.

**JACK:** Emotional denial, I guess. It's better for her ... emotionally, if she gives him a new identity. And a new start or something.

**MARY ANN:** Emotional denial. Yeah, I think that's one of the things I'm suffering from because I—

**ELIZABETH:** Shut up! (*to JACK*) We're talking about a crazy violent drunk. A guy who once took away all our clothes and gave them to Goodwill. A guy who had a nasty habit of waving his loaded gun at us. A guy who tried to burn this house down while we were all asleep in our beds. This is not a guy who deserves a second chance, at least not from me. I mean that's what it looks like, Jack. It looks like he's getting a second chance here that he just doesn't deserve ... So ... what do we do about that.

**JACK:** Well for one thing, I think he has to be watched very closely.

**ELIZABETH:** Yeah and I suppose that's my responsibility. Well forget it. I've got a life. Well, a job anyway ... and other things to worry about. Maybe it's time I let this family solve its own fucking problems!

*She runs out. MARY ANN looks to JACK.*

**JACK:** It's a complicated situation. Everyone has to do what they think is best for them.

**MARY ANN:** What's best for me?

*JACK sighs deeply. Stands. Goes out back.*

*NORA, humming to herself, comes in carrying Christmas lights and goes directly to TOM either at doorway of basement or upstairs.*

*JUNIOR comes in. In soaking jeans. Covered in bubbles. Picks up an apple. Sees the wires being pulled ... Goes to look out the screen door.*

**MARY ANN:** I think I'll go lie down.

**JUNIOR:** See ya.

*TOM has completed wiring a homemade plunger. He has used Christmas tree lights to connect the plunger to the charge down below. The lights trail out across the floor and down into the basement. He takes NORA's hand gently and puts it on the plunger handle, leaving his hand on top of hers. They exchange excited, almost deranged smiles.*

**NORA:** On the count of five?

**TOM:** I can't wait that long.

*And then he pushes the plunger down. An explosion rocks the house. The kitchen window explodes and the screen door flies off its hinges taking JUNIOR down. In the backyard big hunks of grass and dirt, and other debris flying into the air. TOM and NORA look startled.*

**JUNIOR:** (*groans from under the door*) Ah ... man.

*JACK comes rushing back in while MARY ANN and GAIL come running through the house to the kitchen.*

**MARY ANN & GAIL:** Mom!

**JACK:** Nora?!

**NORA:** (*pointing to TOM*) This a man who gets things done.

*TOM, NORA, JACK, MARY ANN and JUNIOR are standing around looking at the kitchen. Suddenly we hear a loud crack. They all turn to see the old maple tree slowly falling towards the car. The tree lands directly on the car.*

**JACK:** Not an auspicious beginning for the new family unit.

*Blackout.*

*Intermission.*

*During intermission, the house is transformed into a safe-zone. Bars are added to the windows. The drawers and refrigerator are padlocked. The door has been replaced by a steel door and a security gate. Sand-bags are stacked in the backyard.*

## SCENE SIX

*MARY ANN is at the envelope-stuffing work station at the kitchen table. But she is not working. She is holding an old doll. Fussing with its clothing. Screen door suddenly jolts open. TOM is in the doorway.*

**TOM:** Whatya doing.

*MARY ANN is startled.*

**MARY ANN:** Nothing. I found this old doll and I was—

*TOM is walking casually toward her.*

**TOM:** You were a selfish little girl, Mary Ann. I was hoping you'd changed a bit. This job produces a base income for this family. People are relying on you to do a serious day's work.

*MARY ANN backs away from TOM. The doll is clutched to her chest.*

**MARY ANN:** I know but—

**TOM:** Don't you think it's time you started considering other people's needs.

**MARY ANN:** Well yes, but—

**TOM:** Because until you do you won't be much good to anyone. Including your baby ... Well?

**MARY ANN:** I ... ah ...

**TOM:** Well?

**MARY ANN:** I ... ah ...

*MARY ANN is staring at the floor. Twisting the doll's body with her hands. TOM stands waiting for an answer.*

*Blackout.*

## SCENE SEVEN

*MARY ANN is asleep at the kitchen table. She awakens with a start. Looks at the doll in her hand. Hides it under the table.*

*GAIL comes into the kitchen carrying a duffel bag. Heads for the door.*

*JUNIOR comes up from the basement. He has been working.*

**JUNIOR:** Hey.

**GAIL:** Hey.

**JUNIOR:** Whatya doin'.

**GAIL:** Movin' out.

**JUNIOR:** Whatya mean movin' out. Since when.

**GAIL:** Since now.

**JUNIOR:** Yeah, but how come you're just telling me. How come you didn't tell me before.

**GAIL:** I didn't know before.

**JUNIOR:** Okay. Yeah but … you know … how come. Aren't you happy.

**GAIL:** No. I'm not.

**JUNIOR:** I'm happy.

**GAIL:** Good for you.

**JUNIOR:** Yeah but—

**GAIL:** Look. I gave the guy a chance. I told him all he had to do was be nice. And act like a real father. And look what happens. More weird shit. All this discipline stuff. It's bullshit. At first I thought, well he's just doin' it to bring us together or something. A project we can all work on. A … thing.

**JUNIOR:** Well maybe it is a thing.

**GAIL:** Yeah but it's not a thing of love. It's a thing of bullshit. I gotta get outta here for awhile. I just gotta … get away.

**JUNIOR:** So like … do you want me to come with you.

**GAIL:** Do you want to come with me.

**JUNIOR:** Not really.

**GAIL:** No?

**JUNIOR:** No ... not really. I kinda like it here. You know ... I do a job. Somebody says "Good job, Junior." I do another job. Somebody says "Good job, Junior." I eat something. Then I get to sleep with you. It's perfect.

**GAIL:** Except I'm leaving.

**JUNIOR:** Yeah. Yeah that's a drag.

**GAIL:** So?

**JUNIOR:** What.

**GAIL:** Do you want to come with me!

**JUNIOR:** No I just said I didn't—

**GAIL:** Asshole!

**JUNIOR:** I mean I do but—

**GAIL:** Yeah but you don't. I mean you're probably thinking, well it's a drag if she goes. But really ... well I'll have the bed all to myself. And people will still be saying "Good job, Junior." And shit like that. So really it's almost, you know ... better. Is that what you're thinking.

**JUNIOR:** No.

**GAIL:** Look at me.

*He does.*

**GAIL:** It is, isn't it.

**JUNIOR:** Yeah. Kinda.

**GAIL:** Asshole.

*She leaves.*

*JUNIOR watches her. Waves a feeble goodbye. Sings a bit of Aerosmith. Goes back down into the basement.*

*MARY ANN sighs. Continues to stuff envelopes.*

*Blackout.*

## SCENE EIGHT

*By candlelight, MARY ANN is sitting at the table. Stuffing envelopes. Trying to do it quickly. Huge piles of envelopes and folded advertisements. Some she stuffs properly. Others she crumples and forces in. Then pounds flat.*

*The light gets turned on. ELIZABETH is standing there with her hand on the switch. Carrying a briefcase. Papers pouring out of it. A trench coat folded over her shoulder. She looks like she has had a rough day. Not tired— sort of unhinged.*

**MARY ANN:** Turn that off. It's not allowed.

**ELIZABETH:** What's not allowed.

**MARY ANN:** We've got rules. One of them is, we don't waste power.

**ELIZABETH:** Gimme a break. Whatya mean rules. Whose rules?

**MARY ANN:** Tim's.

**ELIZABETH:** Who the fuck's Tim?

**MARY ANN:** Tim's what we call Tom, you know, to avoid the painful echoes.

**ELIZABETH:** Is he responsible for all this.

**MARY ANN:** Yes.

**ELIZABETH:** Well I don't like it. I don't like any of it.

**MARY ANN:** That's because you're an outsider. Someone who never comes around anymore. Someone who's not up on the finer points of consumer cooperation. You just don't get it.

**ELIZABETH:** Get what.

**MARY ANN:** We've got rules! We've got jobs. My job is to stuff envelopes with advertisements for drugstores. Actually that's just the first part of my job. The second part is to devise a more efficient way of doing the first part. This requires thinking. Thinking prevents me from worrying. Worrying is anti-productive and "selfish" ... If I worry too much I think they're gonna put me outta my misery. As in, "Ah, she looks so sad. Let's kill her."

**ELIZABETH:** Shut up.

**MARY ANN:** Sure, why not. Soon I'll stop talking forever. Then I plan to stop moving. My ultimate goal is to become invisible. That way I'll get my work done without taking up valuable space. Also I'll feel a hell of a lot safer.

**ELIZABETH:** Shut up.

*NORA comes out of the basement in her rain gear and boots, followed by TOM in similar gear and also a miner's lamp around his hat, followed by JUNIOR wearing just trousers, rubber boots, and his motorcycle helmet. His upper body is bare and covered in mud. They all pick up lunch pails from the counter, wave at MARY ANN and go into the backyard in a line.*

**ELIZABETH:** What was that?

**MARY ANN:** The night shift. Eight at night 'til three in the morning. Six hours sleep . Breakfast. And work again 'til five. One hour for dinner. And two hours of Tim's new political theories. This is just a little break for the happy night shift workers. They take it outside so they won't disturb my work.

**ELIZABETH:** I'm beginning to feel like Gail feels.

**MARY ANN:** How is Gail.

**ELIZABETH:** What do you mean.

**MARY ANN:** She left. We assumed she went to live with you.

**ELIZABETH:** No.

**MARY ANN:** (*stands*) So where is she.

**ELIZABETH:** I don't know.

**MARY ANN:** I'll have to call a meeting of the family unit. This could cause great anxiety for our maternal leader.

**ELIZABETH:** Jesus.

*MARY ANN begins to cry.*

**MARY ANN:** Please, Elizabeth. You don't know what it's like. You're the only one who can help us ... Make him stop! Please!!

**ELIZABETH:** Jesus!!

*TOM comes in from outside. Goes to unlock the fridge. Takes out a carton of milk. Holds it to his mouth. Drinks.*

**TOM:** Hi. How are we doing tonight.

ELIZABETH: We're upset. We seem to have wandered into the wrong house. We seem to have wandered into some perverse social experiment. We think it sucks. We think it should stop. We think if it doesn't stop we'll mangle your face!!

TOM: You don't trust progress?

ELIZABETH: I don't trust you.

*TOM gestures around the kitchen.*

TOM: Things are improving around here. Life is improving. Life is organized and things are working again. The back burner on the stove is working. The light in the refrigerator is working. The broken faucet is working. The broken stairs are repaired. And work on the basement sanctuary is right on schedule. Is there anything that shouldn't be trusted in any of that.

ELIZABETH: Why do you call the basement a sanctuary.

TOM: Why do you call the sanctuary a basement. It's all in your point of view. Take my advice. Change your point of view.

ELIZABETH: I want to talk to my mother.

TOM: Good. She's missed you. I have to get back to work.

*TOM goes into the basement. ELIZABETH goes to the door.*

ELIZABETH: Mom, could you come in here please. Not you, Junior. You just stay put. (*to MARY ANN*) What's Junior doing here anyway.

MARY ANN: Well in theory, he's your brother.

ELIZABETH: Jesus Christ.

MARY ANN: He's not too bad. He just works, eats and sleeps. He says he's had a realization that he's actually a very normal person. And now he just wants to blend in.

ELIZABETH: This is no place for a normal person to blend in.

MARY ANN: Did you notice that the TV and the piano are gone. Tim sold them. Bought five hundred cans of stewed tomatoes. Why stewed tomatoes? High vitamin content. Multiple usage. Long shelf life.

*NORA comes in. Reading a book. And an atlas. She smiles at ELIZABETH.*

**NORA:** Good evening, dear. You've gained weight.

**ELIZABETH:** No I haven't.

**NORA:** You look much heavier compared to your sister.

**MARY ANN:** I think I've lost weight, Mom.

**NORA:** It's for a good cause, dear. Whatever you don't eat has a chance of getting eaten by someone else more needy. That's a political theory.

**MARY ANN:** (*whispering*) A stupid political theory.

**ELIZABETH:** Be quiet.

*NORA points to her book.*

**NORA:** I'm learning about politics.

**ELIZABETH:** That's great Mom. Tell me what you've learned so far.

**MARY ANN:** This is not the time to humour her Elizabeth. This is the time to be direct.

**ELIZABETH:** Go outside.

**MARY ANN:** But I want to—

**ELIZABETH:** Do it!

*MARY ANN leaves.*

**ELIZABETH:** Go ahead, Mom.

**NORA:** Well ... I'm learning how the world operates. You know it's scary. It's complex and scary.

**ELIZABETH:** Is that what all the barbed wire's about, Mom? The bars on the windows? The "sanctuary" you're building down there?

**NORA:** We're just protecting ourselves from looters.

**ELIZABETH:** Mom ... This is crazy.

**NORA:** And we're all working together. Like a family. Tim has helped ... make us a ... By the way, dear, speaking of Tim. I'm thinking of having sex with him. What do you think of that idea?

*ELIZABETH groans and grabs her head.*

**ELIZABETH:** Ah God ... What's going on here. I can't deal with this ... Oh God! I ... I have to ... Jesus I've had a rough day. I lost twelve cases today. That's some kind of record. I ... don't think my mind is on my work. My mind is on my family and you're all fucked ... You know what. I'm not feeling very well. Can I lie down. I'll lie down right here. No! No, I'll go upstairs and lie down. Is that okay. I'll just ...

*She starts toward the stairs.*

**ELIZABETH:** Okay? ... Okay. Just for awhile. I'm ... I'm you know, just ... Oh God ...

*NORA gets up and goes to the basement doorway. She calls down.*

**NORA:** Tim. Oh Tim. Can you come up here for a moment. (*coos softly*) Ohhh, Tiiimm.

*TOM comes up.*

**NORA:** Let's talk. Let's have a nice talk.

*Pause.*

**TOM:** So talk.

*She mumbles something. Smiles. Starts towards him. Mumbles something. Puts her arms around him. Mumbles something. Kisses him. He puts his arms around her. Pulls her in very forcefully.*

**NORA:** Ah ... Tim?

**TOM:** What, you don't like that?

**NORA:** Well I ... I ... kinda ... want to ...

**TOM:** Shush ... no talking ...

*He kisses her passionately. Forcefully.*

*Blackout.*

## SCENE NINE

*The next morning.*

*MARY ANN and ELIZABETH come in to the kitchen. They are carrying boxes of envelopes and flyers.*

**MARY ANN:** I don't think six hours of sleep is enough, do you? Larry used to let me sleep 'til noon sometimes. You know, he'd just take the baby out to the park and play with her ... And I'd just—

**ELIZABETH:** You miss your baby, Mary Ann?

**MARY ANN:** I don't want to talk about it.

*They begin stuffing envelopes.*

*Upstairs. TOM and NORA. NORA is in her bathrobe. Starting downstairs. TOM appears in his pyjamas.*

**TOM:** So ... Nora ... About last night ...

**NORA:** Yes?

**TOM:** You got anything to say?

*NORA thinks about this for a moment.*

**NORA:** Thank you?

**TOM:** Thattagirl.

*NORA comes downstairs ... into kitchen.*

**MARY ANN:** Morning, Mom.

**NORA:** (*distracted*) Thank you. Ah ... yes ... thank you ...

*NORA goes into the basement.*

**MARY ANN:** What's wrong with her.

**ELIZABETH:** Sex.

*TOM comes into the kitchen.*

**TOM:** What are you still doing here, Elizabeth. Don't you have a job to go to?

**ELIZABETH:** I hate my job. I'm thinking of quitting my job.

**TOM:** Really.

**ELIZABETH:** Yeah. I'm thinking maybe I'll join this fascinating experiment in behaviour modification you have going here.

*TOM walks over close to ELIZABETH.*

**TOM:** I sense a threat here. A deep cynicism.

**ELIZABETH:** You do?

**TOM:** I have a lot to accomplish, Elizabeth. And I don't have much spare time. So if you take me on, I'm gonna have to deal with you very quickly. Excuse me, I have to go get my morning papers.

*He leaves.*

**ELIZABETH:** Charming guy.

**MARY ANN:** Do you think he realizes he's going to the store in his pyjamas.

**ELIZABETH:** Do you think he cares. He was always doing shit like that. As if he was daring some poor dope to point it out so he could stomp on him or something.

**MARY ANN:** You really thinking of quitting your job?

**ELIZABETH:** Yeah. I am.

**MARY ANN:** What would you do.

**ELIZABETH:** I don't know. This.

**MARY ANN:** Yeah, right.

**ELIZABETH:** Hey. This is therapeutic work. I might be happier doing this than being a lawyer.

**MARY ANN:** Please.

**ELIZABETH:** Well in a lot of ways it's a dumb life. All my clients are mean stupid pricks. Most of the other lawyers I meet are competitive and nasty. And my friends aren't really friends. They're "colleagues."

**MARY ANN:** You know, Elizabeth. Maybe this isn't the time to get reflective. Maybe you should just concentrate on fixing this mess we're in.

**ELIZABETH:** And everyone I know knows everything about everything. They've all got positions on all the major issues.

And all their positions are right ... Welfare. Daycare.
Education. Nuclear power. Deficits. Abortion. No debate. Just
opinions.

**MARY ANN:** Elizabeth, what are you—

**ELIZABETH:** I mean it's possible that the inability to budge an
inch is what's making the world such a fucked up place. So
really, the danger, as I see it, is throwing the baby out with the
bath water.

**MARY ANN:** I know you think I've deserted my baby! Why don't
you just come right out and say it?!

**ELIZABETH:** Oh please. Get your guilt under control until we
have time to get you professional help. I was speaking about
the situation here. I'm just saying we can't be mentally rigid.
Because certain things are worth retaining. The income from
this job is worth retaining. The knowledge of how to fix
things is worth retaining. Mom's ideal of a better lifestyle is
worth retaining. Only one thing doesn't have to be retained,
if we're careful.

**MARY ANN:** What.

**ELIZABETH:** Tom.

**MARY ANN:** (*whispers*) You mean Tim.

**ELIZABETH:** (*whispers*) I prefer to call him Tom.

**MARY ANN:** How do we get rid of him.

**ELIZABETH:** There are a variety of ways. A long-range strategy to
undermine his influence. A series of compromising situations
we could place him in. An attitude of resistance to everything
that comes out of his mouth. Or we could just kill him.

**MARY ANN:** We'd have to kill him without upsetting Mother.

**ELIZABETH:** We'd have to be inventive.

**MARY ANN:** Or sneaky.

**ELIZABETH:** Or really, really brave.

**MARY ANN:** Is it worth it.

**ELIZABETH:** When he shows his true nature we'll all be in real
trouble. He shouldn't have been allowed to march in here

and set himself up as some kind of chairman of the committee. People who do that are dangerous by nature. Sometimes deranged by nature.

MARY ANN:  I had a nightmare last night. About all the things he did when we were kids. I have them a lot.

ELIZABETH:  So do I. But if we kill him, maybe the nightmares will stop.

MARY ANN:  Just talking about killing him makes me feel better. Maybe if we keep talking about killing him, I mean really get into … details, I can save my marriage to Larry.

ELIZABETH:  Dad had nothing to do with that. A lot of marriages fail. We're not screwed up about men if that's what you're trying to say. I like men. Some of them. I just don't like the ones who show up here. We have to be mature about these things. And we have to maintain our mental health. Like Mom did when Dad left.

MARY ANN:  Like Mom did, more or less, is what you mean.

ELIZABETH:  She did fine. She just didn't learn how to fix the goddamn stairs!

*JUNIOR comes in from the backyard. Carrying a carton.*

JUNIOR:  The tomatoes are here.

*He goes downstairs.*

MARY ANN:  I didn't know he was out there. Do you think he heard anything. Do you think he'll tell.

ELIZABETH:  Not with my fist in his mouth he won't. Listen, Junior's no threat. I know when men are threatening. I have a certain amount of experience, remember.

MARY ANN:  I don't want to talk about that.

ELIZABETH:  Talk about what.

MARY ANN:  That part of your life when you got experience.

*Pause. ELIZABETH is looking at MARY ANN. Hard.*

ELIZABETH:  I'm not sure I know what you're referring to here, Mary Ann. You're going to have to help me out. Describe it. Use a word that describes it. Come on. Just one word. Say it!

MARY ANN:  I can say it. Don't make a big deal about me saying it.

*JUNIOR comes up. Goes outside. Singing.*

**MARY ANN:** Prostitute! You were a prostitute. So there. I can say it. I just don't want to talk about it.

**ELIZABETH:** And what else is new Mary Ann?!

**MARY ANN:** That's right. I never wanted to talk about it. And I still don't.

**ELIZABETH:** Good for you.

*Pause.*

**MARY ANN:** Except I want to say this ... The family was in trouble. We needed money. So you went out and got some. And I think that was a very very brave thing for you to do ... Of course I was disgusted and depressed by it. But that's just me. That's what I do. I get disgusted and depressed. But you did something that took real courage. And I'll love you and respect you forever for that. And that's all I want to say.

*JUNIOR comes back in with another carton.*

**JUNIOR:** I went to pick up the stewed tomatoes. Only guess what ... they're not just stewed tomatoes, they're canned fruit too. It's a gift. It's a gift from Tim cause we're doing so good!

*He goes downstairs.*

**ELIZABETH:** The Santa Claus strategy.

*TOM comes in from outside. Carrying three different newspapers.*

**TOM:** Got 'em.

*MARY ANN lowers her head. Continues working. TOM plugs in the kettle.*

*JUNIOR comes up.*

**JUNIOR:** Hi.

**TOM:** Get that stuff loaded in?

**JUNIOR:** Doin' it now.

**TOM:** Good work. Is it being stacked neatly.

**JUNIOR:** Yeah. The peaches and pears. The mandarin oranges. Everything separate.

**TOM:** Thatta boy.

*TOM sits in the rocker. Opens a paper.*

**JUNIOR:** I just wanted to say thanks. It was a nice thing for you to do… I like canned fruit. I like canned fruit a lot.

*JUNIOR goes outside.*

**ELIZABETH:** All work and no play seems to be making Junior a bit simple-minded.

**TOM:** The happiness found in small things is the only happiness of troubled times.

**ELIZABETH:** Hey that's cute. You come up with that one on your own?

*TOM stands, walks over to them.*

**TOM:** I've seen the spoilers of the world. I know what they look like. I know how they talk. How their talking leads to plotting, the plotting to confrontation.

**ELIZABETH:** Hey. I'm just an envelope stuffer.

**TOM:** And I'm just letting you know that I'm alert.

**ELIZABETH:** Kettle's boiling.

**TOM:** (*he looks*) No it's not.

**ELIZABETH:** Made you look though. (*she chuckles*)

*MARY ANN giggles.*

**TOM:** Mary Ann!

**MARY ANN:** What!

**TOM:** (*stares at her awhile*) Coffee?

**MARY ANN:** Yes, please.

**ELIZABETH:** Me too, please.

*TOM is putting instant coffee in some cups.*

*NORA comes up from the basement. Lost in thought. Goes to window.*

**NORA:** (*to herself*) Canned goods … A lot of canned goods … Thank you. Thank you for the canned goods. (*turns around*) Oh. Hello, Elizabeth.

**ELIZABETH:** Hi, Mom.

**NORA:** Hello, Mary Ann.

**MARY ANN:** Hi, Mom.

**NORA:** (*to TOM*) Hello ah ... I mean ... thank you. (*lowers her head*)

**TOM:** Well, now that Mother's here, Mother can make the coffee. I'll go get dressed.

**NORA:** Thank you. (*lowers her head*)

> *TOM starts off. Stops.*

**TOM:** Mary Ann.

**MARY ANN:** What?! What's wrong. I'm stuffing the best I can.

**TOM:** No, no, Mary Ann.

**MARY ANN:** No, no, Mary Ann what?!

**TOM:** I was just going to say now that your sister's here working on the envelopes maybe you can be doing something else.

**MARY ANN:** What?!

**TOM:** We'll think of something, won't we Nora.

**NORA:** Yes. Thank you. (*lowers her head*)

> *TOM leaves.*

**ELIZABETH:** You look kinda ... awful, Mom.

**NORA:** You don't want coffee, do you.

> *She unplugs the kettle.*

**ELIZABETH & MARY ANN:** No thanks.

**NORA:** Coffee is very overrated as a social beverage. You drink it in gulps. Eventually it kills you. Like everything else. (*looks around*) This place is a mess. How did it get to be such a mess. That wallpaper used to be so pretty.

**ELIZABETH:** What's wrong.

**NORA:** I'm a little worried.

**ELIZABETH:** About Gail?

**NORA:** I worry about Gail all the time. I guess I've become used to worrying about Gail.

**ELIZABETH:** You know something. I worry about Gail all the time too. (*to MARY ANN*) What about you.

**MARY ANN:** Yeah, she's on my list.

**NORA:** It's not Gail.

**ELIZABETH:**  Then what is it, Mom.

**NORA:**  I had a sexual experience last night.

**MARY ANN:**  We know.

**ELIZABETH:**  We ... heard.

**NORA:**  (*a bit embarrassed*) Oh ... Well ... It began in the shower. He soaped me. I soaped him. Then we—

**MARY ANN:**  Mom, you're not going to give us all the details are you?

**NORA:**  Well, if I don't lead up to it properly I don't think you'll understand. The whole thing is about details.

**ELIZABETH:**  We're both experienced Mom. The details tend to be more or less the same.

**NORA:**  Orgasms are wonderful things, aren't they. I'd forgotten. It's been so long. Orgasms are incredibly interesting sensations. That's not the problem.

**MARY ANN:**  Lucky you.

**ELIZABETH:**  Be quiet.

**NORA:**  As for oral sex, well, I can take it or leave it.

**ELIZABETH:**  Oh please Mom, just get to the problem!

**NORA:**  Power. And dominance. And violence. I think if you take away the hugging, and kissing, and the orgasm that's what last night was really about.

**ELIZABETH:**  Did he hurt you.

**NORA:**  Well at one point he looked like he wanted to kill me. I remember that look. Like your father. Tim is much more like your father than he lets on. I think I made a mistake becoming intimate with him. I was just trying to make the situation ... complete. I wonder if it's too late to stop. You see, I don't like looking into his eyes in bed and thinking he could kill me.

*JUNIOR comes in with three cartons.*

**JUNIOR:**  I can carry three of them. I'm getting stronger. This is great. I work. I get stronger. Somebody say "Good job, Junior."

**NORA:**  Good job, Junior.

**JUNIOR:** Perfect.

*He goes downstairs.*

**NORA:** That boy's happy. That boy's rehabilitated. Tim knows how to get things done. And how to rehabilitate criminals. He's brought a lot of improvement to our lives here ... I just wish he didn't want to kill me.

*She goes out, down the hall.*

*MARY ANN and ELIZABETH look at each other. MARY ANN puts her head down on the table.*

*ELIZABETH is just staring off.*

*Blackout.*

## SCENE TEN

*TOM is measuring the floor. ELIZABETH storms in.*

**ELIZABETH:** I want to talk to you, sport.

**TOM:** I'm busy.

**ELIZABETH:** I said I want to talk to you!

**TOM:** And I said I'm busy! I'm fixing the floor. The floor is warped. Haven't you noticed. The floor is a hazard.

**ELIZABETH:** No no fuck all this fixing bullshit. (*grabs the tape measure*) This all fucking stops right now. You've had your second chance and you blew it. You're out of here. You're going!

**TOM:** I'm not going anywhere.

**ELIZABETH:** This family doesn't need you.

**TOM:** No? This family needs me more than the air they breathe. I'm the only one in this fucking family who knows anything about the world out there.

**ELIZABETH:** The only world you know about is the one inside your lunatic skull. I know about the real world. And I can deal with it just fine.

**TOM:** Really. You think so? Can you deal with the future?

**ELIZABETH:** The future? The future's the same as the past and the present. It's tyranny and chaos and bitterness and suffering with just enough joy thrown in to make it endurable.

**TOM:** You're wrong. There's nothing in the future to make it endurable. The future is total shit.

**ELIZABETH:** Nothing is total shit. Only a primitive lunatic asshole could think anything was total shit. Your thinking about the future is like your thinking about everything else. It doesn't go far enough. It doesn't include compassion.

**TOM:** Compassion is a luxury we can't afford. I've got experience.

**ELIZABETH:** I've got experience *and* compassion.

**TOM:** I can fix things.

**ELIZABETH:** So fucking what.

**TOM:** I can motivate people.

**ELIZABETH:** Me too.

*TOM smiles strangely.*

**TOM:** I can kill.

**ELIZABETH:** What?

**TOM:** I can kill. With my bare hands. I can rip flesh. I can take a knife and cut throats, or put it in bellies. When the total shit of the future comes I can look it in the eye and keep it out of this fucking house. I can cheat. I can lie. I can steal. I can beg. I can sneak and grovel and betray and burn things to the ground to protect this family. I am the soldier of the total shit future. I am the provider of the total shit future. I am the basic ingredient for survival.

**ELIZABETH:** You're insane.

**TOM:** Maybe. But I love you. I love this family.

**ELIZABETH:** I don't want your love. This family doesn't need you.

**TOM:** The love of an insane man will be priceless in the total shit future. When the starving millions come to take away our food, do you want to kill them.

**ELIZABETH:** No.

**TOM:** Well I do. I want to kill them. Because I hate them. I hate them already and they're not even here. I hate their weakness. I've seen glimpses of it and it made me sick.

**ELIZABETH:** You can't scare me with that talk.

**TOM:** Sure I can.

**ELIZABETH:** You get power by scaring people with your insane talk. So knock it off. Shut the fuck up. Don't talk to me anymore!

*He grabs her. Throws her against the wall.*

**TOM:** No! You! Don't talk to me! Don't get in my way. This is my family. My house. Get it? Get it?! Get it!? Get it!? ... Get it?!

*Blackout.*

## SCENE ELEVEN

*That evening.*

*JACK and TOM. Two whiskey bottles on the table. One empty. One half full. JACK and TOM sit at the table. Drinking. There's a drunken stillness and strange concentration that they share.*

**TOM:**  A family is a mysterious thing, Jackie. It's beyond your comprehension. A man's got a special responsibility in a family. It's a different responsibility from what a woman's got. It's almost a physical thing. It's a feeling about what you gotta do ... do with your hands and your ... body. There's muscles in a man's body that are made for taking on this ... this responsibility. You know that Jackie. You used to be a man before you became a priest.

**JACK:**  You got it all mixed up, Tom. At some point being a father and a husband stopped being a good thing for you. It became something that made you crazy. And the craziness inside you met up with the craziness out there in the world. And you came up with all these crazy ideas, that are just basically garbage.

**TOM:**  No it's—

**JACK:**  It's garbage Tom. This is dangerous evil shit that you've brought back with you and put in this house. You gotta go.

**TOM:**  They cut off your balls when they made you a priest.

*JACK stands suddenly.*

**JACK:**  Listen to me, you son of a bitch! One way or another, you're going!!

*TOM starts pounding the table with a frustrated mixture of laughter and tears.*

**TOM:**  But they need me! It's better here! I've made it better! It's better! It's better!

**JACK:**  It's not better, you asshole. You're just a fascist prick.

**TOM:**  Can't you see that a little force won't kill anyone. Can't you see that a little scare is good for these people. The stove is working. The goddamn stove is working. I left here ten years ago and the goddamn stove was broken and it took my coming back to fix it. Pitiful. This family is pitiful without me. They need discipline. They need toughness. Can't you see that.

**JACK:** They need nothing you've got to offer!

**TOM:** Ah man, won't you ever get it! Jesus! I told you this years ago!

*With both hands TOM grabs JACK's clothing just below the neck. GAIL appears at the screen door.*

**GAIL:** Hey!

*She comes in.*

*TOM lets go of JACK.*

**GAIL:** I'm back. Somebody should probably say hello or something.

**JACK:** Where have you been.

**GAIL:** I'm fine. Thanks for asking.

*She starts to make a sandwich.*

**GAIL:** (*to TOM*) You looked like you were about to do something really violent.

**TOM:** I can explain.

**GAIL:** I bet. Anyway where I've been is, you know, out in the real world. I rented a room. I got a job. I made a couple of friends. I got relaxed. But then, guess what. My mind let go or something. And a thing that happened to me when I was a little girl came back. (*looks at TOM*) Does anyone want a sandwich.

**TOM:** No thanks … Why are you staring at me. I said no thanks.

**GAIL:** Anyway it just came back and I saw a face. And it belonged to a man I knew. I recognized his voice. And the voice was yelling and spitting out things that weren't real words. He was all stooped over. His arms making circles in the air. And I knew this man was really mad. Then I saw me with the man. And I got so scared I couldn't believe how scared I was. 'Cause I knew it was me he was mad at. And he looked like he wanted to kill me or something.

*TOM looks uneasy. He sits in the rocker. Pretends to read a newspaper.*

**GAIL:**  And people were yelling. Mom was yelling. Elizabeth was yelling "Dad stop. Leave her alone, Dad." Then a bunch more yelling. And pushing. Then Mom jumped on the man. And Elizabeth too. And it was really really messy. And ugly … And no wonder I kinda blocked it out, eh. Was he drunk.

**JACK:**  Yeah he was drunk. And crazy. Crazy drunk. Crazy sober. Sometimes you couldn't tell the difference.

**GAIL:**  Didn't anyone try to punish him.

**JACK:**  Well … yeah. Your mother and I wired his car and tried to electrocute him.

**GAIL:**  Thanks.

**JACK:**  Actually it was just a low voltage charge. We were only trying to scare him.

**GAIL:**  Why didn't you just call the police.

**JACK:**  Your mother wouldn't let me. I … think she felt sorry for him. Anyway he left. We thought for good.

*GAIL takes a bite of her sandwich. JACK stands. Advances on TOM.*

**JACK:**  But he came back three weeks later. Disguised as a human being. A month after that he dropped the disguise, stole everyone's clothes and gave them to Goodwill.

**TOM:**  (*from behind his paper*) Ah, these people didn't appreciate those clothes. They didn't even need those clothes. Who bought those goddamn clothes. The poor son of a bitch who paid for them could give them to anyone he goddamn wanted. And that's the goddamn law.

**JACK & GAIL:**  Shut up!

**JACK:**  We retaliated by chaining him up in the basement for a week. After that there was a temporary cease-fire. War broke out again when he chased your mother out of the house waving his police revolver at her. We arranged a disciplinary action with him tied naked to a tree, hopefully perishing from exposure, just outside the city.

**TOM:**  (*puts the paper in his lap*) Talk about abuse. Talk about victimization. A poor hardworking son of a bitch under a lot of mental stress and does he get compassion and understanding from his family. No! He gets assaulted, abducted, stripped naked, terrified out of his goddamn mind, and tied like a dog to a fucking tree. Is that justice. Or is that going just a bit beyond the fucking limit. Shouldn't it have ended there. Bygones being bygones. I mean I *paid!* It's that simple. I declare the issue closed. Let's move on to nicer things.

JACK: He got free. Made his way back here. And prepared for the cataclysm. It came one night while you were all asleep. He tried to burn the house down. The "poor son of a bitch" tried to burn the house down while his whole family was asleep in their beds! Fortunately Elizabeth woke up and not too much damage was done. But we knew then it was time to get serious about self-defence. We ... put out a contract on him.

GAIL: No way. (*takes a drink of whiskey*)

JACK: We were desperate. We hired one of the local idiots. There was a feeble attempt to fulfill the contract. It failed miserably. And your father disappeared for good.

GAIL: Until now.

JACK: Yeah. Until now.

*She takes a revolver out of her shoulder bag. Points it at TOM.*

TOM: Hey. What do you think you're doing.

GAIL: You gotta go. One way or another you're outta here.

TOM: This is a mistake.

JACK: A family is a mysterious thing, Tim. You gotta take the bad with the good.

TOM: (*stands*) Ah Jesus, can't a guy—

*She fires the gun into the air. TOM staggers back onto one knee.*

TOM: Ah, shit. What's the good of this. This doesn't help. You're just living in the goddamn past. I'm telling you the future is gonna be worse.

JACK: Not for you, asshole.

*JACK goes to GAIL. Staring at TOM he reaches out his hand to GAIL for the gun. She looks at him oddly. Hands him the sandwich. JACK looks at GAIL. Throws the sandwich down. Reaches for the gun. After a bit of a struggle GAIL lets go. Slowly JACK advances on TOM. Pointing the gun at TOM's head.*

TOM:  Ah, Jesus. Am I the only person in the world who reads the newspapers carefully?!

*Blackout.*

## SCENE TWELVE

*JACK is sitting in the rocker. Rocking slowly. Drinking from a bottle of whiskey.*

*ELIZABETH and MARY ANN come in carrying a very long four-by-four wood beam.*

**MARY ANN:** (*to JACK*) Heavy as hell. And we couldn't have it delivered. Oh no, it's not in the budget. So we had to take it on a bus and the subway. I can't tell you how much fun that was.

**ELIZABETH:** Those were the orders.

**MARY ANN:** Yeah. And we obey orders gladly. Some of us are becoming good little citizens of the cooperative consumer republic. Some of us are undergoing personality changes.

*They are struggling to get the beam into the basement. It might be too big.*

**ELIZABETH:** The beams were needed. He explained it to me. It seemed to make sense.

**MARY ANN:** You were supposed to resist.

**ELIZABETH:** I tried. It was hard. This is easier.

**MARY ANN:** Until we're murdered in our sleep. Until we accidentally break a rule, fail to meet our work quota, eat more than our share of canned pears. Then we'll see. Punishment will come. Death will come. The tyrant will come. The dictator. In our sleep. Slit our throats.

**ELIZABETH:** Oh, that's scary. What are we going to do about that. Anyone got a plan. I sure hope so.

*They are still wrestling with the beam ... MARY ANN gives up. Rests it against the counter.*

*NORA and JUNIOR have had an equally hard time just getting their beam into the kitchen from the hallway ... JUNIOR is now just staring at both beams ...*

**JUNIOR:** Don't worry, Mom. I'll just ... I'll just ...

**ELIZABETH:** Get a saw?

**JUNIOR:** Yeah don't worry, Mom. I'll go get a saw.

*JUNIOR goes down into the basement.*

**NORA:**  He's started to call me Mom. It's a bit strange. But I think it's because he's in transition or something. He seems to be changing identities … (*to JACK*) Do you have any thoughts about that.

**JACK:**  No.

*NORA smiles weakly. Sits.*

**MARY ANN:**  (*to ELIZABETH*) Listen I want you to do something about this situation. About the crazy man who is living in our house and getting us to do crazy stupid things because he's got these crazy stupid evil ideas!

**ELIZABETH:**  How about we try something different. You do something.

**MARY ANN:**  What can *I* do.

**ELIZABETH:**  I don't know. Starve him to death with your cooking. Tell about your dreams and fry his brains. Put a knitting needle through his eyes. Drop a sewing machine on his head.

**MARY ANN:**  Oh sure. Try to scare me with that violence stuff. Violence is only one possibility. There are others.

**ELIZABETH:**  Well, consider them all then. Think of every possibility and how it affects this family. That's what I've had to do my whole *fucking* life. And if you need help I'll get you started. Here's your first possibility. What if Tom's right. What if they are coming to get us.

**MARY ANN:**  Who are they.

**ELIZABETH:**  Could be anyone. There are lots of angry people out there. People who need what we've got. Who believe they deserve what we've got as much as we do. And they're probably right if you really think about it. Try to think about it, Mary Ann! Genuinely needy people are coming to rob and hurt this family. And it's your *duty* and your *responsibility* to stop them!

**MARY ANN:**  All right! I give up. Forget it.

**ELIZABETH:**  It can't be forgotten. It's already thought about. It's in the head. It's an idea. It's a possibility. They have to be stopped. And *you* have to stop them. For Mom, for Gail, for me, for yourself. Come on, Mary Ann. Come on, it's up to you, Mary Ann. Please Mary Ann!

**MARY ANN:** No, I can't! It hurts! Just thinking about it makes me hurt. Physically. Here. On my elbows. And here on my collarbone. I've got a pain in my collarbone. So I want you to shut up about it and just … leave me alone.

*MARY ANN sits down.*

**ELIZABETH:** We have to take this beam into the basement!

**MARY ANN:** Fuck it!

**ELIZABETH:** What. You're disobeying?

**MARY ANN:** Yes. I have to! It's scary and it hurts. But I have to!

**ELIZABETH:** There'll be consequences. Are you ready for them!

**MARY ANN:** (*crying*) No! I'm not!

**NORA:** Well, the beams are here. Just two of them. Two less than I thought we'd need. That's progress. That's economy. There's happiness in economy. I think you should look for happiness anywhere you might find it.

**JACK:** Gail's home.

**ELIZABETH:** Is she all right.

**JACK:** Yes. She's fine.

**MARY ANN:** Where is she.

**JACK:** Upstairs. Resting.

**ELIZABETH:** Is she tired.

**MARY ANN:** Why would she be resting if she wasn't tired. (*to JACK*) Why's she tired. I mean she comes home. She goes to bed. What's going on.

**JACK:** She's just a bit tired. Don't worry about her.

**MARY ANN:** Who's worried about her. I'm just getting really annoyed at the behaviour around here. When you come home you're supposed to say hello to everyone. You know. (*to JACK*) Hello. (*to NORA*) Hello. (*to ELIZABETH*) Hello! … I mean it's a basic thing.

**JACK:** What's wrong with you.

**MARY ANN:** Whatya mean what's wrong with me! I'm tired of everyone asking what's wrong with me? (*to JACK*) What's wrong with you! (*to ELIZABETH*) What's wrong with you! (*to NORA*) What's wrong with you!

**ELIZABETH:** Nothing is wrong with her!

**MARY ANN:** Oh. That got a rise, didn't it. Always protect Mom, right? Protect Mom no matter what.

**ELIZABETH:** Leave her out of this.

**MARY ANN:** Sorry. That's what *you* do. I don't do that. I figure we're all in this together. Maybe we're all in this because of her.

*ELIZABETH and MARY ANN are face to face.*

**ELIZABETH:** Shut up!

**MARY ANN:** No!

**NORA:** So Gail is back. That's a good thing isn't it. That means all the girls are home. Safe and sound. Together. There's safety in numbers. Now there's a theory I actually understand.

*JUNIOR comes up with a saw.*

**JUNIOR:** Where's Tim.

**JACK:** Gone.

**MARY ANN:** Gone where.

**JACK:** Just gone.

**NORA:** Gone for good?

**MARY ANN:** Not coming back? Just gone?

**JACK:** Yes.

*Pause.*

**JUNIOR:** Should I go to.

*They all look at him … JUNIOR looks around and goes back downstairs.*

*The women seem dazed. They all sit. ELIZABETH puts her head down on the table.*

*ELIZABETH suddenly lifts her head.*

**ELIZABETH:** Whatya mean he's gone.

**JACK:** He had to go. Something came up.

**ELIZABETH:** Something came up? What the fuck could come up.

*GAIL comes in.*

**GAIL:** Hi. What's goin' on.

**MARY ANN:** Dad's gone.

**GAIL:** I know. Where's Junior.

**JACK:** In the basement.

**GAIL:** Thanks.

*She goes into the basement.*

**ELIZABETH:** (*stands*) Oh my God. What's wrong with us. Do we just let any clown march in here and take over and then just leave. I mean what kind of—

**MARY ANN:** He wasn't just anyone, Elizabeth. He was Dad.

**NORA:** Excuse me.

*NORA goes out back.*

**ELIZABETH:** So that's supposed to make it okay. Because he's our dad he can do just about anything he fucking wants here … Oh my God. (*to MARY ANN*) Did you hear me before. All that "maybe people *are* coming to get us" shit. He must have got to me. Just like before. Nothing changes. Jesus Christ. How long is this going to go on.

*She sits. She puts her head down again.*

**MARY ANN:** (*to JACK*) What are you going to do about this.

**JACK:** Nothing.

**MARY ANN:** Yeah. But this is very confusing stuff. I mean, you know, I'm glad he's gone and everything but don't you think you need to say something now.

**JACK:** What.

**MARY ANN:** Maybe something that puts it all in perspective or something.

**JACK:** How.

**MARY ANN:** I don't know. Maybe say something like well, you know, that's the way life is. And oh well he's just one of life's obstacles, a thing to overcome. Or maybe he's one of life's ... you know ... you know ...

**JACK:** What ... What can I say. Really.

**MARY ANN:** Well okay, but this is going to set me back four or five years. I mean I figure my marriage is pretty well doomed now. I mean I can't commit myself to starting another family when this family here is so ... I mean I can't just go on like nothing happened. That's not my way.

**JACK:** I know.

**MARY ANN:** I'm going to have to ... Well I'm going to have to figure out just how this affects me. And I might have to ask some questions about that. And somebody's going to have to answer them.

**JACK:** I know. Who.

**MARY ANN:** I don't care who. You. Her.

**ELIZABETH:** I'm not answering any more of your fucking questions. Ever.

**MARY ANN:** Sure you are.

**ELIZABETH:** No. I'm not. (*puts her head down*)

**MARY ANN:** I don't care. Somebody will. I mean I won't be ignored about this. I won't.

**JACK:** Great.

**ELIZABETH:** (*lifts her head*) Why come back if you're just going to leave again. Why? Just to cause turmoil? Just to prove who's the toughest? Just to prove who can crush who like a fucking bug.

**MARY ANN:** Yeah. Okay. There's a question. (*to JACK*) Answer that one. Why'd he come back. What did he want from us.

**ELIZABETH:** Okay I'm a bug. I'm crushed.

**MARY ANN:** Me too. I'm a bug too.

**ELIZABETH:** Fuck it. (*lowers her head*)

**MARY ANN:** Yeah. Exactly. Fuck it! (*to JACK*) Unless, you know, you think that's not a good attitude. That maybe under the circumstances there's some other attitude that would be better for me to have right now ... So ... Do you.

**JACK:** Do I what.

**MARY ANN:** Did you stop listening to me.

**JACK:** Yes.

**MARY ANN:** When.

**JACK:** Oh, quite a while ago.

**MARY ANN:** Are you drunk.

**JACK:** Extremely.

*JUNIOR and GAIL come up from the basement.*

**GAIL:** We're going upstairs.

**JUNIOR:** To have sex.

**GAIL:** They didn't need to know that.

**JUNIOR:** But we're a family. We don't need to keep things from each other.

**GAIL:** Yes we do.

**JUNIOR:** But we're a—

**GAIL:** Look this family thing is a pretty new deal for you, Junior. Just trust me on this stuff okay.

*They start off.*

*NORA comes in from the back.*

**NORA:** Everyone stay put. I've got something to tell you.

*They look at her.*

**NORA:** Listen to this. Everything is going to be okay. Don't despair. Things are improving. The man who was here and just left was an improvement on the man who was here before. Sure some of his ideas were strange and ugly and he had some of the same violent tendencies as the man before him did, but overall he was better. He tried to help. Sometimes he even tried to listen. So all I'm saying is don't despair. Nothing happens for no good reason unless you can find no good reason for it happening. And my good reason is

that now when I think of the man who was here I don't have
to think all the way back to when it was so very very bad. I
only have to think back to when it was not as bad. And out of
that not as bad thinking we can all make our way into
something that's kinda okay. And then maybe, you know
what, we can keep going all the way to happiness someday. In
fact I've been thinking a lot about happiness lately. What's
wrong with it anyway. I mean I bet some of you haven't even
tried it out. Maybe some of you need help with it. There are
books about how to be happy, you know. Lots of them. I think
we should buy them all. Every single one of them. Then we
should all read them. Every single one of them. And we
should all do every single thing they say we should do to get
happy. Because happiness is better than despair. It just is. In
the meantime I think we should do something about this
wallpaper. What. Okay. Let's think about it. In the meantime
here's a helpful hint. No here's two helpful hints. One about
happiness. And one about wallpaper.

*Music.*

*Lights begin to fade.*

*NORA is still talking … under the music.*

*TOM appears at the screen door. He is holding a large portable TV.*

*Blackout.*


*End.*

# Escape From Happiness

*Escape from Happiness* was first produced by New York Stage and Film Company in association with the Powerhouse Theater at Vassar College, Poughkeepsie, New York, in July 1991 with the following cast:

**NORA**  Suzanne Shepard
**ELIZABETH**  Jane Kaczmarek
**MARY ANN**  Alexandra Gersten
**GAIL**  Ilana Levine
**JUNIOR**  Joseph Maselli
**TOM**  Mark Hammer
**DIAN BLACK**  Deborah Hedwall
**MIKE DIXON**  Victor Arnold
**ROLLY MOORE**  Dan Moran
**STEVIE MOORE**  James Villemarie

Director: Max Mayer
Set Designer: Tom Lynch
Lighting Designer: Donald Holder
Costume Designer: Paul Tazewell
Production Stage Manager: Ruth Kreshka

*Escape from Happiness* was first produced in Canada by the Factory Theatre, Toronto, in February 1992 with the following cast:

NORA   Frances Hyland
ELIZABETH   Barbara Gordon
MARY ANN   Nancy Beatty
GAIL   Jane Spidell
JUNIOR   Greg Spottiswood
TOM   Ken James
DIAN BLACK   Susan Hogan
MIKE DIXON   J.W. Carroll
ROLLY MOORE   Eric Peterson
STEVIE MOORE   Oliver Dennis

Director: George F. Walker
Production Designer: Peter Blais
Lighting Designer: Michel Charbonneau
Stage Manager: Paul Mark
Production Stage Manager: Ruth Kreshka

*Persons*

**NORA**

**ELIZABETH**, Nora's oldest daughter

**MARY ANN**, Nora's middle daughter

**GAIL**, Nora's youngest daughter

**JUNIOR**, Gail's husband

**TOM**, the father of Nora's daughters

**DIAN BLACK**, a police detective

**MIKE DIXON**, a police detective

**ROLLY MOORE**, a criminal

**STEVIE MOORE**, a criminal

*Place*

The east end of a large city.

*Set*

The worn-down kitchen of an old house. A screen door leading to the backyard. A door leading to the basement. A doorway to the rest of the house. An old fridge and stove, a table, four or five chairs, a broom closet, and a pantry. And all the rest of the usual kitchen stuff.

*Note*

There is an intermission between Scenes Four and Five.

## SCENE ONE

*Lights up very fast. JUNIOR has been beaten up. His clothing is torn. He is bloody. He is on his back on the floor. GAIL has his head in her lap. NORA and GAIL are wearing coats. There are bags full of groceries on the counter and the floor. A couple of chairs have been turned over. NORA is holding a baby wrapped in a blanket in one of her arms. And she is on the telephone*

**GAIL:** Tell them to hurry, dammit!

**NORA:** (*into the phone*) Hurry, dammit! (*hangs up*)

**GAIL:** Junior, what happened. Who did this to you. God Mom, look at him. It looks serious.

**NORA:** He's not hurt badly. If he was hurt badly there'd be a certain kind of smell in the air. Sure he looks weak and torn up, but that's just the way he looks. Can he talk. Ask him if he can talk.

**GAIL:** Can you talk.

*JUNIOR groans.*

**NORA:** Did he say something.

**GAIL:** He made a sound.

**NORA:** That could be a good thing. That could be his way of letting us know he's alive.

**GAIL:** What are you talking about. He's alive. He's breathing, isn't he.

**NORA:** I meant alive in a deeper way. Sure he's breathing. But inside has he given up. Is there hope and lightness in his heart. I'm nervous. I'm not sure I'm saying exactly what I mean.

**GAIL:**  I can't believe this. We were only gone an hour. My first time out of the house in weeks and we come home and find this. Shit ... Junior, who did this to you?! (*to NORA*) Call 911 again.

**NORA:**  No, you can't do that. It annoys them. Or they get confused and suspicious. I've heard terrible stories about their confusion. We'll just have to hope and pray a reliable person took my call. Ask him to make another sound. Ask him if he feels alive.

**GAIL:**  Junior. Can you hear me. Can you say something.

**JUNIOR:**  (*groans*) What. (*mumbles*)

*GAIL has her ear to JUNIOR's mouth.*

**NORA:**  What's he saying.

**GAIL:**  He's saved.

**NORA:**  That's what he said? He said, "I'm saved"?

*GAIL puts her ear to JUNIOR's mouth again.*

**GAIL:**  No. Not saved. Afraid. He said he's afraid.

**NORA:**  That's different than saying, "I'm saved." Emotionally, there's a whole world of difference between those two statements, Gail. Try to be more specific. How can I help if you don't translate properly.

**GAIL:**  Is that what you're doing. Helping?! How. How are you helping.

**NORA:**  I'm ready to help. It depends on his state of mind. If he wants or needs change in his state of mind to sustain life, I'm ready. Ask him if he thinks he's dying.

**GAIL:**  No.

**NORA:**  Ask him. Make it clear. Don't mumble. Separate every word. Make sure he understands. Do it. It's important.

**GAIL:**  You do it. I can't!

**NORA:**  He might lie to me. I'm his mother-in-law. We have an interesting relationship, but I'm not sure it's built entirely on the truth. Ask him if he thinks he's dying. Do it before it's too late, Gail.

**GAIL:**  Junior. Are you dying ... Are you dying?!

**JUNIOR:** (*weakly*) Yes.

> *GAIL screams.*

> *NORA grabs GAIL and pulls her away. She kneels beside JUNIOR.*

**NORA:** Junior! Can you hear me. This is Nora. Your wife's mother. Your child's grandmother. Junior, I want you to do something for your wife and your child. If you don't do it these people you love will be destroyed. You'll be destroying your young innocent family. So Junior, here's what you have to do. You have to get up.

**GAIL:** Mom!

**NORA:** Don't distract me, dear. Junior! Get off that floor!

**GAIL:** Mom, please. He's bleeding. He's probably got internal injuries.

**NORA:** Get up, Junior! You're killing us here! You're killing us with your misery. We need you to get up. Your baby wants you on your feet. Hear her crying for her daddy? (*pinches the baby. The baby cries*)

**GAIL:** What did you just do.

**NORA:** (*whispers*) I pinched her. (*pinches the baby again*)

**GAIL:** Stop that! Stop doing that. What's wrong with you.

**NORA:** Junior, do you hear your baby crying! She's crying because she wants you to get up. She's saying, "Daddy Daddy, please get up. Daddy, please please don't die on that floor!"

**GAIL:** Stop it.

**NORA:** Junior! Daddy! Junior!

> *JUNIOR groans loudly. He tries to sit up.*

**GAIL:** No. Don't make him do this. Junior, lie down.

**JUNIOR:** I gotta get up! (*sits up*)

**NORA:** That's not good enough. Look at yourself. You're on the floor. We need you *off* the floor.

> *JUNIOR is struggling to his feet.*

**JUNIOR:** Gotta get off the floor. Why? Why off the floor.

**NORA:** Because you're alive. You're not dead. The floor is for dying. You have to avoid that floor. Defeat that floor. Rise above that floor! Get up!

**JUNIOR:** Okay. (*staggers to his feet. Weakly*) Okay. I'm up. What now.

**GAIL:** The ambulance is on the way.

**JUNIOR:** I'm dizzy.

**GAIL:** Here. Lean on me.

**NORA:** Stay away from him. He's on his own. Talk to him if you want. Ask him questions he can answer. Simple ones.

**GAIL:** Junior. What time is it.

**JUNIOR:** What? What's wrong with you. Look at me. I'm dying!

**NORA:** Junior! Dance!

**JUNIOR:** What?

**NORA:** Dance. Do a slow dance … Gail, turn on the radio. Turn it on now!

> GAIL *turns on the radio. She begins to search for appropriate music.*

**NORA:** Find some nice music. Be patient, Junior. Music is coming. There. That's good. Now dance, Junior! (*JUNIOR is moving slowly. An ambulance siren sounds in the distance*) Ambulance is coming, Junior. Help is on the way. The police, too. Fire department. Everyone is coming to help. We're not alone, Junior. Life goes on … (*to* GAIL) He's going to be all right.

> *The ambulance is getting closer. Closer.* GAIL *takes the baby from* NORA. NORA *starts to unpack the groceries.* JUNIOR *is still dancing. Lights flashing outside.*

> *Blackout.*

## SCENE TWO

*NORA is sitting across the table from DIAN BLACK. DIAN is a police detective—neatly, pleasantly dressed. She is about thirty-five. MIKE DIXON, her partner, is standing a few feet away, hands in his pocket. He is older, tougher looking. At this moment, he doesn't appear interested in what DIAN and NORA are saying. He is casually looking around the kitchen.*

**NORA:** This is irregular procedure. I'm not an expert in these matters. But I have some knowledge of police procedure, and this is irregular. I'm a citizen who reported a crime. Maybe you're just confused, but it appears I'm being questioned as if I were suspected of something.

**DIAN:** You said you have some knowledge of police procedure. (*long pause*) Well?

**NORA:** I'm sorry. Was that actually a question, dear.

**DIAN:** Yes.

**NORA:** I see. Well were you actually asking me how I got such knowledge.

**DIAN:** Yes. How did you get such knowledge.

**NORA:** My husband was a policeman. (*DIAN looks at MIKE. MIKE nods*) (*to MIKE*) You knew my husband?

**MIKE:** Yeah. Worked the fraud squad with him.

**NORA:** That's nice. I think his two years on the fraud squad were the happiest years of his life. I don't know why exactly. Wasn't for any reason a normal person could understand. He's dead now, of course. Has been for several years. I'm sorry if this comes as a shock to you.

**MIKE:** I saw him on the street last week.

**NORA:** That's a man who looks remarkably like him. He lives here in my house. He behaves like my husband, and to some degree like the father of my children. But my husband is dead. Don't get me wrong. This man isn't really an impostor. He's just dangerously confused. Does any of this help you with your investigation.

**MIKE:** No.

**DIAN:** (*looks at* MIKE. *To* NORA) It's too early to say.

**NORA:** It wasn't too early for him to say. He said "no."

**DIAN:** (*smiles*) Well, he's wrong.

*DIAN and* MIKE *look at each other.* MIKE *shrugs. He begins to look around the kitchen again.*

**NORA:** Well, here we are again. In a state of irregularity. All I've done is call the police to report a crime. My son-in-law is lying in a hospital bed because he was viciously beaten.

**DIAN:** By two men.

**NORA:** Two men. White. One young. One ... older.

**MIKE:** (*has obviously been only half-listening*) Black guys?

**NORA:** No.

**MIKE:** Oriental guys.

**NORA:** No.

*DIAN looks at* MIKE. *She frowns.*

**MIKE:** Asian guys. Guys in turbans. (*gives* DIAN *a what's your problem? look*)

**NORA:** No. White men. I suppose they could have been wearing turbans. But that would have been odd. Odd enough that he certainly would have mentioned it.

**MIKE:** He said they were white? He actually described them as "white."

**NORA:** No. I know them.

**DIAN:** You know them?

**NORA:** Sort of.

**DIAN:** Sort of?

**NORA:** I know them sort of only as white.

**MIKE:** What does that mean. You know them only as white. Sort of. Is there a possibility they could be something else.

**NORA:** I don't think so. Are there criminals running around out there, white criminals who sometimes appear black. Or black criminals who sometimes appear white.

**DIAN:** We think that drugs are involved. Your son-in-law has a history with drugs, doesn't he.

**NORA:** You must be talking about someone else's son-in-law. My son-in-law was a car thief. He has no involvement with drugs. He has a child. And up to the very moment he had his child he was a child himself. I believe I should call a lawyer. My oldest daughter is a lawyer. I could call her. You'd like her. Well perhaps you wouldn't like her, but you'd respect her. She'd insist on that.

**DIAN:** You don't need a lawyer, Nora. You're not being charged with any crime.

**NORA:** Well, that clears that up. You've been so vague. Intentionally vague. Almost arrogant. I know you probably don't think so. I've had police people in my house for dinner. In their hearts they're normal people, most of them. But they have an arrogant manner. You serve them a good meal. They just look at you in a funny way. You try to understand what that look means. Does it mean the food's cold. That there's not enough of it. That they expect you to put it directly into their mouths. I don't know. Maybe you could explain that look to me right now. I mean, it all ties together with our conversation here. And your attitude towards my son-in-law. And perhaps even your attitude towards visible minorities and the way they dress.

**MIKE:** (*approaches slowly*) You were hospitalized once, weren't you. I remember Tom mentioning something. That was a few years back ... So how'd that go. How are you doing these days. Do you ever go back to that hospital.

**NORA:** (*to DIAN*) My husband had me committed once, dear. (*to MIKE*) She didn't know what you were talking about.

**MIKE:** So ... how are you.

**NORA:** I'm fine. I've learned a lot since that happened. First, I learned that I wasn't insane. The doctors in that hospital told me that right away. They talked to Tom. They thought he was insane. They were right. I'm a grandmother now. I got to be a grandmother by bringing my children up to the point where they could have children. It wasn't easy after your good friend Tom deserted us. But that's another story. This is the story of my son-in-law's vicious beating.

DIAN: On the surface, Nora. At first glance. To the uniformed police officers who came here to your house earlier, that's what it probably appeared to be about.

MIKE: But we're different. Our job is to go farther.

NORA: Farther than what. I mean, how far ... can you go.

MIKE: As far as we want.

DIAN: He means ... we have information those policemen in uniform don't have. We specialize in taking that information and applying it in various ways to find possible connections, patterns ... an ... organization of events ... Organizations ... That's the area of our expertise.

NORA: You're experts. I've had quite a bit of experience with experts. So what's your official name. When experts get together they usually give themselves a name.

MIKE: O.C.S.

DIAN: Organized Crime Squad ... And in this house, Nora—the house where you live with your youngest daughter and her child, where a man who looks like your husband also lives— your son-in-law is possibly—make that probably—performing and arranging to be performed, a variety of criminal activities.

MIKE: These are drug-related activities. These are prostitution-related activities, pornography-related activities, money-laundering-related activities ...

NORA: Distantly.

MIKE: What was that.

NORA: Distantly related? Or ... closely related. Distantly related could be just a product of rumour. Neighbourhood gossip. There are dozens of religious fanatics on this street. They report people all the time. They reported me once for abusing my daughters. My daughters had a virus that made their eyes swell up. The fanatics told the police I'd been poking them in the eyes with heated knitting needles. I had to get a letter from a doctor. Show it to the police. Circulate it in the neighbourhood. When they're wrong about people, the fanatics just smile and say, "Better safe than sorry." Of course they're in for a very big surprise. Because they're all going to rot in hell.

*Pause. MIKE and DIAN look at each other.*

**DIAN:** Yes. Well, we don't rely on rumours. We use investigation. Surveillance ... (*looks at MIKE*) Good judgement. You see, Nora, Junior's a ... he's a ...

**MIKE:** He's a crook. He keeps company with other crooks. The beating he received was a payback. A deal went wrong. Money was owed. Junior was to blame. At this moment I'm assuming you know nothing about this. Call it a hunch.

**DIAN:** (*to MIKE*) A hunch? ... Oh yeah, I forgot. You get ... hunches.

**MIKE:** Something wrong?

**DIAN:** (*smiles*) No ... No, I agree. I think Nora doesn't really know much about Junior. (*smiles at NORA*) Even if she believes deep in her heart that she does.

*GAIL comes in from the hallway. She sees MIKE and DIAN.*

**GAIL:** Ah, shit.

**NORA:** Something wrong, dear?

**GAIL:** Yeah. They're still here. Can't you get rid of them. Can't you tell them to just get the hell out. Don't they have something else they could be doing. You know, maybe something useful for a change ... Shit.

*She leaves.*

**MIKE:** Who was that.

**NORA:** My youngest daughter. Gail.

**MIKE:** So what's her problem.

**DIAN:** She hates cops obviously. Right, Nora?

**NORA:** Yes.

**DIAN:** Any particular reason?

**NORA:** Lots of particular reasons. For one thing, she believes being a policeman is what turned her father into a monster.

**MIKE:** Well, that's just stupid. Get her back in here. I'll straighten her out.

**DIAN:** That won't be necessary.

**MIKE:** Says who. Besides, we should question her anyway. Just because I've got a hunch about the mother here doesn't mean I've got the same hunch about her kid.

**DIAN:** I'm afraid he's right, Nora. Gail's involvement will have to be determined at some point. We can assume only so much.

**MIKE:** Listen, we don't have to tell you any of this. What we assume. What we don't assume. We're doing it because you're Tom's wife. And Tom was a good cop.

**NORA:** Tom's dead! And he was a good cop but a lousy father. A neglectful, bitter parent. I'm a good parent, relative to him, anyway. You'll have to remember that if you bring trouble to my family. If you remember that, you'll understand my anger and why I'll be trying to destroy you … I'm sorry I said that. That wasn't me talking. Not really. That must have been some dark part of my soul talking. Forget what I said. You just do your police work and everything will be fine. That's what we have to believe. That the positive will win out. That the dark parts of a mother's soul won't be awakened. (*stands*) In the meantime I'll just go upstairs. I have something productive to do up there. I'm wallpapering the bathroom.

*She leaves. Pause.*

**DIAN:** So?

**MIKE:** So? What.

**DIAN:** What do you make of her.

**MIKE:** She's a fucking flake. They'll be putting a net around her any day. When she talks, my skin crawls. I get a headache. If we have to interrogate her again, you do it alone.

**DIAN:** What's your problem. Does she remind you of someone in your past or something.

**MIKE:** Did I say that. You're out of line.

**DIAN:** Just curious. Is it common for you to have such an emotional personal response to people.

**MIKE:** You're way out of line. They've told me about you. I think we should keep our relationship professional.

**DIAN:** I'm a professional. Don't worry. Didn't I handle that interrogation in a professional manner.

**MIKE:** Not really. No. I thought you were kind of weird with her. Kind of friendly or something. Like you were trying some … new approach. Maybe it's the approach I've been told to watch out for. No one knows exactly what it is. But it's new. And no one likes it.

**DIAN:** I have degrees in sociology and urban planning. Could that be what you're talking about.

**MIKE:** I don't know. Maybe. Why'd you tell me that. What's that prove. It's like you're always trying to impress me or something.

**DIAN:** I think police work is just an expression of my need to participate. A way to use my education to interact fully in the human experience.

**MIKE:** I don't want you interacting with me. Let's get that straight. First of all, I'm married.

**DIAN:** You think I'm interested in you sexually. You're old enough to be my father. Actually, you remind me a lot of my father. Maybe that's why I have these strange, ambivalent feelings about you. Relax. I'm just thinking out loud now.

**MIKE:** Hey, hey! Come on, I was just saying I get enough interaction. I've got a family that does that to me all the time. You're just my partner. We're cops looking for crooks. That's it.

**DIAN:** That's part of it. The rest of it is we're human beings. We need a certain degree of self-awareness, or we can't do our jobs properly. For example, when I ask you for an opinion about a suspect, and you launch into an obsessive whine about how that suspect gives you a headache and makes your skin crawl, I feel it's important to find out why. I think maybe she reminds you of your mother.

**MIKE:** You can't talk to me like that. You wanna know why? Because I don't understand what you're saying. Also, it freaks me out. We've got a job to do here. We can't be freaking each

other out. I'm freaked already. I'm so freaked I can't stand to
be in the same room with you. I'm gonna wait in the car.
(*starts off*)

DIAN:  Hold on a minute. Talking about professionalism, what
was all that about black guys, Asian guys, guys in turbans.

MIKE:  Questions. They were just questions.

DIAN:  Incredibly insensitive questions. Surely you know that our
attitude to racial matters is publicly suspect. You do read the
newspapers occasionally, I assume. Because if you don't, if all
you do is follow your … hunches, well you're just not aware
enough to do your job properly.

MIKE:  Look, just shut up. Don't talk to me anymore. All I know is
I've got a hunch, yeah that's right, a hunch that something's
going on in this house. And I'm gonna get a search warrant.
A good, old-fashioned search warrant.

*He leaves.*

DIAN:  (*throws her arms in the air. She starts off talking to herself*)
Yeah, get a search warrant. Get a couple of attack dogs, too.
Hey, why not get the whole stinking army!

*She is gone.*

*NORA sticks her head in. Looks around. Comes in. She is carrying a roll
of wallpaper. She goes to the screen door. Then over to the table. Sits. She
looks worried. She begins to mumble to herself. Slowly we realize she is
replaying her scene with the two cops. We catch the odd key word,
recognize a gesture, a movement. After a moment GAIL comes back in,
holding TOM by the arm. TOM moves slowly. His head is bowed. He has
a blanket around him. GAIL helps TOM towards a chair.*

GAIL:  Thanks for getting them out of here. The smell of them
was filling the house.

*GAIL helps TOM sit. She gets a box of crackers from a cupboard. Sits next
to him. Gives them to him one at a time. He eats slowly.*

NORA:  They left on their own. In their own good time, I think.
They were so irregular. So full of tension. The world out
there is getting worse by the minute. And the police are
being affected. Their nerves are frayed. Their minds are
disintegrating.

**GAIL:** Why'd you let them in. They had no right being here in the first place.

**NORA:** I was just being polite.

**GAIL:** You let people in this house all the time. Total strangers. Derelicts. Crazy people. You have to stop. This is a good time to stop.

**NORA:** Are you saying they weren't actually the police, that they were just crazy people pretending to be the police.

**GAIL:** No. What I'm saying is smarten up. It's time to just stop trusting everyone. Cops included. They're out to get us.

**NORA:** Everyone? Is everyone out to get us.

**GAIL:** No! Yes! Yes. Just assume everyone's out to get us. And if those cops show up again, keep them out. Call someone.

**NORA:** I'll call Elizabeth. She'll know what to do.

**TOM:** Who's Elizabeth.

**GAIL:** Elizabeth is your oldest daughter, Dad. She's a lawyer.

**NORA:** Gail. Please. I've asked you a hundred times not to call this man Dad.

*She goes to the fridge. Starts to clean it out and rearrange things.*

**GAIL:** I'm not having this argument with you anymore, Mom. If you don't want to admit he's your husband that's your business. But he's my father. He's Mary Ann's father. And he's Elizabeth's father.

**TOM:** Mary Ann?

**GAIL:** Your other daughter. You see, Dad, it goes like this … Try to pay attention, I'm getting sick of telling you. Elizabeth is the oldest, then Mary Ann. Then me. I'm Gail. I'm the youngest.

**TOM:** Why don't the other two ever come around.

**GAIL:** They come around when you're asleep, Dad. They don't like you.

**TOM:** Was I mean to them.

**GAIL:** Yes, you were.

**TOM:** Was I mean to you.

**GAIL:** Yes. You were mean to me, too.

**TOM:** But you're here all the time.

**GAIL:** I forgave you.

**NORA:** You forgave him? You took a total stranger and made him into your flesh and blood. It was an act of incredible imagination and perhaps even generosity. But Gail, I have to ask you, where is it all leading. What good can come from it.

**TOM:** (*points to NORA*) She'll never forgive me.

**GAIL:** You got that right.

**TOM:** Does she know I'm dying. Maybe if we tell her I'm dying she'll forgive me.

**NORA:** Tell him I know he's dying. And I'm sorry. He's a human being. I feel genuine sadness over the dilemma of death as faced by all human beings. But also tell him that's beside the point.

**TOM:** There's misery in this house. I can feel it. Is it because of me. It usually is.

**GAIL:** Junior was hurt, Dad.

**TOM:** I know Junior. He brings me soup.

**GAIL:** Junior was beat up by a couple of guys. We don't know why.

**TOM:** Bastards. Were they bastards.

**GAIL:** Yeah. And now the cops are on our back. They think Junior is involved with these guys in some criminal gang or something.

**TOM:** Bastards. Bastard cops. Bastards.

**NORA:** Don't let him get started.

**TOM:** Bastardization! I've had experience with all those bastards. The crooks, and the cops, and their bastardization of the simple, real world that was constructed by simple, real people. I like Junior. He brings me soup, and unsalted crackers. (*stands*) If you see him, send him my best. I've got to go back to bed now. I'm upset. (*starts towards the door to the hall. Stops*) Junior's not here?

**GAIL:** No, Dad. He's in the hospital.

**TOM:** If I need soup, who'll bring it to me.

**GAIL:** I will.

**TOM:** Good. And crackers … And some juice. The fizzy kind. With a straw, if it's no trouble.

*He leaves.*

**NORA:** Go watch him. Make sure he doesn't go into my bedroom.

**GAIL:** He knows where his room is.

**NORA:** Go watch.

*GAIL goes out to the hall.*

**NORA:** He forgets. He *says* he forgets. Sometimes he's in my bed. Under the covers. Naked. I have to sleep down here in the living room. I'm getting scared. Do you think he wants a sexual experience.

**GAIL:** Well, not tonight. He's in his own room.

*MARY ANN and ELIZABETH appear at the screen door.*

**MARY ANN:** Is he gone.

**GAIL:** Yes.

**ELIZABETH:** Go check.

**GAIL:** I just did. He's gone to his room. For the night.

**ELIZABETH:** Go make sure.

**MARY ANN:** Go make sure he's not listening at his door. That he's actually gone to bed.

**GAIL:** No.

**ELIZABETH:** Go check, Gail.

**MARY ANN:** We're not coming in until someone goes up there and tells us he's in his bed.

**NORA:** Please, Gail. We need them to come inside. We can't talk about the things we need to talk about through the screen door.

**ELIZABETH:** Look, we're not staying out here indefinitely. We're leaving.

**MARY ANN:**  She's right. We're leaving. Or we're coming in. But we're only coming in if someone actually goes up there and checks him out.

**NORA:**  (*to GAIL*) Please, dear.

**GAIL:**  Unbelievable. (*she goes out*)

**NORA:**  This should only take a second. How are you both.

**ELIZABETH:**  Fine.

**MARY ANN:**  I'm okay, Mom.

**NORA:**  How's your daughter, Mary Ann.

**MARY ANN:**  She's great, Mom. She misses you. She said to give you a "beeeg kiss." She said, "I miss gwamma. I want gwamma."

**ELIZABETH:**  Shut up!

**MARY ANN:**  That's what she said.

**ELIZABETH:**  She said gwamma?

**MARY ANN:**  Yeah.

**ELIZABETH:**  Well, she's four years old. Teach her how to say it properly.

> *GAIL comes back.*

**GAIL:**  He's in bed. He wants split pea.

**ELIZABETH:**  He wants what?

**GAIL:**  Soup. He likes soup. That's basically all he likes.

**NORA:**  You can come in now. (*They come in. ELIZABETH heads for the telephone. Takes a pad from her briefcase. Punches in her code. Writes down her messages*) Will you make his soup for him, Gail.

**GAIL:**  That's what I'm doing, Mom. That's why I opened the cupboard. That's why I took out this can.

**NORA:**  (*to ELIZABETH*) Junior usually makes his soup. But Junior … Well Junior is … You better tell them, Gail.

**GAIL:**  I told them already, Mom. I called them and told them. That's why they're here.

**MARY ANN:**  Where's your daughter.

**GAIL:**  Upstairs. Asleep. Where's yours.

**MARY ANN:** At home. What do you mean. She's at home, of course. She's asleep too. What do you mean, Gail. What are you getting at.

**GAIL:** Nothing. Relax. You asked about mine. I asked about yours.

**NORA:** That's what sisters do. They ask each other things.

**ELIZABETH:** How come Dad only eats soup. Is he getting worse.

**GAIL:** Yeah.

**MARY ANN:** Has he seen a doctor lately.

**NORA:** Now why would Gail want to talk about that. Talk about a man who, to be kind about it, may or may not be her actual father, when her actual husband is lying in the hospital fighting for his life.

**MARY ANN:** His life?

*ELIZABETH hangs up the phone.*

**GAIL:** No. He's going to be all right. Broken arm. Ribs. Cuts and stuff. Mom, why do you do that. Say outrageous exaggerations like that.

**NORA:** To get attention, perhaps. To bring the truth into focus. To provide a topic for discussion. To get things rolling. Something like that. Tea anyone? Sit down. Everyone sit down. Except you, Gail. You just continue making the man upstairs his soup. And make sure you serve it at just the right temperature. I know you will, though. I know you deeply respect his needs. (*to MARY ANN*) She deeply, deeply respects his needs ... for some reason.

**MARY ANN:** She feels sorry for him, Mom.

**ELIZABETH:** Yeah, Mom. She's like you that way. She has sympathy for the diseased and dying.

**GAIL:** He's my father.

**ELIZABETH:** So what. He's my father, too. And do you see me taking care of him. I'd like to throw him off the goddamn roof.

**MARY ANN:** You see, Mom, we all feel our own way about him. Elizabeth hates him. I'm afraid of him, and Gail feels sorry for him. And that's okay. It has nothing to do with you. It's not directed at you. Any of it.

**NORA:** He's in my house. He eats my food. Uses my furniture. And my bathroom. Occasionally sleeps in my bed.

**GAIL:** By accident.

**NORA:** So *she* says. But, well, I'll give her that one. That one is too distressing to discuss in detail. We'd have to explore the darkest part of human sexuality.

**ELIZABETH:** Mom, please.

**NORA:** I know. I know. That man upstairs says he is your father. And you all have a tremendous inner need to believe him.

**ELIZABETH:** And you have a need not to believe him. We respect that, Mom.

**MARY ANN:** We agreed to that, Mom. We agreed to let you not believe. And you agreed to let us believe.

**NORA:** But from an historical perspective, Mary Ann—it's hard. Historically, your actual father deserted us and left us in a wretched hole of poverty and debt. And then ten years later a man just ... shows up. The man upstairs. Why? It's a simple question. But the answer could be historically terrifying. It scares me. I can't sleep. I'm thinking of taking pills. Lots of pills.

**GAIL:** Oh, stop it. You're fine. You don't see him much. You never talk to him. You can deal with it. He stays. I want my kid to know her grandfather. I want her to have roots.

**NORA:** Okay. Forget it. *I'm fine* ... if she says so—

**ELIZABETH:** (*to GAIL*) Whatya mean roots. She doesn't need roots from that jerk. He's her grandfather, but he's slime.

**MARY ANN:** Anyway, she's got us. We're her roots.

**GAIL:** You're never here.

**MARY ANN:** We're here.

**GAIL:** You sneak in at night for a few minutes. Give Mom a hug, then piss off. When's the last time you saw Gwen.

**MARY ANN:** Who's Gwen.

**GAIL:** Gwen's my daughter's name, you asshole.

**MARY ANN:** Please be nice to me. I've made so much progress in the last few months. I'm a much stronger, more independent person. But I believe my strength and independence are entirely dependent on people being nice to me. So does Clare.

**GAIL:** Who's Clare.

**ELIZABETH:** Her therapist.

**MARY ANN:** My friend ... My therapist and my friend. Mom. I have something to tell you.

**GAIL:** Not now. (*to ELIZABETH*) Please don't let her get started.

**MARY ANN:** I have knowledge. It's important knowledge, and I want to share it with my mother. With you too, Gail.

**GAIL:** No. Look. I guess you guys have forgotten why I called you. You know. Junior. The crooks. The cops.

**ELIZABETH:** Don't worry. I'm looking into it. I've called my contacts on the police force.

**NORA:** I thought everyone on the police force hated you, dear.

**ELIZABETH:** Most of them ... Ignorant, neanderthal bastards can't take a little constructive criticism.

**NORA:** (*to GAIL*) Elizabeth has recently been publicly critical of the of the police in several sensitive areas.

**MARY ANN:** We know. We're all real proud of her.

**GAIL:** Right. But now we've got to—

**ELIZABETH:** Don't worry. When I've got time I'll call my contacts back. See what they found out.

**MARY ANN:** Mom. Gail.

**GAIL:** When you've got time?

**MARY ANN:** Gail. Mom. Listen. I have to share this knowledge with you. I've always shared my knowledge with you. All of you.

**ELIZABETH:** And that's what's made us the people we are today.

**MARY ANN:** Elizabeth is a lesbian.

ELIZABETH:  What.

MARY ANN:  You're a lesbian. And you're proud of it. And I'm proud of you for being proud. And now Mom and Gail can be proud of you, too.

ELIZABETH:  Mary Ann, what are you doing.

MARY ANN:  I'm outing you.

NORA:  What, dear.

MARY ANN:  I'm outing her. She's been in the closet. I'm helping her get out. She's a lesbian. Say it loud and clear. She's a lesbian. She's a lesbian! Clare told me to do it. Someone did it to Clare, and it was the best day of her life. So I'm doing it to you Elizabeth. You're a lesbian. You have sex with women. Lots and lots of women. Right?!

ELIZABETH:  (*to NORA and GAIL*) Let's talk about Junior.

NORA:  We went to see him in the hospital.

GAIL:  There were two cops guarding his door. I mean come on, they think he's some kind of criminal mastermind.

NORA:  I'm worried, Elizabeth. The beating was unprovoked. They broke in and beat him for a reason Junior doesn't know.

ELIZABETH:  Or isn't telling.

GAIL:  He doesn't know! Okay?! We got that straight? We can move on from that?!

ELIZABETH:  Yeah. Okay. He doesn't know.

MARY ANN:  (*pointing at ELIZABETH*) Lesbian!

ELIZABETH:  Look, what's your problem.

MARY ANN:  It won't work unless you admit it. Admit it, and let us all hug you and love you. Lots and lots and lots.

ELIZABETH:  If I admit it, do you promise not to hug and love me lots and lots and lots.

MARY ANN:  Whatever.

ELIZABETH:  Okay.

MARY ANN:  Say it.

ELIZABETH:  I'm a lesbian.

**MARY ANN:** Tell Mother.

**ELIZABETH:** Hey, Mom. I'm a lesbian.

**NORA:** I know, dear.

**ELIZABETH:** She knows.

**MARY ANN:** She knows? For how long.

**ELIZABETH:** Forever, you silly cow. You're the only one in this family who didn't know.

**MARY ANN:** Why. Why am I the only one who didn't know. Why. Tell me.

**ELIZABETH:** Guess.

**MARY ANN:** No. Tell me. Why didn't you tell me. How come Clare had to tell me.

**ELIZABETH:** Your therapist told you I was a lesbian?

**MARY ANN:** Yes. Clare told me. She says you're famous in lesbian circles. You're a famous lesbian. She told me to be proud of you. So I am. Not that I wasn't before. But now I am, too. But more so.

**ELIZABETH:** Why? Why more so?

**MARY ANN:** Because it was hard.

**ELIZABETH:** What was hard.

**MARY ANN:** Being a lesbian.

**ELIZABETH:** Get another therapist.

**MARY ANN:** Wasn't it hard.

**ELIZABETH:** Your life's falling apart. You've been a basket case for almost twenty years, and you sit around talking to your therapist about me … Amazing … Now tell them. Stop talking about me, and tell them what's new with you.

**MARY ANN:** Not yet.

**ELIZABETH:** Tell them. Or I will. And I won't make it all sad and gooey like you will.

**MARY ANN:** I'm leaving my husband.

**GAIL:** Again?

**MARY ANN:** I have to. I'm at a crossroads. How many times does a person come to a crossroads.

**GAIL:** If they're like you, about every three months.

**NORA:** What about your daughter. Is she with Barry.

**MARY ANN:** Larry. Yeah. He loves her. He'll be good to her. He understands my needs. He understands me.

**GAIL:** Great. Maybe he could explain you to us.

**ELIZABETH:** I asked him once. Actually, I begged him to explain to me what makes her tick. He just shook his head and whistled. And then he made the sound of a loon.

**MARY ANN:** You should talk to Clare. She could explain me to you. She explained me to me … Okay. This is the thing. I'm a kindred spirit of all the victims of the women's holocaust. A once powerful gender-species decimated by the religious patriarchy because they were terrified of their feminine strength.

**GAIL:** What the hell is she talking about. And why is she talking about it now!

**ELIZABETH:** (*smiles. To MARY ANN*) A witch. Are you saying you're a witch.

**MARY ANN:** I would have been a witch if the witches hadn't been decimated. (*to NORA*) The way it is now, I don't belong anywhere. I'm at a crossroads, though. I'm ready to belong somewhere. And the thing is, I've always admired Elizabeth so much. Elizabeth has always been my strength. So I'm thinking maybe I'll become a lesbian, too.

**ELIZABETH:** You see, that's why I never told you. I knew you'd pull some kind of wacky shit like this. This is not something you choose.

**MARY ANN:** I think you might be wrong. Clare showed me some statistics.

**ELIZABETH:** All right. It's something *you* shouldn't choose. And do you know why. Because all your choices are *wrong!*

**MARY ANN:** That's not fair!

**GAIL:** (*suddenly bangs the pot of soup down on the stove, hard*) Okay! That's it. That's enough! I mean, come on. Junior's in the frigging hospital. And there are cops swarming all over our lives here.

**NORA:** Mary Ann. I don't like saying this, but you leave me no choice. You could go to hell and rot there for eternity if you don't stop deserting that child of yours.

**MARY ANN:** I'm not deserting her. I'm at a crossroads!

**GAIL:** (*bangs the pot*) Hey! Shut up! Shut your stupid mouth! I didn't call you here to listen to this garbage!

**MARY ANN:** It's my life!

**GAIL:** Your life is a joke! (*starts to bang the pot over and over again*)

**ELIZABETH:** Okay! Okay! That's enough! I haven't got much time. I've got two *ex parte* restraining orders in chambers, a gender bias submission that was due yesterday and a poor sick bastard I'm trying to get committed! I'm very, very busy! Let's deal with this Junior thing, whatever it is.

**GAIL:** You're always very, very busy. If you can't spare the time to help your family, get the hell out!

**ELIZABETH:** Listen, kid. Watch your attitude. I'm here, aren't I?!

**MARY ANN:** And so am I!

**NORA:** But that could be a mistake, Mary Ann. You're here. But is there somewhere else you should be instead. Perhaps somewhere in the vicinity of the innocent, little child you brought into this world.

**MARY ANN:** Please, Mom. Don't keep doing this.

> GAIL *throws her arms up. She goes to the table. Sits. Puts her head down.*

**ELIZABETH:** She's your mother. She's just expressing an opinion.

**MARY ANN:** But it's so morally loaded. Isn't it. It's so dense with … guilt. And stuff. Guilt and remorse. She can say whatever she wants, but she can't—

> TOM *appears at the doorway.*

**TOM:** Hey, where's my soup.

**MARY ANN:** Oh my God.

> *She runs into the basement.*

**TOM:** Where's she going. Who is she.

**ELIZABETH:** Get him out of here.

**TOM:** Who are you.

**ELIZABETH:** Get him out of here. Or I'm history.

**GAIL:** (*looking up*) Go back to bed, Dad. The soup is coming.

**TOM:** Is this woman one of mine. She looks like me, I think. Shouldn't we be introduced.

**GAIL:** This is Elizabeth, Dad. Your oldest daughter. You know her. You've just forgotten.

**TOM:** Sure. I remember now. I've forgotten. (*to ELIZABETH*) Hi. How you doin'. Come here. Give me a hug.

**ELIZABETH:** Okay. That's it. I'll be out back. Let me know when this clown's back in his bed. You've got five minutes.

    *She goes out back.*

**NORA:** Tell him to leave, Gail. Tell him he's causing turmoil.

**TOM:** Well, that's obvious! I forget things but I'm not, you know …

**GAIL:** I'll be right up, Dad.

**TOM:** The thing about soup is the temperature. You know, just like the porridge in "Goldilocks." Think of me as Baby Bear. That's what I always tell Junior. Any word about Junior.

**GAIL:** He's going to be fine. Thanks for asking.

**TOM:** Well, as long as he dresses warmly and puts his wages in the bank. If he does that, Alaska can be a friendly, profitable place. Besides, the world needs that pipeline. You should be proud of Junior for helping to build it. When his plane gets in send him upstairs and we'll have a little chat.

    *He leaves.*

**NORA:** Everything he says has a purpose. Don't ever let him convince you otherwise. That man has a reason for being here, and a reason for everything that comes out of his mouth.

    *GAIL has a small tray prepared. She goes to the counter. Pours the soup into a bowl on the tray.*

**GAIL:** He's sick. He's got a disease that's done something to his mind. That's all there is to it. I'll take him his soup. Tell his other loving daughters it's safe to come back.

*GAIL leaves. NORA goes to the basement door.*

**NORA:** Mary Ann. You can come up now. (*goes to the screen door*) Elizabeth. It's all right. He's upstairs. (*goes to the table. Sits. Pours herself some tea*) Mary Ann! … Elizabeth!

*A moment's pause. From the basement, MARY ANN appears. Behind her with a hand over MARY ANN's mouth, is STEVIE MOORE. He is holding a gun.*

**STEVIE:** Okay, lady. Stay real calm. Stay calm, and I don't hurt her.

*He takes MARY ANN to the screen door. Yells out.*

You out there? Okay. Come in … Come on, come on. (*to NORA*) Okay, stay calm.

*The screen door opens. ELIZABETH appears. Behind her is ROLLY MOORE. He has his arm around her throat. A gun to her head.*

**ROLLY:** Did you tell everyone to stay calm.

**STEVIE:** Yeah.

**ROLLY:** Are they. Are they calm.

*MARY ANN passes out in STEVIE's arms.*

**STEVIE:** I don't know for sure. But I think so. I think they're calm. Look at them … What do you think.

*STEVIE lays MARY ANN against a cupboard.*

**ROLLY:** Yeah. I guess. Okay. (*to NORA*) You're the mother, right. We know you. (*to STEVIE*) Did you tell her the thing.

**STEVIE:** Yeah … No.

*ROLLY cuffs STEVIE.*

**ROLLY:** (*to NORA*) Okay, this is the thing. You've got something of ours. We want it back. That's the thing.

**STEVIE:** The thing is also, we're ready to kill.

**ROLLY:** Yeah. That's part of the thing, too. We're ready to kill. You understand us so far?

**NORA:** Yes.

**ROLLY:** Okay. So far so good. (*to STEVIE*) What do you say.

**STEVIE:** Yeah. I say that, too. So far so good.

**ROLLY:** Okay.

*STEVIE and ROLLY look at each other. Nod. GAIL comes in, breast-feeding the baby who is wrapped in a blanket. A long pause.*

**GAIL:** Great. Just great.

**STEVIE:** Oh, man. Dad, she's got a baby.

**ROLLY:** I can see that.

**STEVIE:** I can't do bad things to a baby. No way.

**ROLLY:** Yeah. Okay. No one ever asked you to hurt a baby. Stay calm. Everyone! Stay calm.

**GAIL:** I know you guys. You're the guys who put my husband in the hospital.

**NORA:** Gail. We don't have any opinion about the identity of these two men. These two men could leave now, and it would be like they were never here.

**ROLLY:** Except we need something you've got. And the thing is … The thing is—

**STEVIE:** I can't, Dad. Not in front of a baby. We might have to use maximum force here. And I don't know. I just don't know.

**ROLLY:** Hey, stay relaxed. You know. Calm down. Okay. Okay this is the thing … We're leaving. (*to NORA*) Like you said. We were never here.

**STEVIE:** Yeah. We were never here. But we'll be back.

**ROLLY:** Yeah we have to come back. Because the thing you've got, we need it. I don't know. Maybe you don't even know you've got it. It's a … strange thing.

**STEVIE:** Yeah. But we can't get into that now.

**ROLLY:** Right. Now we're leaving.

*They look at each other. Nod. Let the women go. Back up. Go out the screen door. ELIZABETH goes to the sink. Fills a glass with water.*

**GAIL:** Did you see that. Those assholes had guns. Didn't I tell you. This is a serious situation we've got here. Maybe next time I call a family meeting to discuss this situation we can stick to the fucking point!

*ELIZABETH walks past MARY ANN without stopping. She throws the water in MARY ANN's face. MARY ANN wakes up suddenly. ELIZABETH continues to the telephone. Picks up the receiver.*

**GAIL:** What are you doing.

**ELIZABETH:** Calling the police?

**GAIL:** No.

**MARY ANN:** Yes.

**GAIL:** No!

**ELIZABETH:** Mom?

**NORA:** I have mixed feelings. Give me a minute to think about it.

*They are all looking at her. GAIL hands the baby to MARY ANN.*

**GAIL:** Mom, we don't need the police. They're all pricks. I don't trust them. No way do I trust them. We can handle this ourselves. If we just put our heads together, and forget all that other shit, and try to concentrate on this one fucking problem, we can do it on our own. We can, Mom! Goddammit!

**NORA:** I'm thinking. In the meantime, Gail, if you don't mind a bit of advice. Now that you're a young mother with an innocent child you should try to watch your language. Every time we run into a bit of trouble your language deteriorates and eventually winds up in the gutter. It's not the words themselves that bother me. But they show that inside you've given up. That you feel trapped. Had a failure of the imagination. And that's no state of mind a young mother should be in. A young mother should be positive at all costs. No matter what the world throws at you, remain positive, remain buoyant, light ... Light as a feather. In fact, that's good advice for all of you. Remain light as feathers and everything will be fine.

*Pause.*

**GAIL:** (*looks at ELIZABETH. Gestures feebly*) You better call the police.

**ELIZABETH:** Okay.

*ELIZABETH is dialling. MARY ANN is trying to get the baby's attention, making little noises for her. NORA is looking around at all her daughters. Smiling. GAIL is shaking her head, sadly.*

*Blackout.*

## SCENE THREE

*DIAN and MARY ANN. DIAN is sitting at the table, nibbling on a sandwich that MARY ANN has made for her. MARY ANN is busy icing a chocolate cake and occasionally rearranging the condiments in front of DIAN.*

**MARY ANN:** Is this family doomed. I used to ask myself that question all the time. Are we forever doomed. Forever on the brink of destruction. Under some enormous shadow. Has God constructed a gigantic, mean-spirited shadow full of noxious, evil vibrations, emanating poisonous soul-killing rays, that has one job and one job only. To hover over this family and keep us doomed. And then one day I asked myself, why would God single out this family. And I knew right away that God wouldn't. God just made the shadow. And like everything else that God made, the shadow has a mind of its own. The shadow picked this family to hover over. I figured all this out a while ago, and it came as a great relief. You see, I didn't have to wonder anymore how we'd displeased God. I could forget about God for a while—which is always a great relief for me, seeing how I feel basically that God hates me—Mustard?

**DIAN:** No thanks.

**MARY ANN:** Anyway, I could forget about God, and concentrate on the shadow, and what possibly motivated it. You see, the shadow is fate. And our fate, the fate of this family, has some enormous grudge against us. So I figure we have to appease it, make amends, make some kind of huge, almost mythic, apology. We have to find a way of apologizing for something we don't know we did. So it has to be symbolic. It has to symbolize in some way everything bad each one of us has ever done as an individual or as part of a group. It's an almost impossible task. But we have to do it soon. Because we're doomed. Unless we make the shadow, you know, go away. Events are unfolding here that prove we're running out of time. Right now I'm making a chocolate cake, but inside what I'm really doing is apologizing. This cake is an apology for all the times I know that people I loved or people I hardly knew needed some special little treat, and I didn't have the energy to make them one. Just a little thing. But you see this huge, symbolic apology will actually be made from thousands and thousands of little things just like this ... This cake ... This chocolate cake, and oatmeal cookies, and blueberry pancakes, fudge, a nicely pressed pair of slacks, a bit of change to someone in need, taking care of a friend's cat, smiling on the subway. These are the things that are going to save this family.

**DIAN:** You're an awful lot like your mother.

**MARY ANN:** A chip off the old block. Yeah. Sort of. What do you mean.

*NORA comes in from upstairs.*

**NORA:** (*to DIAN*) Your partner said to tell you he'll be right down. He searched the entire upstairs. He has a search warrant.

**DIAN:** Yes, I know.

**NORA:** Right now he's in that man's room. Talking. He thinks he knows him, of course. What can I do about it.

**MARY ANN:** Bake a cake. Fix a chair. Give someone a hug. The little things.

**NORA:** That's right, dear. The little things. (*they hug each other*) Did you call your daughter yet, Mary Ann.

**MARY ANN:** Yes, Mom. She's fine. She misses me.

**NORA:** I'm sure she misses you. But it's also possible she's beginning question your reliability.

**MARY ANN:** Well that's a chance I'll have to take.

*MIKE comes in, laughing.*

**MIKE:** Same old Tom. The same basic guy. Still breaks me up. Don't know why ... (*to DIAN*) Upstairs is clear.

**DIAN:** What about the basement.

**MIKE:** You don't need to remind me about the basement. I was on my way to the basement. (*to NORA*) Where's the basement.

*NORA points.*

**MIKE:** I suppose you want to come with me. (*laughs*) You know, to make sure I don't plant anything.

**NORA:** If it's all right.

**DIAN:** Go ahead.

**MIKE:** You're giving her permission. *I* was talking to her. But *you're* giving her permission.

**DIAN:** She doesn't actually need permission.

**MIKE:** You're saying that. You're saying that in front of her.

**DIAN:** Yes. I am.

**MIKE:** Okay. Okay if *you* say so. (*to NORA*) Come on ...

*MIKE goes downstairs. NORA waves at DIAN. Goes downstairs.*

**MARY ANN:** Would you like a piece of chocolate cake.

**DIAN:** No, thank you. Would you mind answering a few questions for me.

**MARY ANN:** I don't like questions. I'd rather just give you things. If you don't want any cake, maybe I could make you another sandwich ... or a casserole ...

**DIAN:** They're not hard questions. I'm just looking for a little clarification.

**MARY ANN:** Oh my God. Clarification. I'm no good at that at all. Maybe in a year or two. Right now I'm just working on saying anything that comes into my mind. You know, unblocking myself. Maybe you could wait till my sister Elizabeth gets here. She's an expert on clarification.

**DIAN:** Elizabeth. She's the lawyer?

**MARY ANN:** Yes. A lesbian lawyer. We're very proud of her. She overcame so much to be what she is. Well, look around. This family has nothing. We used to have a bit. The usual amount a family like ours has. But our father took it all away when he left. Of course he came back eventually, but he didn't bring anything with him. And now, well he's a vegetable. Sort of. That's what they tell me. I don't know for sure, though, because I never see him. He scares me. It's odd about my father. When he deserted us, everything just fell apart. Who would have thought he had that kind of power. Not me. Before he deserted us, I barely gave him a second thought ... Except when he was doing something loud and horrible. But we were talking about Elizabeth ... Why.

**DIAN:** Elizabeth seems to be a very important part of this family.

**MARY ANN:** She's our weapon. She's the thing that protects us. I mean, if we're threatened.

**DIAN:** Like now.

**MARY ANN:** Like now. And then. Whenever.

**DIAN:** That's a heavy responsibility to take on.

**MARY ANN:** She can handle it.

**DIAN:** Mary Ann. Here's the problem I have. The men who broke in here, the men who beat up Junior ... Your mother seems to know these men ...

**MARY ANN:** That's actually a question, isn't it. I'm supposed to answer that, I can tell.

**DIAN:** Just try to make that clear for me. And then maybe I'll have a piece of cake or something.

**MARY ANN:** Okay. My mother hires people. Men mostly. Derelicts. Fallen men. Criminals even. She hires them to do handiwork around the house. She just finds them, we don't know how. They come here and work. She talks to them. Pays them. Talks to them some more.

**DIAN:** So she wouldn't really know much about them. Their names, or ... how to find them ...

**MARY ANN:** No. She doesn't ask them questions like that. She just talks to them. Would you like that cake now.

**DIAN:** Sure. You know, Mary Ann, this is a very rough neighbourhood. It's a dangerous environment you're living in here. Perhaps your family should try a more realistic approach in dealing with it.

**MARY ANN:** (*cuts a piece of cake. Puts it on a plate*) Realistic? Oh. I think I know what you mean. We've tried that. It doesn't seem to work for us. It was very real when I was a kid. My dad was here. There was anger and violence. Hopelessness. I think what we do now is better. It's more like Mom than Dad. And Mom's way is more ... well ...

**DIAN:** Innocent.

**MARY ANN:** (*laughs*) Innocent? No ... Hopeful.

*NORA comes up.*

**NORA:** He found something. I'm a little worried.

*MIKE comes up. Carrying two large garbage bags. Each about half full.*

**MIKE:** (*to DIAN*) They were hidden in a hole in the wall. Behind a work bench.

*MIKE puts the bags down. DIAN goes over. Looks in them.*

**DIAN:** Did you know about these bags, Nora.

**NORA:** No.

**DIAN:** So you don t know what's in them.

**NORA:** No. I mean, I suspect it's something of substance. Some substantially evil thing. I picked that up from the … substantially evil way your partner smiled at me.

**MIKE:** Hey!

**NORA:** (*to MARY ANN*) I'm a little worried about the neighbourhood fanatics. Break-ins. Police cars. I bet they're passing around a petition at this very moment.

**DIAN:** Drugs.

**MARY ANN:** Oh my God.

*MARY ANN goes to NORA. Puts her arms around her neck. Hangs on.*

**DIAN:** Hundreds of thousands of dollars worth of drugs. I think you'll have to come with us, Nora, so we can straighten this out. I'm sorry.

**MIKE:** You're sorry. You're telling her you're sorry.

**DIAN:** That's right. Come on, she didn't know they were there.

**MIKE:** (*goes to DIAN*) You're saying you don't think she knew. You're saying that right in front of her. Where the hell were you trained. Disneyland?

**DIAN:** I'll deal with you later!

**MIKE:** I'll deal with you later! (*to NORA*) Turn around. Put your hands behind your back.

*MIKE is trying to handcuff NORA. But MARY ANN still has her arms around NORA and is turning her around. MIKE is turning with them.*

**DIAN:** No cuffs.

*DIAN is trying to restrain MIKE.*

**MIKE:** We're in a war here. You ever hear about it. It's called the war on drugs. Drugs are the main thing now. It's what we're all about. It's our reason for friggin' living, and she's a suspected drug dealer.

*All four of them are tangled and turning.*

**DIAN:** I said no cuffs! Now get your hands off her or I'll have your head!

*DIAN groans and pulls MIKE away from NORA and MARY ANN. She is poking him in the chest and backing him up. MIKE is trying to resist. Trying to control his temper.*

**DIAN:** I've got friends. Friends high up. (*poke*)

**MIKE:** Back off.

**DIAN:** You know, the ones you resent. The ones you talk about behind my back. (*poke*)

**MIKE:** Get your hands off me. Back off.

**DIAN:** The ones you say gave me my job because I screwed their brains out. (*poke*)

**MIKE:** Back off. I'm warning you.

**DIAN:** I think you should assume these friends will do anything for me! (*poke*)

**MIKE:** Hey, you were warned. Now back the fuck off.

*He pokes her. She grabs him by the collar. He grabs her by the collar.*

**DIAN:** If I ask them, my friends will take your badge and shove it so far up your ass your spleen will think it's under arrest!

**MIKE:** You talk to me like that?! In front of them?! I gotta say fuck you! I really do! (*shakes himself free. To DIAN*) Fuck you. (*to NORA and MARY ANN*) And fuck you, too. (*picks up the garbage bags. To NORA and MARY ANN*) No, to you I'm sorry. (*to DIAN*) But to you, definitely, fuck you!

*He leaves.*

**DIAN:** (*trembling slightly. Searches her purse. Finds a small plastic tube*) Lip balm. Do you mind.

**NORA:** No.

**DIAN:** (*applies the lip balm, strenuously*) That was ugly, wasn't it. Sorry you had to witness that. Obviously my partner and I are having problems maintaining a relationship. There are just so many many differences between us. Age, sex, levels of intelligence. The conflicts run very deep. The relationship is deteriorating rapidly.

**NORA:** Would you like a cup of tea, dear.

**DIAN:** No.

**MARY ANN:** Cake?

**DIAN:** No. Thank you . .. We should go now, Nora. Back to the office. Talk this thing through in detail. You'll be back in no time.

**MARY ANN:** I want to come too.

**NORA:** No you don't, dear.

**MARY ANN:** You're right. I *want* to want to come. But I don't really want to come at all.

**DIAN:** (*to NORA*) Do you need a coat ... or a sweater.

**NORA:** No ... Should I call my daughter Elizabeth, though. She's a lawyer.

**MARY ANN:** She's the lesbian, remember. You'd like her. Not that I think you're a lesbian. Not that there's anything wrong with being a lesbian. I'm thinking about it myself. I just meant she was ... well, you know what I meant.

**DIAN:** No. But it's all right. Come on, Nora. You can call Elizabeth from my office.

*NORA goes to MARY ANN.*

**NORA:** Maybe you could cook supper.

**MARY ANN:** I would anyway. That's what I do when I run away from home, remember. I come here and cook things.

**NORA:** I've been thinking, Mary Ann. It's possible you aren't a good mother. It's possible you're just average. Maybe you could go home and just be a good, average mother. Think about that while you're cooking. I'll see you soon.

*NORA and DIAN leave. MARY ANN looks around. Lost. She goes to the table. Sits in a chair. Puts her head in her palms.*

**MARY ANN:** (*looks up suddenly, a puzzled look on her face*) When I said she'd like Elizabeth because Elizabeth is a lesbian what

*did* I mean. Really. I think I meant Elizabeth is *great.* She'd
like her because she's great. Why do I say lesbian instead of
great ... I don't know. But maybe I don't really want to be a
lesbian. Maybe I just want to be ... great ... Do I have to be a
lesbian to be great ... I'll ask Elizabeth. She wasn't always a
lesbian. She wasn't always great, either. What came first. The
lesbianism or the greatness. When did she become
lesbianistic. Is that a word. Use it in a sentence. Never mind.
It's beside the point. Just ask her. Okay. Yeah. Of course, she
hardly ever listens to me. Unless I cry. When I cry she listens.
Okay. Yeah. I'll cry. It's demeaning. But I'll do it. Because I
need to know. I mean, I'm working things out here.
Important things. Yeah.

    TOM *appears at the hallway door.*

**TOM:** I'm starving to death.

**MARY ANN:** Oh dear. (*she stands. Hurries towards the basement door.
Leaves. Reappears*) No. No. I can do better than this. I can.
(*looks at* TOM. *Smiles weakly*) Hi.

**TOM:** Hi.

**MARY ANN:** You're hungry?

**TOM:** (*lowers his head*) I'm starving to death.

**MARY ANN:** Would you like some chocolate cake.

**TOM:** Not soup?

**MARY ANN:** I can do soup. Soup is all right, too. I'll ... make you
some. From scratch. I'm good at soups. It'll take some time.
Can you wait.

**TOM:** No.

**MARY ANN:** Okay. Have the cake now. Here. I'll cut you a piece.
No. Here, take it all. Here's a fork. Take it.

**TOM:** (*takes the cake*) It's big.

**MARY ANN:** Yeah.

**TOM:** But there's a piece missing.

**MARY ANN:** Is that okay.

**TOM:** I don't know. Maybe. Maybe not. Who are you, anyway.

**MARY ANN:** Mary Ann.

**TOM:**  My daughter?

**MARY ANN:**  Yeah.

**TOM:**  I've gotta ask you a question.

**MARY ANN:**  Oh ... okay ... I guess.

**TOM:**  How you doin'. How's your life. Are you having a good life. Have you recovered.

**MARY ANN:**  Ah ... From what.

**TOM:**  Me ... I guess. Recovered from me. The things I did. I did some bad things to this family. I think I had a ... I had a ... I had a—

**MARY ANN:**  Problem. You had a problem.

**TOM:**  Drinking.

**MARY ANN:**  Drinking. Yeah. And a vicious temper. And awful impatience. But, well ... I'm okay. Sure, I'm fine now. That was your question? So ... I'm basically ... well, I've got some things to work on ... some choices I have to ... but basically—

**TOM:**  I'm tired.

*He leaves. MARY ANN sits down. Lowers her head on to the table. Keeps it there a moment. Sits up.*

**MARY ANN:**  Soup.

*She stands. Goes to the cupboard, the fridge, assembling ingredients for vegetable soup. GAIL and JUNIOR come in through the screen door. GAIL is helping JUNIOR, who has a slight limp, an arm in a cast and sling, and various cuts and bruises on his face. ELIZABETH is right behind them carrying a small suitcase.*

**GAIL:**  Hi ... Well, here he is. Look at him. Disgusting, isn't it. If I get my hands on those creeps I'm going to rip their faces off.

**ELIZABETH:**  What good will that do.

*She heads for the telephone. Punches in her code. Takes out a pad.*

**GAIL:**  It will make me feel terrific. That's what. You know, sometimes you just have to lash out, Elizabeth. You just have to lash out to keep yourself from going nuts. I learned that from you, Elizabeth. That's how you used to be before you became so ... busy.

**ELIZABETH:** What's your problem. You've been sniping at me all day. You were taking shots all the way home in the car.

**JUNIOR:** Can I sit down.

**MARY ANN:** Let me help you.

**JUNIOR:** Hi, Mary Ann. Why are you looking at me like that. I look pretty bad, eh.

**MARY ANN:** You probably just need some food. (*makes herself busy*) Lots and lots of food.

**JUNIOR:** Could I have a glass of water.

**GAIL:** Sure, honey. I'll get it.

**MARY ANN:** I'll get it.

**GAIL:** I said I'd get it! … Look at him. Pathetic or what. He's probably going to lose his job, too.

**JUNIOR:** Ah, no. You think so?

**GAIL:** Your foreman called. He said the police were by the plant. They told him some bad stuff about you. I'm going to go talk to him later. Maybe I can fix it.

**JUNIOR:** Maybe I should talk to him.

**GAIL:** Yeah? What would you say.

**JUNIOR:** Ah, I don't really—

**GAIL:** Well, until you can think of something, leave it to me. (*to MARY ANN*) Where's my baby.

**MARY ANN:** Still asleep, I think.

**GAIL:** What do you mean you think. Haven't you been checking on her.

**MARY ANN:** I checked her a while ago.

**GAIL:** When.

**MARY ANN:** I don't know.

**GAIL:** Well, was it ten minutes, an hour, two hours.

**MARY ANN:** I don't know!

**GAIL:** Too much. I feel like I'm in one of those science-fiction movies where I'm the only human being, and everyone else is some kind of plant life.

**MARY ANN:** I feel that way sometimes, too. Only the opposite.

**GAIL:** There. That's an example of what I mean. Nothing you say makes any sense to me. In fact nothing makes much sense to me these days. I'm married to a guy who has bad luck following him around like it's a close friend. And my oldest sister here, who I used to trust more than anyone, has turned out to be the biggest disappointment in my life.

*GAIL grabs the phone from ELIZABETH. Hangs up.*

**ELIZABETH:** Ah, come off it. I'm not responsible for all your problems. Where the hell do you get off blaming me.

**GAIL:** I'm not blaming you for the problems, Elizabeth. I'm blaming you for not helping to solve them. Are you a member of this family or not.

**MARY ANN:** She's changed, Gail. She's a changed person and she's trying to deal with it. It's because she's—

**ELIZABETH:** If you say I'm a lesbian again I'm going to take you upstairs and drown you in the bathtub.

**MARY ANN:** Are you saying you're *not* a lesbian.

**ELIZABETH:** Who I sleep with isn't the issue. Its never the issue. It's always never the issue. Why are you trying to make it so important. I sleep with women *and* men, if you must know. I sleep with anyone I like. I find nice, sexy people and I sleep with them.

**GAIL:** When you can spare the time.

**ELIZABETH:** Ah, gimme a break.

**GAIL:** Go ahead. Talk some more about yourself. Talk about your personal life, your love life. Like it's some big deal. Like we really care. I've got to go check on my baby.

*She leaves.*

**ELIZABETH:** Unbelievable. Why is she on my back like this. What the hell is her problem.

**JUNIOR:** She's upset.

**ELIZABETH:** I'm upset.

**MARY ANN:** I'm upset, too! You were supposed to be a lesbian. You were supposed to have made a choice. But no. You sleep with anyone just because they're nice! What kind of choice is that. That's not courageous. That's not politically ... important. Anyone can do that. Even I can do that.

**ELIZABETH:** No! No you can't. You can't even sleep with your husband. So go to hell!

**MARY ANN:** Don't talk to me! I'm busy. I'm cooking. And I'm re-examining my life! (*she is cutting vegetables*)

**JUNIOR:** Where's Mom.

**MARY ANN:** At the police station.

**ELIZABETH:** What's she doing there.

**MARY ANN:** The police took her there.

**ELIZABETH:** Why.

**JUNIOR:** Is she under arrest.

**MARY ANN:** I don t think so.

**ELIZABETH:** (*to JUNIOR*) Get serious. (*to MARY ANN*) What do you mean you don't think so. You don't know for sure?

**MARY ANN:** That's right. Not for sure.

**ELIZABETH:** Could you make a guess.

**MARY ANN:** No. Not really. They said they just wanted to question her. But that could have been a trick. Something they just said so she wouldn't make a fuss.

**ELIZABETH:** They can't do that. If she was under arrest they'd have to tell her.

**MARY ANN:** That's what you say about that now. Who knows what you'll say about it tomorrow. Maybe tomorrow you'll say they can arrest anyone anytime. Men. Women. Anyone who is sexy. And nice!

**ELIZABETH:** Shut up!

**JUNIOR:** Question her about what.

**MARY ANN:** About what they found when they searched the house.

**ELIZABETH:** They searched the house? You let them search the house?

**MARY ANN:** They had a warrant. Mom said it looked official.

**JUNIOR:** What did they find.

**MARY ANN:** Drugs. In the basement.

**ELIZABETH:** What are you talking about?!

**MARY ANN:** Hundreds of thousands of dollars worth of drugs in two garbage bags.

*JUNIOR groans. Puts his head down on the table.*

**ELIZABETH:** How the hell did they get there.

**MARY ANN:** How am I supposed to know. Questions I can answer are one thing. Questions like that I don't feel bad for ignoring.

**ELIZABETH:** Oh God, you're too much, Mary Ann. And you didn't think any of this was worth mentioning when we first got here. Cops come here with a warrant, search our house, find bags full of dope, take our mother away, and you just go about your business like usual. You just cook something!

**MARY ANN:** Dad's hungry.

**ELIZABETH:** *Who's* hungry?

**MARY ANN:** Dad. I talked to him. Yes. I know we promised we never would, but I couldn't help it. I was trying to be a better person. Make apologies.

**ELIZABETH:** You're apologizing to him? You've got that kind of ass-backwards, haven't you.

**MARY ANN:** Not in the mythic, larger—

**ELIZABETH:** Shut up. We'll deal with that later. (*starts off*) I'm going after Mom. She's probably scared half to death. (*stops*) Where'd they take her. Downtown to headquarters? Why am I asking you that. You don't know, do you. You didn't friggin' ask, did you. Did you?!

**MARY ANN:** That's right! I didn't! I'm sorry!

*ELIZABETH grabs MARY ANN.*

**ELIZABETH:** When I get back I'm going to do something to you, Mary Ann. I'm going to change your outlook on life. I'm going to crawl inside your brain and alter your entire personality. The neurotic idiot child you are now is going to cease to exist. Say goodbye to her forever! … Shit!

*She goes out the back. JUNIOR lifts his head.*

**MARY ANN:** (*kind of thrilled*) That's how she used to talk to me. Remember.

**JUNIOR:** Yeah.

**MARY ANN:** You look worried.

**JUNIOR:** Aren't you.

**MARY ANN:** About Elizabeth? No. I like it sort of when she talks to me like that. I can't explain it. I'm sure it's not healthy, but what can I do.

**JUNIOR:** No I meant aren't you worried about your mother being in jail.

**MARY ANN:** Oh yeah. But I can't think about that. I'd die.

*GAIL comes back in.*

**GAIL:** She was hungry. She was lying there ... hungry. (*to JUNIOR*) You know that sad, hurt little look she gets.

**MARY ANN:** Why didn't she cry.

**GAIL:** She doesn't cry.

**MARY ANN:** Not even when she's hungry. Why not.

**GAIL:** I don't know. Maybe she just trusts us. Maybe she thought, "Hey, they're all responsible adults. One of them is bound to look in on me before I starve to death."

**MARY ANN:** Well, if I were you I'd teach her how to cry. Adults can let you down. They aren't perfect ... I think adults are expected to do too much, anyway. Why can't we—

**GAIL:** Why do you do that. I was just being sarcastic. Just trying to make a point. Why can't you just let me make my point without launching into one of those long, complicated ... things. You're getting more like Mom every day.

**MARY ANN:** I know!

**GAIL:** In some ways. Just in some ways. I mean, Mom cares more about kids. Mom would never neglect a kid.

**MARY ANN:** (*starts to cry*) I know! I know!

*Pause.*

**GAIL:** I looked in on Dad. He says you're making him soup. He's fantasizing, right.

**MARY ANN:** No. I'm doing it.

**GAIL:** Really ... He says you talked to him.

**MARY ANN:** A little.

**GAIL:** Really ... Do you want to talk to him some more. He needs company. I could finish the soup.

**MARY ANN:** It's vegetable. Not out of a can. From scratch.

**GAIL:** I think I can manage that, Mary Ann. Do you want to go up and see him.

**MARY ANN:** I don't know. Maybe I said all I've got to say to him right now.

**GAIL:** You could read to him. He likes that. There's a pile of books beside his bed ...

*Pause. MARY ANN is staring at the floor.*

**GAIL:** Come on, Mary Ann. What's it going to be. Are you going all the way with this one or not. Are we going to be living in the past forever with this guy, or are we going to make a little progress here ... Mary Ann, he's dying. Do it for the same reason I do it. So that when he's dead you won't feel so shitty. You'll feel it was basically okay with him for a while at least. Not great. But okay.

*Pause.*

**MARY ANN:** Yeah.

*She leaves.*

**GAIL:** That's a breakthrough. You know, just when you've written her off she surprises you. She's always done that. Sometimes at the last moment ... You know, just when your hands are around her throat, and you're about to apply serious pressure.

**JUNIOR:** I like her. I've always liked her.

**GAIL:** What's wrong. That look on your face. Are you in pain.

**JUNIOR:** Come here. Sit down. Here. On my lap.

**GAIL:** What about your ribs.

**JUNIOR:** Don't worry.

**GAIL:** Nah. I don't want to hurt you, honey. I'll sit next to you. (*she does*)

**JUNIOR:** But you see, I'd kind of like to hold you.

**GAIL:** Are you going to cry.

**JUNIOR:** No.

**GAIL:** That's what you say when you're going to cry. That you want to hold me.

**JUNIOR:** Yeah. I know. But I'm not. Just sit on my lap.

**GAIL:** Okay. But let's be careful. (*she sits on his lap. Puts her arm around him*) What's wrong. Something real terrible I bet. You had another one of those dreams where I meet someone with money and style, and take off with him.

**JUNIOR:** Your mother's in jail.

**GAIL:** Oh. Right. Sure.

**JUNIOR:** The cops found some drugs in the house. I guess they think she's been dealin'.

> *GAIL starts to laugh. Harder. Really hard. Rolls off JUNIOR on to the Floor. Sits up. Points at him.*

**GAIL:** I love you. You always know when I need to laugh.

**JUNIOR:** No, seriously. The drugs were in the basement. In green garbage bags. Hundreds of thousands of dollars worth.

> *GAIL pounds the floor. Laughing almost hysterically. Falling back.*

**JUNIOR:** No, seriously ... Gail ... We've got a real problem here. Come on. Really.

> *Lights start to fade. GAIL's laughter continues into the ...*
>
> *Blackout.*

## SCENE FOUR

*JUNIOR, MARY ANN and TOM are at the table. TOM has a blanket around him, his head is bowed. JUNIOR is feeding TOM soup. He has to lift TOM's head for each spoonful. MARY ANN has her elbows on the table, her head in her hands. She's staring at TOM, smiling a little. After a while, GAIL comes in from the hallway, pushing the baby in a stroller.*

**GAIL:** I'm off. I won't be long.

**JUNIOR:** Where are you going.

**GAIL:** I told you. To talk to your foreman.

**JUNIOR:** You can leave the baby here, if you want.

**GAIL:** Are you kidding ... Anyway this beautiful little girl is going to save your job. I'm going to pick her up, let that foreman of yours look into her eyes and see if he can fire you then. You don't mind me doing this, do you. I mean, it won't make you feel weak, or unmanly, or something stupid like that.

**JUNIOR:** Just save my job. That's the only important thing.

**GAIL:** I love you. Are you coming, Mary Ann.

**MARY ANN:** Where are you going.

**GAIL:** How do you do that, Mary Ann. How can you be in a room and not hear a word that's said.

**MARY ANN:** Practice. Where are you going.

**GAIL:** I've got something to do. And then I thought we'd go shopping.

**MARY ANN:** Grocery shopping?

**GAIL:** Whatever. Do you have any money.

**MARY ANN:** I took some of our life savings. Larry always agrees to let me do that when I leave.

**GAIL:** Larry is a very generous, understanding man. Larry might be Jesus Christ come back to earth. Did you ever think of that.

**MARY ANN:** He's got faults like everyone else. So you can't make me feel bad saying things like that. I'm beyond guilt anyway. I'm in some other place now.

**GAIL:** Yeah. Where is it.

**MARY ANN:** (*shrugs*) It's the place ... in the place ... where I have to be.

**GAIL:** Let's not talk to each other for a while. Let's just go shopping.

**MARY ANN:** Okay. (*stands*)

**JUNIOR:** Was that Elizabeth again on the phone.

**GAIL:** Yeah.

**JUNIOR:** Something wrong? She got Mom away from those cops, didn't she. They didn't try to take her back or anything.

**GAIL:** She just wanted me to know they had something to do before they came home. She wouldn't tell me what. She sounded really really ticked off. Like the old Elizabeth. It's great to hear her like that.

**MARY ANN:** Yeah. It is, isn't it. I wonder why.

**GAIL:** Let's go. (*to JUNIOR*) See ya. (*JUNIOR waves*)

**MARY ANN:** Do you think we've got a hang-up about Elizabeth. You know the kind of thing where we know she's our sister but we really think she's our mother or something like that.

*GAIL opens the back door. Pushes MARY ANN through. Follows her.*

*JUNIOR stands.*

**JUNIOR:** Great. The cops think someone is dealing dope out of this house. This house right here. People we're supposed to love are living in this house ...

*TOM mumbles.*

**JUNIOR:** What? I can't hear you. Lift your head. They're gone.

**TOM:** I'm afraid they might come back. If they come back and see me normal they'll make me leave. (*lowers his head*)

**JUNIOR:** They're not coming back. Lift your head. We have to talk. The people in this house are in deep trouble.

**TOM:** (*lifts his head*) Yeah. I know. Did you put drugs in our basement ... for some reason.

**JUNIOR:** No. I thought you did for some reason.

**TOM:** Then it's a mistake. (*lowers his head*)

**JUNIOR:** A mistake? Someone's going to jail. In my bones I feel it. Someone in this house is gonna do some time over this. Whatya mean a mistake. That's gotta be the wrong word. Think about it. A mistake is like … an accident. Those garbage bags didn't get down there by accident. Please lift your fucking head! I need your help!

**TOM:** (*lifts his head*) I mean a mistake in our strategy. Someone figured out what we were doing, and did it to us for some reason.

**JUNIOR:** Who the hell could figure out what we were doing. I mean, I was actually doing it, and I could hardly understand it myself.

**TOM:** Look, you have to stop underestimating these crooks. I warned you about that right from the start.

**JUNIOR:** No, you didn't. You just threw me in. Right into the middle of a bunch of low-life scum.

**TOM:** They're scum. But they've got experience. Experience can make stupid people smart. Experience is a kind of replacement for intelligence.

**JUNIOR:** Not close up. Not when they open their mouths and talk to you. You've put me in a position where I've had to listen to a lot of scum talking right at me. Real close, you know? Guys who mug, steal, break and enter. Guys who rent their sisters out for twenty dollars an hour. They trusted me. They showed their, you know, inner thoughts. And their inner thoughts are stupid! So stupid they make me want to puke. God, man. They're everywhere. And I'm right in the middle of them.

**TOM:** That's right! That's my point, goddammit! This neighbourhood is going down the toilet. And no one else seems to be doing anything about it. Goddamn cops, social workers, goddamn press. Bastards. I don't know. Maybe the bastards don't have enough at stake. But this is where my family lives. I owe it to them to fix their neighbourhood. Okay. Let's get to work! (*stands suddenly*)

**JUNIOR:** What? Calm down. Sit down. We're not doing anything. Not until we figure out what we've already done.

**TOM:**  I owe my family. You know I owe them! (*he is agitated.*
*Moving around*)

**JUNIOR:**  Yeah. I know. But that's not—

*TOM approaches JUNIOR quickly.*

**TOM:**  Do you! Do you really know?!

*TOM grabs JUNIOR by the shoulder of his broken arm.*

**JUNIOR:**  (*groans*) Yeah. I really do. I do!

**TOM:**  I hurt this family. I was a frigging monster. I have to make
amends for all the bad things I did to them. I have to
apologize in a really major way!

*TOM is staring into space. Squeezing JUNIOR's shoulder.*

**JUNIOR:**  Don't get too worked up, man.

**TOM:**  Do you know what I did? I tried to burn this house down
once. I tried to burn it down while they were all asleep in
their beds ... So I guess I tried to kill them. What do you
think. Does that sound like attempted murder. Attempted
goddamn mass murder!

**JUNIOR:**  Yeah. But try to calm down a little.

**TOM:**  They didn't even have me arrested. Nora felt sorry for me.
God, man. What a lucky bastard I was. I owe them. I've got to
fix this part of the world where they live. This little part of the
world is theirs. I've got to make it better. I do!

*TOM starts to move around again. JUNIOR stands. Gently approaches*
*TOM.*

**JUNIOR:**  Maybe you don't. Maybe it's too much. Maybe there's a
limit to what you can do, you know, a line ... and you've
crossed it. I've been thinking about this. Maybe you just have
to talk to them. Let them see that you're basically all right
now. Just be yourself.

*TOM turns on JUNIOR.*

**TOM:**  Myself?! That's not enough! (*he grabs JUNIOR*) You know
that! That's not enough. Goddammit!

*JUNIOR loses his balance. Falls. Groans loudly. Grabs his broken arm.*

**TOM:**  Ah, damn! Are you all right.

**JUNIOR:**  Holy shit. I can't believe what's happening to my life.

**TOM:** I'm sorry ... You see, I can't be myself. This is the self I can't be. They'd never trust me. And who could blame them. They'd toss me out in a minute. (*sits. Puts the blanket around himself*) I'm here because I don't look threatening to them. (*lowers his head*) And that's the way it has to stay.

**JUNIOR:** (*getting up slowly*) So that's it? You've only got two speeds? You're either gonna rant and rave or sit there like a zombie. Can't we get you somewhere in between those two things. And can't we get you out of the past. Sort of here and now. And sort of normal. Because these people here are in deep shit right *now*. That's the real thing you've got to come to grips with. Not that other stuff. The house burning thing. The drinking. That's yesterday's shit. Today we're in this new shit. I mean, come on, I'm probably gonna lose my job. I'm the only person in this house with a real job. Mom still stuffs envelopes, but there's no real money there. She won't take anything from Elizabeth. Why. I don't know. And there's the baby now, and Mary Ann's here. Maybe for good. Maybe her husband won't take her back this time. I don't think he likes her much, anyway. I think he just liked her cooking. Which is a plus for us. I mean, if she concentrates on it, and doesn't leave out important ingredients, her cooking can be really good. And she hardly eats anything herself. So, overall Mary Ann is a plus. But it's still dire. Overall, it's a really dire thing we're in and we—

**TOM:** Look, I'm sorry to interrupt. But what the hell are you talking about. What's Mary Ann's cooking got to do with this. I thought you wanted to work out a solution here. This is no time to go haywire. You can't let your mind run around in circles like that. (*JUNIOR puts his head down on the table*) Okay. You're upset. We're both upset. And scared. Being scared is a hard thing for a, you know ... a man to admit. Okay, maybe not for you. But for me it is. It's the pressure. A ... you know ... a man has all this pressure to prove things. So he gets worked up. It's the pressure of self-imposed leadership. Okay, it's bullshit. But it's genetic.

**JUNIOR:** Someone's coming.

*Noises outside.*

**TOM:**  Meet me here tonight. When they're all asleep. Together we'll work out a plan to save these people.

**JUNIOR:**  Okay. But it's got to be a plan that makes sense. Something I can understand.

**TOM:**  And something that won't put too much pressure on us.

*TOM lowers his head. JUNIOR lowers his head, too. NORA and ELIZABETH come in. They are pushing a shopping cart, with something large inside it, covered with a blanket.*

**ELIZABETH:**  What's he doing down here. Tell him to go away.

**JUNIOR:**  He was just leaving. Tom … Go upstairs. Upstairs, Tom. I'll bring your soup up in a minute. (*TOM nods, rises slowly, leaves*) (*to ELIZABETH*) I'm sorry about that. I was just … I mean he asked me to … tell him a story.

**NORA:**  Really. What kind of story. A war story?

**JUNIOR:**  Just a story. I made one up. I'm not very good at that stuff … What's in the cart.

**ELIZABETH:**  I decided to go on the offensive. (*ELIZABETH pulls the blanket away. She and NORA tip the cart and ROLLY falls out on to the floor. ROLLY's feet and hands are bound. And he has an old rag stuffed in his mouth*) You should recognize this man, Junior. He's one of the guys who beat you up.

**JUNIOR:**  (*stands*) Excuse me. I gotta go to the bathroom.

*He leaves.*

**NORA:**  Was that an unusual response for Junior to have, Elizabeth.

**ELIZABETH:**  It's Junior, Mom. He responds … the way he responds. Help me get this guy in a chair. (*they are getting ROLLY settled in a chair*) Okay, asshole. We're going to make you comfortable. Then I'm going to ungag you and ask you a few questions. The same questions I asked you in that alley. If you answer them this time I won't have to use this again. (*points to a can of mace strung around her neck*)

**NORA:**  (*to ROLLY*) Please don't make her use that … that … What's it called again, Elizabeth.

**ELIZABETH:**  It's mace, Mom.

**NORA:** Please don't make her use the mace again, mister. It was so upsetting to watch you writhe around like that.

**ELIZABETH:** Don't worry, Mom. He's going to be a good little asshole this time, aren't you fuck-face.

**NORA:** You're the expert on these things, Elizabeth. But do you really think calling him names like that is helpful.

**ELIZABETH:** It helps *me*, Mom. It makes me feel good. Don't worry. I'm sure he's been called worse. Right, ass-wipe?

*ROLLY nods.*

**ELIZABETH:** (*takes some rope from her pocket. Ties ROLLY to the chair*)Good little asshole. Here, let me take this piss-soaked rag away. How did such a disgusting piss-soaked rag come to be the only thing in the vicinity suitable for sticking in your mouth. Well that's life, eh. That's what some of my friends might call karma. Karma can be a really ugly experience for dirt-bags like you … There. Feel better?

*ROLLY is making gagging sounds. Wiping his lips with his tongue. Groaning.*

**NORA:** Can I take that rag away, Elizabeth. Or will you be needing it later.

**ELIZABETH:** Depends. Just leave it on the floor for now … (*to ROLLY*) Okay, stay calm! (*smiles*) Are you ready for that first question, shithead.

**ROLLY:** Yeah.

**ELIZABETH:** What's your name.

**ROLLY:** Rolly. Rolly Moore.

**ELIZABETH:** You're a crook, aren't you, Rolly.

**ROLLY:** Whatya mean.

**ELIZABETH:** You found that question difficult to understand?

**ROLLY:** Come on. You ask if I'm a crook. What am I supposed to say. "Yeah?" What good can come to me for saying "yeah" to a question like that.

**ELIZABETH:** I have to know who you are, Rolly. What you're up to. So I'm asking about how you make your living. You make your living by breaking the law. Right?

**ROLLY:** Sometimes.

**ELIZABETH:** Sometimes. So what are you saying here, Rolly. You occasionally do straight work.

**ROLLY:** I'm not a young man. I can't always take the tension of doing crime. I need calmer things to do every once in a while. Ask her. I worked for her once.

**NORA:** Yes. He helped me make my garden.

**ROLLY:** I carried rocks. It was hard. But I didn't complain.

**NORA:** Yes. You did. You complained a lot. And I think you stole my wheelbarrow.

**ROLLY:** Come on. Hey. (*to ELIZABETH*) Is that what this is about. Jesus, you people gotta be kidding. A wheelbarrow. What's that cost, twenty bucks, I mean—

**ELIZABETH:** Hey! Take a good look at me. I'm a busy woman. I don't have time for your bullshit. If I have to keep listening to your bullshit you're going to get hurt!

**ROLLY:** She brought it up. She was the one who brought up the thing about the wheelbarrow.

**NORA:** That's true, Elizabeth. I did. (*to ROLLY*) She's upset. I'll tell you why. She believes the police are making plans to charge me with a very serious crime.

**ROLLY:** That's too bad.

**ELIZABETH:** All right! All right. Mom, why don't you go see how Junior's doing.

**ROLLY:** Why does she have to leave. I'm a little nervous to be left alone with you. I'm sorry to offend you. But I'd feel a lot better if she stayed.

**NORA:** Is that good, Elizabeth. Is it good or bad if he feels less nervous. You're the expert.

**ELIZABETH:** Go ahead, Mom. We'll be fine.

**NORA:** Please, Elizabeth. Don't do anything you can't live with later.

*She leaves.*

**ELIZABETH:** (*looks at ROLLY. Smiles*) I can live with a lot. By most people's standards that is. An awful lot. (*leans into him. Close*)

Now, you're probably going to try to dance around this for a while. Buy some time to help your little brain find its way out of this mess. I'm a very, very busy woman. I've got a law practice to keep going, and an apartment I've been trying to finish painting for six months. But I'm going to have to stay here listening to some extreme amounts of bullshit from you unless we find a way to cut right to the issue ... Now, where's that piss-soaked rag. Ah, there it is. (*ELIZABETH picks up the rag. Sprays it with mace. Grabs ROLLY's nose, and when he opens his mouth, she shoves the rag in. ROLLY gags*) Believe it or not, a part of me hates doing this to you. You're a pathetic bastard. I see guys like you every day. Messed up. Stupid. Defenceless. Beaten up by everything and everyone. You even get beaten up by the police. And that pisses me off. They have no right, no right at all to punish you physically ... But this is different. I'm not the police. I'm not a representative of the state. I'm just a member of a family. A family you've messed with! You see, this is personal. This is a deeply personal thing. This is not sanctioned by the government. And therefore there's a limit, a restriction on the damage that can be done here. The only thing that can be damaged here is you. And basically, I think that's okay. Because really, all I'm doing is ... defending my family.

> *ELIZABETH removes the rag. ROLLY gags. Coughs. Licks his lips. Starts to cry.*

**ROLLY:** Ah, Jesus.

**ELIZABETH:** Why did you beat Junior up.

**ROLLY:** Ah, Jesus. That was awful. I can't ... breathe ...

**ELIZABETH:** Why did you break in here and beat Junior up. Why?!

> *She holds the rag close to his mouth.*

**ROLLY:** He ripped me off!

**ELIZABETH:** Bullshit.

**ROLLY:** Honest. We had a deal. We made a deal. Then we made a time for a meeting. He was supposed to bring his man to the meeting. His suit man. It was a simple thing. The usual thing. Except when they showed up they were armed. They had serious weapons in their possession. I was not prepared. I don't do crimes with weapons. I'm against it, you know, on principle.

**ELIZABETH:** I told you I don't want to hear this bullshit!

**ROLLY:** They ripped me off. They took my merchandise. That's the simple truth, man. Two big bags full of top-grade stuff. Beautiful stuff. Explicit. You know, *real* explicit.

**ELIZABETH:** (*backs away. Lowers her head*) Ah, shit. (*she goes to the hallway door. Yells upstairs*) Junior! Junior get down here. Now! (*ELIZABETH starts to pace. Stops. Looks at ROLLY. Shakes her head*) The word is illicit by the way. Not explicit. Illicit.

**ROLLY:** Ah, no. I'm sorry. But I think it's explicit.

**ELIZABETH:** Listen, I know the word, asshole. The word to describe your drugs is illicit.

**ROLLY:** Drugs? It wasn't drugs. I don't touch drugs on principle. Also, that's for younger guys. I'm talking porn. Pornography. Real first-rate stuff. You know—explicit.

**ELIZABETH:** What are you talking about.

**ROLLY:** My business is pornography. I'm the king of it. Ask anyone. Been doin' it for years. Some good years, a few bad years. But that's what I do. I sell pictures of naked people doing things to other naked people. And videos. Videos you can't get in any store. The market is huge. And it's growing. I don't know why. There must be a reason for it, you know, a need. I'm just helping people with a need they've got. I don't know, it's a strange—

**ELIZABETH:** Okay. Shut up. Keep your mouth closed.

**ROLLY:** Okay.

*Long pause.*

**ELIZABETH:** I believe you. I think you're telling the truth, you disgusting little pile of vomit.

**ROLLY:** Thank you.

**ELIZABETH:** Not that it helps me one stinking little bit. Not that I understand how pornography turned into drugs and wound up—(*NORA comes in*) Where's Junior.

**NORA:** Gone. I think he went out through a window. And he took the man upstairs with him. What's going on here, Elizabeth. Has this Rolly person implicated Junior in some crime. You can tell me. I know you probably don't want to worry me. You're generous like that. But—

**ELIZABETH:** You're going to have to be quiet for a while, Mom. I'm thinking.

**ROLLY:** Can I go now.

**ELIZABETH:** No.

**ROLLY:** Can I go later.

**ELIZABETH:** No. Probably not.

**ROLLY:** Well, I have to go sometime. You're not making any sense. Sooner or later I gotta go. I mean, what else can I do. I can't just stay. What's the point in that.

**ELIZABETH:** I might need you.

**ROLLY:** Why. I told you all I know. He did that to me. So I did that to him.

**ELIZABETH:** I might need you! If all this comes together in the worst possible way. You know, in a meaningless, arbitrary, pathetic, ugly, destructive way with no true purpose, and nothing but sad and wretched consequences—well, I might need an outlet for that! I might need to kill someone. That might be you! I mean, why not you! I mean, why the hell is this happening to my family. So why the hell shouldn't you die!

*She's shaking ROLLY.*

**ROLLY:** (*to NORA*) Could you help me out here. Maybe calm her down a bit.

**NORA:** Not when she's like this. Maybe later. Maybe when she's had a little sleep.

**ELIZABETH:** Good idea. Sleep. Just a little nap. To clear my head. Wake me in thirty-five minutes. (*starts off*)

**NORA:** I will, dear.

**ELIZABETH:**  (*stops*) Gag him, Mom. You have to gag him. And don't let him go. I know in your heart you've already forgiven him for whatever he's done. But if you let him go, I'll just have to go get him again.

**NORA:**  I know, dear.

**ELIZABETH:**  And could you call my office for me, Mom. Tell them I won't be in for a couple of days.

**NORA:**  I'll say you're ill.

**ELIZABETH:**  I am ill, Mom. I'm really, really ill.

*She leaves.*

**ROLLY:**  You could let me go. I think that'd be okay.

**NORA:**  I have to trust Elizabeth on this. Elizabeth is sometimes the only thing this family has going for it in the struggle.

**ROLLY:**  What struggle.

**NORA:**  The struggle. You know. The one out there. (*standing at the counter looking for something in a drawer*)

**ROLLY:**  Oh yeah. The struggle out there is ... really something. (*starts to cry*) That's my struggle, too. The one out there. That's the one where everyone and everything doesn't make sense. And everything you do is wrong. And they find out. And—

**NORA:**  You can't talk anymore. Talking doesn't help you anyway. I've noticed that. Talking just makes you wallow and cast blame. I found some tape in the drawer. I'm going to put a piece over your mouth. It's better than the rag. I'm sorry about the rag, I really am. But this tape is better. (*she rips off a piece. Puts it across his mouth. She gets a chair to put next to him*) I'm going to talk to you now. Talk to you for a long time. Until I get tired and have to go to bed. You have to listen closely and try to understand what I'm saying to you. There's a little trick you can use. When I'm talking don't pretend I'm not really talking about you. Don't let yourself believe I'm saying these things about someone else. Someone neither of us knows. For example. If I say you feel worthless and afraid, you can't say to yourself that's not true. And then not listen when I suggest all the reasons you feel worthless and afraid. Because if you do, you won't understand when I get to the part when I talk about all the ways you can maybe stop feeling worthless and afraid. So that's the trick. Try to understand. And don't pretend. All right. Get ready. Are you ready. (*ROLLY nods*) Good for you. *(lights start to fade)* First. You were born. Right away you shared some experience with everyone else in the world. Everyone in the past, everyone rich and poor, and smart and average. That's a fact. You were born. You were alive in the world. So far so good ...

*Lights fade. NORA is still talking, but the audience can't hear her.*

*Blackout.*

*Intermission.*

## SCENE FIVE

*ROLLY alone. Still tied up. Eyes wide.*

*TOM and JUNIOR come in from the screen door.*

**TOM:** Okay. Go make sure they're all asleep.

**JUNIOR:** Are you sure this is a good plan.

**TOM:** Well, it's better than doing nothing.

**JUNIOR:** Are you sure. Maybe doing nothing is better. Maybe it's the best we can do right now ... Okay. So let's do that instead.

**TOM:** Get a hold of yourself. Try to act like a ... you know ...

**JUNIOR:** A what. Try to act like a what.

**TOM:** Forget it. Go check on them.

*JUNIOR starts. And passes ROLLY.*

**JUNIOR:** (*to ROLLY*) Look what you did to my arm, asshole.

*He leaves. TOM goes to ROLLY.*

**TOM:** Okay, listen to this, insect. I'm going to untie you. If you make a move to escape I'll be forced to hurt you. The ugly part of me wants to hurt you anyway, so I won't need much of an excuse to cause you grievous bodily harm. Understand?

*ROLLY nods.*

**TOM:** Good. (*TOM starts to untie ROLLY*) We heard you talking to Elizabeth, insect. We were hiding outside the window here. We heard you deny knowledge of those drugs. Maybe you were telling the truth, maybe you weren't. We'll determine that when we get you to a more secluded place. But someone set us up. If it wasn't you, it was your kid. To save your life, insect, you might have to lead us to your kid. Do you think you'll be able to make that decision when the time comes.

*ROLLY nods.*

**TOM:** That's what I thought.

*JUNIOR comes back in.*

**JUNIOR:** They're all asleep. How you doin'.

**TOM:** Getting there.

**JUNIOR:** Elizabeth isn't going to like this. She went to a lot of trouble to hunt this guy down and bring him here. I mean, look at all the rope she bought.

**TOM:** Yeah. She thinks ahead. She's committed to a job well done. God, I admire her. If she's ever talking to me again I'm going to tell her that.

**JUNIOR:** You know what, man. I don't think that's ever gonna happen. We're finished in this house. This guy told Elizabeth we were doing business with him. That means we're *both* outta here. They don't really need us anyway. They'll be fine without us. Better.

**TOM:** Get a hold of yourself. You can't talk that way. We have a part to play in this family. We do.

*TOM has finished untying ROLLY.*

**JUNIOR:** Yeah? What.

**TOM:** We're working that out. That's part of what we're doing. Look, don't fall apart on me here. Think about all of the good things we've done.

**JUNIOR:** Yeah? What were they.

**TOM:** Come on, get a hold of yourself. We've done plenty. We ripped off that gang of break-and-enter artists, and we made them think they'd been ripped off by that other gang of break-and-enter artists. They had a nice little battle about that. Put a few of them out of action. And that guy with the pit bull …

**JUNIOR:** The pimp?

*TOM pulls ROLLY up.*

**TOM:** No! The pimp had the Doberman! The guy with the pit bull had the old Dodge van and that crack house. He doesn't have that crack house anymore.

*They all start off.*

**JUNIOR:** Oh, right. 'Cause of the pimp with the Doberman. We took money away from the break-and-enter artists, and paid some of those girls to leave that pimp—

**TOM:** Which made it look like the guy with the pit bull in the Dodge van was looking to move into the prostitution business. And bingo!

**JUNIOR:** The crack house gets burned to the ground! It was great.

**TOM:** Yeah, it was. Feeling any better?

**JUNIOR:** A little. Someday we gotta get rid of all those friggin' dogs around here. I mean, especially with the baby ...

*They are gone. NORA comes in. Goes to the door. Watches a moment. Turns.*

**NORA:** It's better this way.

*ELIZABETH comes in. Hair tousled. Blouse outside her skirt. Barefoot.*

**ELIZABETH:** Mom, I said just thirty-five min—Hey! Where is he. Where's my prisoner.

**NORA:** Junior and the man you call Dad took him. It's better this way.

**ELIZABETH:** They had no right! He was mine. I wasn't finished with him. I just left him down here to stew for a while. (*she is agitated. Moving around*)

**NORA:** Junior and the man you call Dad know about these things. They both have past lives with criminal content. They've probably made plans with that Rolly person that will resolve this whole dilemma. I'm a little worried about Junior. If something bad happens let's pray it happens to the man you call Dad.

**ELIZABETH:** Typical bullshit! I do the hard work. Someone else gets the glory. It's the same thing at work. This is the same crap the senior partners are always pulling. I work sixty-five hours a week. I've got a family that's in more or less perpetual crisis, and all I want out of life, I mean *really* all I want, is just one stinking even break!

**NORA:** Maybe you should get some more sleep, Elizabeth.

**ELIZABETH:** Come on, Mom. I had that little rodent on the edge of collapsing. Telling me things he didn't even know he knew. Junior and Dad aren't the only ones who know about guys like that. I've spent my whole life around guys like that. I'm the expert here! Me! They had no right to interfere!

**NORA:** Are you hungry. Thirsty. Do you want to play a game of cards. (*quickly takes a deck of cards from a drawer*)

**ELIZABETH:** I thought he was dying! How could he have taken anyone anywhere. He's a drooling, mumbling mess!

**NORA:** That was a trick of course, dear. A disguise. I suspected it. This confirms it. If nothing else good comes out of this, we'll all discover the true nature of the man you call Dad.

**ELIZABETH:** (*slams the cards down. Stands*) He is my dad! That's why I call him Dad, Mom. Because he is!

*MARY ANN comes in, wearing a bathrobe and slippers. Looking angry.*

**NORA:** Hello, Mary Ann. What's wrong. Trouble sleeping?

**MARY ANN:** Gail sent me down. All this shouting is waking up the baby.

**NORA:** I'm not shouting.

**ELIZABETH:** She means me.

**MARY ANN:** That's right, Elizabeth. I mean you. What's wrong, Elizabeth. Did you have a hard day. Did someone question your right to change your mind about something. Perhaps question your ability to make a choice and stick to it.

**ELIZABETH:** Ah, Jesus Christ.

**MARY ANN:** That's right, Elizabeth. I haven't forgotten. I never forget. And certain things, I never forgive.

**ELIZABETH:** Go back to bed.

**MARY ANN:** You go back to bed. I don't do things because you tell me to anymore. I've discovered recently that you can be very wrong about things. Dad, for example. You were wrong about him. He's nice. I like him. There. What are you going to do about that.

**ELIZABETH:** Didn't I tell you before if you didn't stop acting and talking like an idiot I was going to do something about it.

**MARY ANN:** I remember words to that effect. But so what. I'm not afraid of you anymore. And do you know why. You're

inconsistent. Seriously inconsistent. Mom, I have something
to tell you. Elizabeth is *not* a lesbian. Elizabeth will sleep with
anyone. She hasn't made any hard decisions at all.

*ELIZABETH has her teeth clenched. She is approaching MARY ANN.*

**ELIZABETH:** Please go back to bed.

**MARY ANN:** No.

**ELIZABETH:** I don t want to hurt you.

**MARY ANN:** I don't care if you want to hurt me or not. I'm on a
voyage of self-discovery. I can't be stopped. You're part of
that voyage. Getting to the truth about you. There are other
things on this voyage, of course, but I'm dealing with you
right now. Dealing with things is all I care about.

**ELIZABETH:** Really. You don't care about the police, or the drug
charges, or any of that.

**MARY ANN:** Those aren't actually my problems. I can only deal
with myself. My personal self. My unconscious self. Clare
taught me that.

**ELIZABETH:** Then Clare should be killed. I'll do it. Give me her
address. Give it to me! Now!

*ELIZABETH makes a wild grab for MARY ANN. MARY ANN backs away.*

**NORA:** Who is Clare.

**ELIZABETH:** The devil!

**MARY ANN:** My therapist!

*ELIZABETH grabs MARY ANN. Puts her over her shoulders.*

**MARY ANN:** Okay, okay. Clare also taught me the value of the
apology.

*ELIZABETH puts MARY ANN inside the broom closet. Closes the door.*

**MARY ANN:** (*from inside the closet*) I know I've hurt people and
disappointed people myself. The two of you, for example. So,
as well as taking care of myself in an inner way, I'm taking
care of others in an outer way. That's why I cook for you.
That's why I fixed the strap on your briefcase, Elizabeth.
Before I went to sleep I fixed it and put it back beside your

bed. You don't have to thank me. I didn't do it for thanks! I did it for mythic reasons! Symbolic reasons! The reasons of dreams!

**ELIZABETH:** You're nuts! You're out of your goddamn mind!

*MARY ANN comes out of the closet holding a box of Bisquick and a muffin pan.*

**MARY ANN:** Says who?!

**ELIZABETH:** Me! Me! And her. (*points to NORA*) She'd say it too, if she wasn't so nice, and if she wasn't your mother. Everyone would say it. Everyone on the planet who had to listen to you for more than five seconds!

*GAIL comes rushing in.*

**GAIL:** Hey, hey come on! The baby! Your voice is bouncing off the walls.

**MARY ANN:** Sorry.

**ELIZABETH:** She means me!

**GAIL:** Yeah. What's wrong with you, anyway.

**ELIZABETH:** What makes you think something is wrong with me. I mean, you were on my back before for not getting involved in this family's problems like I should. So now I'm involved. And … this … is … what … I'm … like … when I'm involved!

**GAIL:** Keep your voice down!

**MARY ANN:** Yeah. There's no reason to shout. I express very personal, upsetting feelings without shouting. You can do the same.

**ELIZABETH:** (*throws her hands up in the air*) I need a drink. (*starts searching through the cupboards*)

**GAIL:** Hey. Where's that guy who was tied up here before.

**MARY ANN:** Oh, yeah. I didn't notice.

**ELIZABETH:** (*mocking*) "Oh yeah. I didn't notice." I'm a good person, but I didn't notice. I cook for people, do things for people, tell people what their problems are, but I don't notice anything … My name is Mary Ann, and I'm looking for a job. Do you have anything a semiconscious idiot with a lot of opinions could do ... Where's that bottle of scotch. It used to be under the sink.

**GAIL:** (*to NORA*) So where is he. The guy.

**NORA:** Junior took him.

**GAIL:** To the police?

**ELIZABETH:** We don't think so. That would not be our first guess.

**GAIL:** Yeah. So where did he take him.

**ELIZABETH:** Our first guess would be some unpopulated and heavily wooded area just outside the city. Somewhere the ground isn't too hard for digging. Where's my scotch. Who took my scotch. I left it under the sink. It's not there.

**MARY ANN:** Are you that messed up, Elizabeth. You leave bottles in places. Do you leave them everywhere you visit.

**ELIZABETH:** No. Just anywhere you might be.

**NORA:** I took it, Elizabeth. I threw it out. I thought it belonged to someone else. You know ... (*points upstairs*)

**MARY ANN:** The baby?

**GAIL:** What's she talking about, Mom. She's saying Junior took that guy out to the country to kill him. Is that right.

**NORA:** Is that what you were saying, Elizabeth.

**ELIZABETH:** (*looking in other cupboards now*) It was just a guess. You wouldn't have any other alcohol in the house would you, Mom. No of course not. Not since Dad got drunk that last time and tried to kill us all. That was a stupid question, Mom. I'm sorry for asking. How about rubbing alcohol, lighter fluid, glue.

> GAIL *goes to* ELIZABETH. *Starts to follow her around.*

**GAIL:** So, why would Junior want to kill that guy.

**ELIZABETH:** He's one of the guys who beat him up.

**GAIL:** Yeah. I know that. But that wouldn't be enough of a reason. What are you getting at.

**ELIZABETH:** Relax. It was just a guess. I could be wrong. I'm wrong sometimes. Right, Mary Ann? Hey Mom, where's that stuff you spray on frying pans. I hear you can get a buzz off that.

**MARY ANN:** Stop her, Mom. She's doing that thing she does. When she's overloading. I don't like it.

**NORA:** Elizabeth, you're scaring your sisters.

**GAIL:** Elizabeth. I want you to stop for a moment.

**ELIZABETH:** In a moment. In a moment I'll stop for a moment. Right now I need something. A little something.

**MARY ANN:** You better stop her, Gail.

**ELIZABETH:** (*mocking*) "You better stop her, Gail." (*searching frantically now. Pulling things out of the cupboards*) Stop her before she says something, does something, finds something. She's doing that thing she does, Mom. What thing, dear. The thing she does when she's falling apart, Mom. Had it up to here, Mom. Right up to the nose. Almost full. Almost filled right up. Just can't take much more ...

*GAIL grabs her. ELIZABETH shakes her off.*

**ELIZABETH:** Get off me. Get the fuck off me. I'm on a mission here. A mission of self-fulfillment. This one's for me, Mom. I'm enjoying this. I'm going to rip this home apart, Mom. I think it's time you moved, anyway. Moved everyone, the whole family. My family. The one I'm responsible for!

*GAIL grabs her. MARY ANN is moving closer to them.*

**GAIL:** (*to MARY ANN*) Help me!

**ELIZABETH:** Let me go! You have to let me go. I gotta go. Let me go you little bitch before I rip your scalp off.

**GAIL:** (*to MARY ANN*) Help me!

**MARY ANN:** Okay.

*MARY ANN grabs ELIZABETH. They are both trying to put her on the floor.*

**ELIZABETH:** Ah, shit. This won't work. This will only make me mad. Jesus. Get away from me. Get off me. You're trying to kill me. Aren't you. You want to kill me. I know you do. Ah, here's some hair. What happens if I just pull a little.

*MARY ANN screams.*

**ELIZABETH:** I like that sound. I like that sound a lot.

*MARY ANN screams.*

**MARY ANN:** Let go!

**ELIZABETH:** You let go!

**GAIL:** Don't! Don't let go. We've almost got her down.

*ELIZABETH grabs GAIL's hair. Now she has them both by the hair.*

**ELIZABETH:** You've got miles to go before I'm down, kid. I'm absolutely indestructible. Right, Mom. I'm a rock. Aren't I, Mom. A rock. A rock doesn't go down.

**GAIL:** Trip her!

**MARY ANN:** How?!

**GAIL:** Just trip her. Put your foot out!

**ELIZABETH:** How about another little pull on the hair, sis!

*MARY ANN screams. GAIL screams.*

**MARY ANN:** I hate you! Stop that!

**GAIL:** Ouch! Shit! Trip her!

**MARY ANN:** I'm trying!

*The three of them are swaying back and forth. ELIZABETH in the middle. A tangle of arms and hands.*

**ELIZABETH:** They're weak, Mom! Very weak. Gail talks tough, but she's really a pussycat. And Mary Ann's, well Mary Ann's a shadow … My shadow. And my pussycat. Look at them. Mom. I'm still up. I'm still standing. If you need a daughter to rely on, Mom, I'm the one. Call me anytime. Call me night or day. (sings) "Call me. Don't be afraid to just call me." But you do, don't you. You call me. You all call me, and call me, and call me …!

*Finally MARY ANN succeeds in putting a foot behind ELIZABETH. GAIL pushes. ELIZABETH falls. They fall on top of her.*

**GAIL:** Okay! We've got her. Don't let go.

**MARY ANN:** Don't you let go!

**GAIL:** Okay, Mom. Do it!

**MARY ANN:** Hurry, Mom. We can't hold her much longer.

*NORA is nodding. She gets down on her knees beside them.*

**GAIL:** Quick, Mom!

*NORA opens up the bottom two buttons of ELIZABETH's blouse. Leans over. And starts to blow on ELIZABETH's stomach, giving her a huge raspberry. ELIZABETH's groaning and yelling gradually subside and slowly turn into laughter. The laughter grows. MARY ANN and GAIL sit back on the floor. NORA continues to blow on ELIZABETH's stomach. ELIZABETH is laughing hysterically.*

**GAIL:** It still works.

**MARY ANN:** Thank God.

**NORA:** (*stands*) Are you all right now, dear.

**ELIZABETH:** I'm fine, Mom. (*giggles*) I love that. Do that again.

**NORA:** Maybe later ... I'm going to put the kettle on.

**MARY ANN:** (getting up) I'll make toast.

*Pause. ELIZABETH is sighing happily.*

**GAIL:** Elizabeth.

**ELIZABETH:** What, honey.

**GAIL:** I'm really worried about Junior.

**ELIZABETH:** Oh. (*sits up. Hugs GAIL*) He's all right. He's fine. I was just being pissy. They probably took that guy and handed him over to the cops.

**GAIL:** Really. You really think so.

**ELIZABETH:** Yeah. I really do. (*hugs her tight*) I love you.

**GAIL:** I love you, too. I'm sorry you're such a frigging mess.

**ELIZABETH:** So am I.

**GAIL:** Maybe you should stop practising law. Stop doing all that political stuff you do. Take a vacation or something.

**ELIZABETH:** Yeah. Maybe you could come with me. Take a little break from motherhood. And we'll go some place soft and warm.

**MARY ANN:** Can I come too.

**ELIZABETH & GAIL:** No.

**MARY ANN:** I know you don't mean that.

**GAIL:**  Yes—

**ELIZABETH:**  We do.

**MARY ANN:**  No, you don't. I know you don't. I'm coming. Wherever you go. I'm coming. You love each other. But you love me, too. I know that. I'm confident about that. They love me, don't they, Mom.

**NORA:**  Of course they love you. They were taught to love you. I paid special attention to that part of their education. I knew there would be times it would be easier not to love you. Because of your ... well, because of your—

**MARY ANN:**  Gee, Mom. When I asked you if they loved me I was only kidding. I feel like crying.

**NORA:**  Why.

**MARY ANN:**  Well, because of what you just said. That's sad. That you had to teach them to love me. That's so very sad.

**ELIZABETH:**  (*getting up*) She's going to tell Clare about that, Mom. Clare is going to have a lot to say about what that means.

**MARY ANN:**  Clare loves me.

> *ELIZABETH goes over. Puts her arms around MARY ANN.*

**ELIZABETH:**  No, Mary Ann. We love you. Clare just thinks you're very interesting.

**MARY ANN:**  What do you want on your toast.

**ELIZABETH:**  Cocoa.

**MARY ANN:**  No way. I hate that. That's disgusting.

> *ELIZABETH grabs MARY ANN by the hair.*

**ELIZABETH:**  It's my toast, Mary Ann. You asked me. I told you. Put cocoa on my toast. Lots of cocoa. Okay?

**MARY ANN:**  Sure ... Gail? ... Jam? Marmalade?

**GAIL:**  I've got to go back to bed.

**MARY ANN:**  You can't. We're all here. The four of us. We're never together anymore just the four of us. It's the family.

**GAIL:** The family has grown a bit since you last looked in on it, Mary Ann. I've got to get up with the baby. (*starts off*) Goodnight. (*stops. Looks at ELIZABETH*) Is there something you're not telling me about Junior.

**ELIZABETH:** No. Junior's fine. Don't worry about him.

**GAIL:** Because he's my life, you know. A large part of it. If he's going down the drain, so am I.

**ELIZABETH:** Trust me. Go upstairs. Get your daughter. Get in bed. Hug her. Go to sleep.

*ELIZABETH hugs GAIL. GAIL leaves.*

**NORA:** (*to MARY ANN*) You're sad, aren't you. Feeling guilty about leaving your daughter. Gail is going up to sleep with her daughter, and this makes you feel empty, hollow, hard ... Doesn't it, Mary Ann.

**MARY ANN:** Yeah, Mom. A bit. I guess. So?

**NORA:** So what, dear.

**MARY ANN:** So, what should I do.

**NORA:** I wouldn't give you advice about that, dear. You're the expert about your own life. Besides, you have so many things on your mind. Things I could barely understand even if I had the desire to listen to them. Things more important than your only child, the child you brought into this world. Things you've recently found out at ... at that place where you said you are ... Where was that place again, dear.

**MARY ANN:** Crossroads. I'm at a crossroads. Your toast is in the ... thing. I'm going to bed. (*starts off. Stops*) I am, though. I really am at a crossroads ... Dammit.

*She leaves.*

**ELIZABETH:** She'll go home to her daughter, Mom. She always does.

**NORA:** But why does she leave in the first place.

**ELIZABETH:** Her father deserted *her.* Maybe she's just repeating a pattern.

**NORA:** Why. Why is she repeating a pattern ...

**ELIZABETH:** You have to stop worrying about her, Mom. She just basically has a difficult time living. The only solution would be to put her out of her misery ... Harden your heart, put her in a sack and drown her like a kitten ... That was just a joke, Mom.

**NORA:** I know, dear ... And I know Mary Ann could never actually be happy. She'll never be ... lighthearted.

**ELIZABETH:** Anyway, I don't think Mary Ann's in any worse shape than the rest of us.

**NORA:** She deserts her child! There's nothing worse a mother can do. Don't be stupid! (*pause*) I'm sorry.

**ELIZABETH:** That's okay.

**NORA:** I have to tell you something, Elizabeth. It's about that man you call Dad ... Guess what. I know he really is your dad. I'm not insane about that. That's good news isn't it, Elizabeth. So far so good. And I actually had a very good reason for not acknowledging him. For the first time in years I had something he needed. Needed badly ... Do you want to know what it was. Recognition! The power of simple recognition ... Of course, I just stumbled across this power. But once I had it I used it without remorse. You see, when he first came back after what ... ten years?

**ELIZABETH:** Yes.

**NORA:** Yes. Ten. Anyway, when he came back a terrible thing happened. I saw him. And right away I wanted to kill myself. I thought I'd rather be dead than go through any more awful experiences with him. Of course, I couldn't do that because of you and your sisters. I couldn't leave you alone with him. So I came up with another way. I just pretended he was a total stranger. I don't know where I got the idea, but it seemed to work all right. I didn't have to have anything to do with him. And you girls could have a father if you needed one.

**ELIZABETH:** Why are you telling me this, Mom.

**NORA:** Circumstances change. The needs of people change. What this family needs now is something more clear. Clearer roles. Lighter burdens for ... some of us. (*starts off. Stops*) You know, Elizabeth, I have a theory about why bad things keep happening to this family. Do you want to hear it.

**ELIZABETH:** (*sighs*) Sure, Mom.

**NORA:** I think we believe that we don't deserve to be happy. We're running away from happiness. We think we need to struggle, and suffer, and work really hard before we can just stay still, and let happiness catch up and surround us. What do you think about that theory, Elizabeth.

**ELIZABETH:** It scares me, Mom.

**NORA:** Oh. Then just forget about it. I could be wrong ...

*NORA gestures, shrugs. She wants to say something soothing. ELIZABETH turns away.*

**NORA:** Goodnight, Elizabeth.

**ELIZABETH:** Goodnight, Mom.

*NORA hesitates. Then leaves. ELIZABETH wraps her arms around herself Shudders. Looks around. Begins to clean up some of the mess she made earlier.*

*Blackout.*

*Later. ELIZABETH is at the table, her head down. TOM,*
*JUNIOR and ROLLY come in. TOM has ROLLY by the scruff of the neck.*
*They are all dirty and wet.*

**ROLLY:** Please, please let me go. I did what you asked. I tried to help you find my kid Stevie. I took you to all our special places. Why won't you let me go.

**JUNIOR:** (*whispering*) Shut up. (*to TOM*) Who is that over there. Oh no. Is that Elizabeth.

**TOM:** It's okay. She's asleep. If we're quiet we won't—

**ROLLY:** She's waiting! She's been waiting for me! She can't wait to get her hands on me. Let me go!

**JUNIOR:** Shush!

*TOM whacks ROLLY on the head.*

**ROLLY:** Geez! That hurt!

**JUNIOR:** Shut up. Shut your mouth!

**ROLLY:** He hurt me. Geez! He hit me with his knuckles. I'm dizzy.

**TOM:** (*calmly*) Look. I'm trying not to really hurt you. I'm trying to control a really ugly, violent urge I've got to take away your face.

**ROLLY:** Take away my face? What's that mean.

**JUNIOR:** What should we do.

**TOM:** Tie him up again.

**JUNIOR:** What good will that do.

**TOM:** We didn't accomplish anything by taking him so the least we can do is put him back where he was.

*They start to tie him up.*

**ROLLY:** Oh no, don't do this. There's no purpose in this. Look, the truth is the women in this house are kinda spooky. The mother—she's a nice lady, I guess, but she just wants to talk to me all the time. She talked to me for hours. She said things that really bothered me. Really personal things about

me. Like she knows me or something. Knows all about my
life. It's spooky. And this one here. The one you call
Elizabeth. She's something else. She's like a monster of some
kind. She comes across as some kind of evil thing from some
other planet. No offence. I know you're related. But she's
worse than guys I've met in prison who kill people with saws.
You can't give me back to her! You keep me!

TOM: She hunted you down. You belong to her.

JUNIOR: We just borrowed you.

ROLLY: (*crying*) I can't stay. It's spooky here! While I was sitting
here before, these two other women came in, with a baby in a
stroller. They just came in, saw me all tied up, and just smiled
at each other and went upstairs. Like having a frigging
prisoner in the kitchen, some guy tied up like a frigging dead
pig, was a normal thing. I can't stay here. I can't, I can't, I
can't!

> TOM whacks ROLLY hard. ROLLY is unconscious. They continue to tie
> him up.

JUNIOR: Did you have to do that.

TOM: Yeah. That's the least I had to do. I've told you, I've still
got these ugly things inside me. Things that get stirred up by
stuff like this. By scum like this. I'm trying hard to change,
but sometimes—

JUNIOR: Can we talk about this later. Let's just get out of here
before Elizabeth wakes up.

TOM: She must be a tired person to sleep through all of that. Do
you think she works too hard. I've heard them talking about
her. Nora and Gail. They say she's working herself to death.

JUNIOR: Look. We have to talk about this later. I'm depressed.
This whole thing is really depressing.

TOM: And confusing. Why aren't things working out better for
us. Why wasn't his kid at any of those places.

JUNIOR: And why were those places so disgusting. Do you think
they really live in that sewer. Who can live in a sewer, man. Or
that bush by the railway tracks. I mean a bush, man. They had
a little clearing inside a bush. Talk about depressing.

TOM: Get a hold of yourself.

**JUNIOR:** Stop telling me to get a hold of myself. That doesn't help. Try to say something that helps. Anything.

**TOM:** Okay. He's all tied up. Just the way he was. Let's get out of here.

**JUNIOR:** Okay.

*Their backs are to ELIZABETH. She sits up suddenly. Eyes wild.*

**ELIZABETH:** Stay exactly where you are!

*JUNIOR and TOM jump. ELIZABETH stands. Walks around them. Looking at them.*

**JUNIOR:** (*to TOM*) We should explain to her. She looks like she definitely wants an explanation.

**ELIZABETH:** Be quiet, Junior. I want this man here to talk. This man here who's not supposed to be able to talk. This man here who is supposed to be sick. Dying.

**JUNIOR:** (*to TOM*) She wants to hear it from you. (*to ELIZABETH*) Can I go upstairs, then.

**ELIZABETH:** Stay where you are. (*to TOM*) Go ahead.

**TOM:** I … don't know where to start. How much did you hear. I mean, when did you wake up.

**ELIZABETH:** I wasn't asleep.

**JUNIOR:** (*whimpers*) I'm feeling a little sick to my stomach.

**TOM:** Cut that out. Act like a … you know.

**ELIZABETH:** A what?

**TOM:** Let Junior go upstairs, Elizabeth. You and I can work this out. Junior is nervous. Aren't you.

**JUNIOR:** Yeah.

**TOM:** And he's making me nervous.

**ELIZABETH:** He stays. If anyone is leaving it's you. And I don't mean upstairs to your cozy room. Now what in God's name are you up to! Speak!

**TOM:** Okay. So first, you're probably wondering why I seem better all of a sudden.

**ELIZABETH:** No. I've figured that out. Skip to the part where you explain everything bad that's happened to this family lately, and how you're responsible.

**JUNIOR:** See that look in her eyes. I've seen that look before. Tell her before she does something!

**TOM:** Okay! Okay, yeah … (*to ELIZABETH*) I had a plan.

**JUNIOR:** I just want to make that part clear. *He* had a plan. Okay?

**TOM:** It was a plan I got all of a sudden. It was a good plan, but it came from a bad place in me, I think. From guilt. From all the bad—

**ELIZABETH:** Yeah, I got it. What was the plan.

**TOM:** At first it wasn't a plan. It was just a feeling. I heard about what was going on in this part of the city. I read about it in the newspapers. I saw how things were deteriorating. The crime, the awful victimization—

**ELIZABETH:** Okay. Be quiet. That's enough.

**TOM:** No, but I haven't—

**ELIZABETH:** I said that's enough! I got it. I know what you did.

**JUNIOR:** She's amazing. You didn't tell her, really. But she knows. She's unbelievable.

**ELIZABETH:** No. I just know him. Know how his mind works. He went into his protector mode. He hatched some plan to clean up the neighbourhood.

**JUNIOR:** Amazing.

**ELIZABETH:** And he sucked you right into the middle of it.

**JUNIOR:** Right. Right into the middle. I got sucked in.

**ELIZABETH:** You idiot!

**JUNIOR:** Right again!

**TOM:** We infiltrated. We developed a complex and daring plan to make contact with all the criminal elements in this neighbourhood. And then by trickery and theft make them think they were being double-crossed by each other. And that would start a war.

**JUNIOR:** A crime war.

**TOM:**  A war in which they would all be destroyed or made totally ineffective. Like I said, it was a complex plan.

**JUNIOR:**  I never really understood it.

**TOM:**  It was beyond understanding. It was designed to operate on momentum. It was a plan that came from deep inside me. From my experience and my heart.

**JUNIOR:**  A plan of love, really.

**TOM:**  And anger and regret.

**JUNIOR:**  And fear. At least for me. Fear was a big part of the plan.

**ELIZABETH:**  But that old standby "stupid" was the biggest part, right?

**TOM:**  We each had a part to play. I was the money man. The suit man.

**JUNIOR:**  I worked the streets.

**TOM:**  He did pretty good. I'm proud of him in many ways. (*to JUNIOR*) I haven't told you that till now.

**JUNIOR:**  Thanks.

**ELIZABETH:**  But something went wrong! What was it!

**JUNIOR:**  We don't know.

**TOM:**  We think we were set up. I know we can find out who did it. But it will take time.

**ELIZABETH:**  You've got six hours. Is that time enough.

**JUNIOR:**  I don't think so. It usually takes us a few hours just to talk about what we're going to do, and then the first thing we do is usually wrong, so we have to—

**TOM:**  Elizabeth. Why do we only have six hours.

**ELIZABETH:**  (*stares at TOM. Speaks very clearly*) I cut a deal with the cops. They gave me until eight o'clock this morning to come up with the person or persons who put those drugs in our basement. Failing that they are going to arrest my mother and charge her with possession for the purpose of trafficking.

**JUNIOR:**  Really?

**ELIZABETH:**  Really.

**JUNIOR:** (*to TOM*) We can't let that happen.

**ELIZABETH:** (*turns to JUNIOR*) Don't look at him when you say that. He can't help you. He's a total screw up. (*to TOM*) Aren't you. Aren't you?!

**TOM:** I ... just wanted—

**ELIZABETH:** What, what did you want?!

**TOM:** To help! But I was isolated. Wasn't allowed to be in the family. Had to pretend to be sick ... All that made me not think straight.

**ELIZABETH:** Sad ... Jesus. (*to JUNIOR*) That's his excuse. He wasn't allowed in the family so his mind got cloudy. What's yours.

**JUNIOR:** I don't know. I didn't know he had a cloudy mind. Maybe having the baby made me extra worried. Maybe it made me cloudy, too.

**ELIZABETH:** (*to TOM*) You're a plague. And a curse. You're a life-long, enormous, black hole of misery to this family.

**TOM:** I'm trying to change. I just ... Well, you see, I ... (*mumbles something*)

**ELIZABETH:** What. What did you say.

*TOM goes to JUNIOR. Whispers in his ear.*

**JUNIOR:** He loves you.

**ELIZABETH:** What?!

*TOM whispers in JUNIOR's ear.*

**JUNIOR:** He loves this family.

**ELIZABETH:** He loves us. He loves us?! Amazing! Can you imagine what he'd do to this family if he hated us. The mind boggles. I don't know, could be anything ... Little nuclear devices shoved up our assholes!

*A knock at the back door. DIAN is standing there.*

**DIAN:** Hi.

*They all look at each other. JUNIOR starts to cry.*

**DIAN:** We got a call about a prowler around your house ... Can I come in.

*ELIZABETH goes to ROLLY. Sits on his lap. Puts an arm around his neck.*

**ELIZABETH:** Sure.

*DIAN comes in.*

**DIAN:** Thanks. I thought it might give me a chance to see how you were getting along with our little problem. Any solutions to that yet.

**ELIZABETH:** What about the prowler.

**DIAN:** I looked around. Seems fine. So ... you didn't answer my question.

**ELIZABETH:** We have 'til eight o'clock. That was the deal.

**DIAN:** Pretty stupid deal if you ask me. That was my ex-partner's idea. Deadlines. How primitive can you get ... Anyway that was the last stupid idea I could take. I asked to work alone. I mean the guy's a throwback.

**ELIZABETH:** What are you doing here. Really.

**DIAN:** There's no reason to be hostile, Elizabeth. I mean come on, I haven't even asked you about your hostage here.

*ELIZABETH gets off ROLLY's lap. Goes to JUNIOR. Gives him a quick whack. JUNIOR stops crying.*

**DIAN:** Because I know people need plenty of space to wheel and deal when they're trying to solve complex problems like this. I mean this could be a matter entirely within the family, and it's obvious the human interaction in this family is *extremely* complex. But you still didn't answer my question. Are you any closer to finding out who put all that illegal substance in your basement.

**ELIZABETH:** We're working on it.

**DIAN:** Hi, Junior. How's the arm.

**JUNIOR:** All right.

**DIAN:** (*to TOM*) You must be the father. We haven't met. (*puts out her hand*) Dian Black, O.C.S.

**TOM:** Hi.

*They shake.*

DIAN: You guys look kind of messed up. And you don't smell so good, either. Been down in the sewers, have you. Searching for a rat? No, no don't answer that. I was just thinking out loud.

ELIZABETH: Why don't you just go away. I told you I was working on it.

DIAN: Well, I'm glad you're working on it, Elizabeth. But there could be forces at play here beyond your knowledge. I'm about to stick my neck out here, Elizabeth. And you have to appreciate all the implications involved in me doing that, vis-à-vis my career, vis-à-vis my personal safety.

TOM: What's wrong with you. You talk like you're on drugs.

JUNIOR: Yeah.

DIAN: Shush. I'm talking to the brains in the family now. Right, Elizabeth? Your hostage here is a dead end. He's just a victim of Junior's shenanigans. That's right! We know about the avenging angels here. We know. And we don't care. Not the people I work for anyway ... But hey, wait a minute ... my ex-partner, he might feel different. (*to TOM*) You know him, don't you Tom. You know Mike Dixon. (*takes out her lip balm. Applies it casually*)

TOM: We worked together for a while. A long time ago.

DIAN: You see, this is leading somewhere, Elizabeth. Ever do anything to him that might deserve a payback, Tom. No, don't answer that! Just think about it. You get my drift, Elizabeth? You see how I'm opening up the possibilities here? I mean if a cop, a certain kind of cop, or a number of cops, are very very annoyed with someone, well ... well, revenge may be too strong a word, but—

ELIZABETH: It's me, isn't it. This was a set-up to pressure me. To neutralize me.

DIAN: How did you do that. Get into the middle of my thought process like that. No one has ever done that. Wow. Okay. We have to be careful now. Vis-à-vis our personal safety and our careers. Maybe we should talk about this alone, in another room.

ELIZABETH: It's me. Shit!

**DIAN:** I can help you with this, Elizabeth. But we have to be discreet.

**ELIZABETH:** I'm not sure I want your help, Dian. So go fuck yourself. I think I owe my family an explanation.

**TOM:** You don't owe me anything, honey. Let's just call it even.

**ELIZABETH:** (*to JUNIOR*) Did you hear what he just said.

**JUNIOR:** He didn't really mean that, Elizabeth … (*to TOM*) How the hell can you be even, man. Did she try to burn the house down and shit like that.

**TOM:** It was just an expression!

**ELIZABETH:** Unbelievable.

**JUNIOR:** I wouldn't mind an explanation, Elizabeth.

**ELIZABETH:** I was just getting really sick and tired of defending people who'd had their brains beaten out in the back seats of cruisers, in the basements of police stations. So I complained. And I tried to organize other people, lawyers mostly, so they could complain too.

**DIAN:** Bad timing, Elizabeth. You caught the police force at a particularly sensitive moment, is what I think. They've received so much negative press.

**ELIZABETH:** This is criminal conspiracy we're talking about, Dian.

**DIAN:** Maybe. But is there a possible deal here, Elizabeth. Do you have a message you want me to take downtown vis-à-vis you taking a slightly less public approach in your campaign against police brutality. Or do we let your mom go to jail. Come on, Elizabeth. You know how it works! Make an offer for chrissake!

*Pause.*

**ELIZABETH:** I'm willing to talk about it.

**DIAN:** A good faith negotiation without prejudice, is all I think they're looking for here.

**ELIZABETH:** I'm willing to talk about it.

**DIAN:** Can I use the phone.

**ELIZABETH:** Sure. Go ahead.

**DIAN:** This has to be a private call, Elizabeth. Is there another one somewhere.

**ELIZABETH:** In the hall upstairs.

**DIAN:** Thanks. I feel good about this. I think this is going to work for us, Elizabeth.

*She hurries off.*

**JUNIOR:** (*to ELIZABETH*) Do you really think she's trying to help us.

**ELIZABETH:** I don't know. She's hard to read.

**TOM:** She doesn't talk like a cop. Maybe it's a woman thing.

**ELIZABETH:** Jesus. What's that supposed to mean.

**TOM:** Some woman sees some other woman in a tight spot. So she, you know, feels something about that only a woman could feel.

**ELIZABETH:** You mean something human? Like sympathy? Look, don't answer that. I don't want to talk to you anymore. I didn't mean to talk to you in the first place. I forgot.

**TOM:** I'm glad you forgot. I enjoyed talking to you. Whatever happens, I'll always remember these last couple of minutes.

*STEVIE suddenly appears at the basement door. Holding a gun.*

**STEVIE:** Okay. Hands up. Up high. Really high. Come on!

**ELIZABETH:** How did you get into our basement again. We put bars on that window.

**STEVIE:** So what. You think bars mean anything to me? I do this for a living for chrissake.

*TOM takes a step towards STEVIE.*

**TOM:** Do you want me to take that weapon away from this insect, Elizabeth.

**ELIZABETH:** Stay out of this. (*to STEVIE*) What do you want.

**STEVIE:** Whatya mean what do I want. I want my dad. You can't just take a guy's dad away like that. Look at him. He's been tortured or something. You rotten bastards ... Untie him ... Come on, untie him!

**ELIZABETH:** (*to JUNIOR*) Do it.

*JUNIOR starts to untie ROLLY.*

**STEVIE:**  Hey, not the guy with the broken arm, man. That'll take hours. You think I'm stupid? I want someone with two arms to untie him. You rotten bastards. Look at him. I hate the way he looks. Wake him up. Slap him or something.

**TOM:**  My pleasure.

*TOM takes a step.*

**STEVIE:**  Hey, I heard that, you pig. Okay, I changed my mind. Splash him with water. Come on. You. The woman. Get water. Splash him. You. The guy with two arms. Untie him. Well, what are you waiting for. Do it. Do it, you pigs!

*TOM is approaching STEVIE. STEVIE is backing away.*

**TOM:**  Okay. Look, I'm going to do what you ask. But I'm warning you, for your own safety, to be careful how you talk to us.

**STEVIE:**  Jesus! He's threatening me. I've got a gun. But he doesn't care. He wants to hurt someone so bad he doesn't care about guns or anything. What's wrong with you people. You're all crazy-mean. Jesus!

**ELIZABETH:**  (*moving to get a pot, which is sitting on the stove beside a burner. To STEVIE*) You're getting yourself all worked up here. Why don't you just put that gun away. We'll give you back your dad. And the two of you can just ... leave.

*She throws a pot of liquid on ROLLY. He starts to stir. ELIZABETH begins to untie him.*

**STEVIE:**  Oh right. I'll put the gun away. Like I trust you or something. I saw you kidnap my dad. I saw you spray him with that stuff. That was horrible, man. Seeing your own dad roll around and puke like that.

**ELIZABETH:**  Really. So why didn't you try to help him.

**STEVIE:**  Well I'm here now, eh. I had some business to take care of, but I'm here now.

**ROLLY:**  (*opens his eyes. Sees ELIZABETH. Screams*) Keep away from me! Keep her away! What's this. What'd she put on me. Some kind of oil. She's gonna burn me up! Help me!

**STEVIE:**  Relax, Dad. Stay calm.

**ROLLY:** Don't let her burn me up.

*STEVIE moves to ROLLY's side.*

**STEVIE:** Don't worry, Dad. It was just … soup. (*to ELIZABETH*) You poured soup on him. Why. I ask you to splash him with water, and you pour a pot of soup on him. You're a pig!

**TOM:** Look, didn't I warn you about that kind of talk.

*TOM takes one step towards STEVIE.*

**STEVIE:** I'm sorry, okay?! (*starts to cry*) Ah, man. You're just lookin' for an excuse to hurt me, aren't you.

**ROLLY:** Hey. Stevie. It's you. (*he is free. Stands*)

**STEVIE:** Yeah, Dad. I'm here.

*ROLLY cuffs STEVIE on the head.*

**ROLLY:** So what took you so long. Eh?! You know what I wish. I wish you were a girl. In my older years I wish I had a daughter instead of you. A daughter would have been here earlier. A daughter would take care of me in my older years. Look at her. She's a daughter. Look at all the shit she goes through for her loved ones. Why can't you be like that you little bastard.

*ROLLY cuffs STEVIE repeatedly.*

**STEVIE:** Come on, Dad. Watch it. Watch out. I've got a gun I'm trying to aim at these people. This gun is the only thing that's keeping these crazy people away, Dad. You're going to make me drop it.

**ROLLY:** Hey that's real! Who said you could have a real gun. Since when is a real gun a thing we use. Why didn't you bring one of the toy guns we usually use.

*ROLLY starts to cuff STEVIE again.*

**STEVIE:** I mean it, Dad! Watch out. Okay. Okay. Fuck it. I'll just drop the gun. Then you'll see what happens to us here! (*DIAN comes in*) Hey, it's you. What are you doing here.

**DIAN:** (*lifts a gun from her side*) Put that gun down, Stevie.

**STEVIE:** I'm confused by this. Why are you here.

**ELIZABETH:** You know her?

**STEVIE:** Yeah. I know her.

**DIAN:** Put the gun down. And you can go. Both of you. You can just walk away.

**ROLLY:** She's talkin' like a cop. Is she a cop.

**STEVIE:** She's—

**DIAN:** Hey! Shut up! Put the gun down and leave. Or I'll use my weapon.

**ELIZABETH:** Who is she, Stevie. Who do you think she is.

**STEVIE:** I feel like I'm in an awkward situation here. I just came to get my dad.

**DIAN:** And now you've got him. So leave.

**ELIZABETH:** I want to know how you know her, Stevie.

**DIAN:** If you make him tell you that, Elizabeth, you'll be putting us all in a very unfortunate position. (*to ROLLY and STEVIE*) Get the hell out of here!

*MIKE swings around the basement door. Gun up.*

**MIKE:** Everyone stay very still. (*to STEVIE*) Drop your weapon. Do it now!

**ROLLY:** Now, he's a cop for sure. Drop it, Stevie.

*STEVIE drops his gun. MIKE turns to DIAN. Points gun at her. She points her gun at him.*

**MIKE:** Dian. I want you to drop your gun, too.

**DIAN:** That's not going to happen, Mike.

**JUNIOR:** Oh, this looks bad. This is weird. Two cops pointing guns at each other. (*starts to sob*)

**TOM:** What's going on here, Mike.

**MIKE:** Can't talk now, buddy … I think my ex-partner here wants to kill me.

**ELIZABETH:** Is that right, Dian.

**DIAN:** It crossed my mind … Look, Mike, I think I know why you're here. But for the good of the force we better work together on this.

**STEVIE:** Can me and my dad leave.

**MIKE & DIAN:** Yes.

**STEVIE:** We can go, Dad.

**MIKE:** That's right, Dad. You can go. You can disappear back into your hole. But you have to forget everything you saw here.

**DIAN:** And everyone you saw here.

**MIKE:** (*to ROLLY*) You got that?

**ROLLY:** What about our merchandise. I'm sorry to bring it up. But it's all I've got in life. I don't have a pension, or anything.

**STEVIE:** It's okay, Dad. You mean the videos, right? I've got them

**ROLLY:** Yeah? So they were right about you. You pulled a switcheroo. You brought drugs to that meeting in the alley. You sneaky little bastard. Who said you could sell drugs?!

*He cuffs STEVIE.*

**STEVIE:** I didn't bring drugs to that meeting, Dad. I was given the drugs later.

**ELIZABETH:** Who gave you the drugs, Stevie.

**DIAN:** He can't answer that question. People might get hurt if he answers that question. The best thing right now is for him and his dad to leave!

**MIKE:** (*to ROLLY*) Did you hear that.

**ROLLY:** Yeah.

**MIKE:** So why the fuck are you still here?!

*MIKE is advancing on ROLLY and STEVIE. ELIZABETH puts herself in front of ROLLY and STEVIE.*

**ELIZABETH:** Stay away from them. They belong to me … Stevie, I want you and your dad to stay a little longer. I'll make it worth your while.

**STEVIE:** Is that an offer.

**DIAN:** (*pointing her gun at ELIZABETH*) Back away, Elizabeth.

**ELIZABETH:** You're aiming your weapon at me. What malfunctioning part of your brain is telling you to do something like that, Dian.

**DIAN:** You're interfering in police business.

**ELIZABETH:** You're in my mother's kitchen you demented bitch!

*MIKE suddenly cuffs ROLLY.*

**MIKE:**  Why the fuck are you still here. (*he cuffs* STEVIE) How many fucking times do I have to ask you that question. (*he cuffs them both. Fast*) How fucking stupid are you, anyway. Are you so stupid you like pain.

**TOM:**  Hey, Mike. Not in front of my kids. Not in my house.

**MIKE:**  Can't be helped, buddy.

*He grabs* ROLLY *with one arm.* STEVIE *with the other.*

**ROLLY:**  Okay, okay, we're leaving.

**STEVIE:**  But she made me an offer, Dad. It could be a good one. What's a little beating. A little pain. Screw you, cop. I'm gonna tell this lady the truth about those drugs.

**MIKE:**  Sure you are.

*He knees* STEVIE *in the groin.* STEVIE *doubles up.* MIKE *grabs* STEVIE's *hair. Smashes his head into the refrigerator.* STEVIE *crumples to the floor.*

**ELIZABETH:**  Ah, Jesus. I told you he belongs to me. Leave him alone!

*TOM grabs* MIKE's *shoulder.*

**TOM:**  Okay, that's enough, Mike.

**MIKE:**  I told you to stay out of this.

*MIKE swings at* TOM. *TOM ducks. Grabs* MIKE's *arm and twists it behind his back. Pushes* MIKE *face first over the kitchen table. Takes his gun away.* ELIZABETH *is moving towards* DIAN. *And what happens next happens very, very fast.*

**ELIZABETH:**  Junior.

**JUNIOR:**  What.

**ELIZABETH:**  Attack!

**JUNIOR:**  What.

**ELIZABETH:**  Attack, Junior. Kill!

**JUNIOR:**  What?! Who?!

**ELIZABETH:**  Her. Now, boy. Attack. Kill. Go for the throat.

**JUNIOR:**  Come on, Elizabeth. Give me a break here.

**ELIZABETH:**  Look, I'm telling you to kill her or suffer the consequences!

**JUNIOR:**  Okay, okay!

*JUNIOR moves towards DIAN, growling wildly. DIAN turns to face JUNIOR.*

**DIAN:** All right, that's far enough. I'll use my weapon.

*ELIZABETH has moved quietly and quickly behind DIAN. She grabs her in a bear hug, trapping DIAN's arms. Lifts her off the ground.*

**ELIZABETH:** Junior, get her gun!

*JUNIOR grabs DIAN's gun.*

**DIAN:** Elizabeth, it's still not too late to make a deal.

**ELIZABETH:** Sure.

*ELIZABETH throws DIAN to the floor. Grabs the gun from JUNIOR. Puts her foot on DIAN's head, pressing it to the floor. Points the gun at DIAN's head.*

**JUNIOR:** Good trick, Elizabeth. All that Junior attack and kill stuff. I was supposed to be like a mad dog, right. I didn't get it at first. Where did that come from, Elizabeth.

**ELIZABETH:** My subconscious I guess. Don't worry about it.

**JUNIOR:** It's just that if that's how you really feel about me I'm a little—

**ELIZABETH:** (*points gun at him*) I said don't worry about it!

**JUNIOR:** Okay, okay …

**TOM:** What now.

**ELIZABETH:** Well, now we find out which one of these cops has set us up. And which one is just trying to cover up the set-up. Rolly, why aren't you picking your son off the floor.

**ROLLY:** Fuck him.

**ELIZABETH:** (*points gun at him*) Do it!

**MIKE:** I'm cooled down now, Tom. You can let me up.

**ELIZABETH:** (*points gun at him*) Keep him where he is.

**DIAN:** You people are in over your heads. You people have crossed the line.

*ELIZABETH stamps the floor near DIAN's head. DIAN curls up in fear. ROLLY has STEVIE on his feet.*

**ELIZABETH:** How you doin', Stevie.

**STEVIE:** You know something? I don't give a fuck how I'm doing! That's how I'm doing!

**ELIZABETH:** You were going to tell us something.

**STEVIE:** You were gonna make me an offer. I wanna hear what it was.

**ELIZABETH:** (*points gun at him*) Your life.

**ROLLY:** Tricked again. I coulda told ya.

**STEVIE:** (*to ELIZABETH*) You won't use that.

**ROLLY:** Sure she will. She's meaner than any of them. And we're nothing to her. We're sewage. (*to ELIZABETH*) Aren't we. Shit floating in the dark. Big, fat, floating turds!

**STEVIE:** Come on, Dad. Calm down. Have a little, you know, self-respect. I say let her shoot. Fuck her. Fuck them all. How about it.

**ROLLY:** Yeah. Yeah, okay. Fuck you. We've been abused one too many times. We're gonna show you something here. We're gonna show you some class. Kill my kid. Go ahead. Kill him.

**STEVIE:** (*starts to cry*) And you too, Dad. Tell her to kill you, too. Come on, Dad.

**ROLLY:** Yeah, okay. The hell with it. Kill us both. (*starts to cry*) Come on. Whatya waiting for you big, mean, spooky woman!

*They are approaching ELIZABETH arm in arm. Crying.*

**STEVIE:** Yeah. Come on!

**ROLLY:** Come on!

**ELIZABETH:** (*lowers the gun*) A thousand dollars.

**ROLLY:** What.

**ELIZABETH:** I'll give you a thousand dollars. All Stevie has to do is tell me which one of these cops hired him to plant those drugs.

**STEVIE:** Okay, that's more like it. That's an offer we can live with.

**ROLLY:** Where's the money.

**ELIZABETH:** I don't have it on me. I'll get it to you.

**STEVIE:** Yeah. Like we trust you or somethin'.

**ELIZABETH:** (*mocking*) Yeah. Like you got a choice or somethin'.

**ROLLY:** She's right. Tell her.

**STEVIE:** Should I.

**ROLLY:** If I didn't think you should, would I tell you you should.

*He cuffs STEVIE.*

**STEVIE:** Okay, okay. It was her. The lady cop.

**DIAN:** You're making a big mistake.

*ELIZABETH stamps the floor. DIAN curls up in fear.*

**STEVIE:** But I didn't know she was a lady cop. I thought she was a lady crook. She told me she was connected to the big-time. She contacted me. Told me she wanted a favour. (*to ROLLY*) This was after we broke in here, but had to leave 'cause of the baby—

**ELIZABETH:** Get on with it!

**STEVIE:** Okay, she told me she wanted me to break in here again. Find our merchandise, and put the drugs there instead. If I did this I would be given things. Money. Good references. Future business dealings. Things like that. I could give you the details.

**ELIZABETH:** That's not necessary. You can go now.

**STEVIE:** That's it?

**ROLLY:** We can go?

**ELIZABETH:** Yeah.

**ROLLY:** And you'll get that thousand dollars to us.

**ELIZABETH:** Yes, I will.

**STEVIE:** Oh, sure you will. But you know what. I don't care. Fuck you! And everyone here! And fuck the things you're all doin'! Whatever they are! That's what I say. (*to ROLLY*) Right?

**ROLLY:** Sure. I say that, too. But I'd still like the money.

**STEVIE:** If we get the money, that's a good thing, I agree. But you still gotta say fuck them.

**ROLLY:** Okay. Yeah. Fuck you! And the things you're doin'! 'Specially to us!

**STEVIE:** Now all we gotta do is leave with some class.

**ROLLY:** Come on.

*They leave.*

**ELIZABETH:** Okay. Everyone up.

*ELIZABETH and TOM back away. MIKE and DIAN get up. TOM hands MIKE's gun to ELIZABETH.*

**TOM:** Here. You gotta excuse me. I'm not feeling very well. (*starts off*)

**ELIZABETH:** Are you faking illness again.

**TOM:** No … This stuff reminds me too much of other stuff. And the other stuff reminds me of … other stuff … Bastards.

*He leaves. ELIZABETH hands guns to JUNIOR.*

**ELIZABETH:** Here. Take the bullets out of these for me, will you.

*JUNIOR sits at the table.*

**ELIZABETH:** Why did you do this to my family, Dian. Is it because you're insane.

**DIAN:** You were planning to seriously damage something to which I owe a high degree of loyalty. You understand loyalty. Think of the police force as my family and it'll all make perfect sense to you, Elizabeth.

**ELIZABETH:** My family is made up of human beings. You're loyal to an institution. I'll visit you in the asylum some day and explain the difference.

**JUNIOR:** These are unloaded. Can I go upstairs now, Elizabeth. I want to see my wife and daughter.

**ELIZABETH:** Sure. Go on. Give them both a kiss from me.

*He leaves.*

**DIAN:** (*takes out her lip balm*) Isn't that lovely. Everyone's all cozy and tucked in their beds. But who's out there protecting them while they sleep. Who stands guard and keeps the scum from the door.

**ELIZABETH:** Who are you, Dian. What are you.

**DIAN:** A committed social servant. Look, you had to be stopped. I'm truly, truly sorry I had to involve your mother. But a police force damaged and soiled in the public's eye is not going to be an effective player in the ongoing societal conflict! (*begins to apply her lip balm furiously*)

**ELIZABETH:** (*to MIKE*) Are you listening to all this.

**MIKE:** Yeah.

**ELIZABETH:** So what do you make of it.

**DIAN:** What are you asking him for?! I'm the only one with vision! With imagination. I see the big picture. I see the big picture with details. Details that contradict what you see in the big picture. You think that's easy?! It's scary! It makes you do scary things sometimes!

**MIKE:** You're nuttier than a fruitcake.

**DIAN:** This woman here was out to destroy the force!

**MIKE:** I don't know what force you're talking about. The one I work for just gives you a book full of laws and tells you to arrest anyone who breaks them. It's simple, really.

**DIAN:** (*mocking*) "It's simple, really." It's not simple. You think it's simple because you're rigid and stupid. I know it's not simple because I'm flexible and extremely intelligent.

**MIKE:** Why do you think I followed you here. I mean if you're so smart how come a bozo like me could figure out what you were up to. You know how? Hunches.

*DIAN screams.*

**DIAN:** Walk away, Mike. Let me cut a deal with Elizabeth. She'll back off to keep her mother out of jail. The police force will be saved any more unfortunate publicity.

**MIKE:** No.

**DIAN:** It's the best solution.

**MIKE:** No. No can do.

**DIAN:** "No!" "No can do" ... Why not, asshole?! Why the fuck not?! (*she is very mobile. Very agitated. Much lip balm is being applied*)

**MIKE:** Because I've got a better plan! I got it while I was listening to you talk like a fruitcake. I came here to try and cover up your crazy scheme. But now what I want is for you to leave these people alone. Let Elizabeth make all the fuss she wants. And let the police force deal with her any way, any goddamn legal way it can.

**DIAN:** Damn you! Damn you guys. Cut me some slack here. I'm the kind of cop this city needs now. I'm creative. I can arrange solutions to difficult problems in non-linear ways. I am the future! You big, dumb jerk. And I'm tough. I'm tough, too. I'm that rarest of human beings. A caring, sensitive, intelligent adult who also happens to love law and order!

**MIKE:** Go home, Dian. Have a bath. Take a pill. Write a letter of resignation.

**DIAN:** I'm not quitting. I don't care what you say. In fact, I'm asking to be made your permanent partner. We're engaged in something here, Mike! It's big, this thing we're engaged in! Big and contradictory. It's new and old. Woman and man. Daughter and father. Smart and dumb. Really really smart! And really really dumb! (*she grabs his cheeks. Gives him a long hard kiss*) See you tomorrow, partner.

*She rushes off out the screen door. Pause.*

**MIKE:** (*sighs. Gestures feebly*) Ah, I'm really sorry about all—

**ELIZABETH:** I only need to hear an official confirmation that all charges pertaining to those drugs, against my mother or any other member of this family, are dropped. Can you give that to me.

**MIKE:** Yes. I can.

**ELIZABETH:** Thank you. And now pay attention, Mr. Policeman. I'm going to continue my campaign against police brutality. I'm going to bring your beloved police force to its knees. I'm going to start with that insane bitch. And then I'm going to destroy anyone who was even remotely involved in what she was doing to me and my family, and if that includes you, tough fucking luck!

**MIKE:** Did you say something about police brutality? Well, you just keep right on complaining. I hate it when those awful police get brutal. I mean who the hell are they to get brutal. All the nice people they get to deal with. All that love and affection they get from that wonderful scum out there. Why the fuck would anyone want to get brutal with that wonderful innocent harmless scum. So you just make a stink about that. I'm right behind you. Goddamn right I am!

*He leaves. Slams the door behind him. ELIZABETH watches him leave.*
*JUNIOR, then GAIL, carrying the baby, then MARY ANN, come in behind*
*ELIZABETH.*

**ELIZABETH:** (*turns*) What are you doing down here.

**GAIL:** Junior woke us up.

**JUNIOR:** I started thinking you might need some help. I thought
we should all face it together. Whatever happened.

**MARY ANN:** Did something happen.

**ELIZABETH:** We found out who set us up.

**JUNIOR:** It was that lady cop.

**GAIL:** We were set up by a cop? All my worst fears are coming
true. We should think about moving to the country.

**MARY ANN:** Set us up? How. Why. I don't get it. Is someone going
to explain it to me.

**ELIZABETH:** Do you want someone to explain it to you.

**MARY ANN:** I don't know. Let me think about it.

*NORA comes in. They all look at her.*

**NORA:** Is everything okay now, Elizabeth.

**ELIZABETH:** Yes, Mom.

**NORA:** I'm not going to jail.

**ELIZABETH:** No, Mom.

**NORA:** Good. That's good … Tom and I have been talking. I
decided to talk to him. Don't make a fuss about it. I had my
reasons. He told me what he'd tried to do and why. He said
he just wanted to help. And I've decided to believe him …
Anyway. He wants to ask you all something. He's right out
there in the hall. Come on in, Tom.

*TOM comes in.*

**NORA:** Go ahead, Tom. Just ask right out loud.

*ELIZABETH turns away.*

**TOM:** (*quietly*) Can I stay.

*Pause.*

**NORA:** I don't think they heard you.

**JUNIOR:** I heard him.

**MARY ANN:**  So did I.

**GAIL:**  She means Elizabeth.

*ELIZABETH turns to face TOM.*

**TOM:**  (*to ELIZABETH*) Can I stay.

**ELIZABETH:**  Would that accomplish anything.

**TOM:**  We'd be together. We'd be a family.

**ELIZABETH:**  And you think that would be a good thing. You think something positive would grow out of that. I mean, what kind of family do you think we'd be with you ... that we weren't without you. Stronger? Meaner? Better prepared to deal with the shit of the world? We know how you feel about that world full of shit out there. You've been telling us about it since we were kids. Obviously you haven't changed your mind. You still think we need protection. You still think that's your job.

**TOM:**  I can't help that.

**ELIZABETH:**  You still think we're weak.

**TOM:**  No. I don't.

**ELIZABETH:**  Sure you do. You make all your decisions about us based on a feeling of superiority.

**TOM:**  I don't think you're weak. I just think you've got a different kind of strength.

**ELIZABETH:**  Yeah? So what kind is it.

**TOM:**  The kind that keeps you together. It's ... (*mumbles something*)

**NORA:**  Love. He said love. I heard him.

**GAIL:**  So did I.

**TOM:**  The strength of love ... I need that. I want some of that, is all I'm saying. I want to be able to give over to it.

**ELIZABETH:**  So how do you plan to do that.

**TOM:**  I don't really have a plan. I just want to stay. If I stay here with you I figure there's a chance for me. If I go out there alone again I won't last. The shit in my brain will meet the shit in the world and there'll be an explosion.

**ELIZABETH:**  So we're supposed to keep you here to keep you safe from the world. To keep the world safe from you.

**TOM:** Yeah. I guess so ... But also ... so I can love you. And so you can love me. I need you all to love me so bad I can taste it. Really. I can taste the need.

**ELIZABETH:** Where do you think love comes from.

**MARY ANN:** Maybe that's enough for now, Elizabeth. Who can answer questions like that.

**GAIL:** Leave her alone. She has to do this. This is what she does.

**ELIZABETH:** (*to TOM*) The kind of love you're talking about. Do you think it's going to rub off on you.

**TOM:** If I let it ... yeah.

**ELIZABETH:** You think its what ... hugging, kissing ... being nice?

**TOM:** That'd be a good start.

**ELIZABETH:** You think it's just hanging around together. Maybe going on a picnic. Maybe going skating like we used to when we were kids. We don't need you to go skating with us anymore. That would just be a luxury. At best, that would be ... a good time. We don't need you to show us a good time. We don't need you to be nice to us. If you stay we only need one thing from you ... respect.

*Long pause. They are staring at each other.*

**GAIL:** Use another word. Respect is such a sucky word, Elizabeth. It just embarrasses everyone.

**ELIZABETH:** I don't care. It applies. Do you know what I mean, Dad. Do you have any idea what that word means. Why I used it.

**TOM:** I do respect you. All of you. Look what you've made of yourself, Elizabeth. You're a lawyer.

**ELIZABETH:** You're proud! We've survived. We're your women and we're chips off the old block ... Well we've done more than survive. And I don't need you to be proud of me ... You've got to do better that that. A lot better.

*She leaves. Pause.*

**MARY ANN:** Dad? (*waves*) I could make you a list. I agree with most of what Elizabeth said. But I think what you really need is a list. Something you can carry around. Something

that's ... real. You know, a list of things like ... no lying, no
pretending, no using your "man voice" just to get your way.
Stuff like that. Do you think that would help.

**TOM:**  Maybe.

**MARY ANN:**  A list of things you can do, and a list of things you
probably shouldn't. Just suggestions maybe. Nothing too
strict. There's some paper upstairs, I'll bet. I'll go do it now.

**TOM:**  That's very nice of you, Mary Ann.

**MARY ANN:**  Oh no, I have to help. I have to do what I can. That's
usually not much, and sometimes it's not anything, but ... I
still have to do it.

*She leaves.*

**GAIL:**  Dad?

**TOM:**  Yes, honey.

**GAIL:**  I love Elizabeth and Mary Ann a lot. But it would be okay
with me if you ignored them. And just tried your best ...
Come on Junior, let's go to bed.

**JUNIOR:**  Great. I want to sleep for a week.

**GAIL:**  You can't. You've got to go talk to your foreman tomorrow
morning.

**JUNIOR:**  You saved my job?

**GAIL:**  Unless you do something else really stupid. What *have* you
been doing anyway. Are you going to tell me about that, what
ridiculous things you and my dad have been up to?

**JUNIOR:**  Sure. But you won't like it. You might get really mad.

**GAIL:**  Yeah. Or I might just laugh. (*they start off, arms around each
other. GAIL stops*) Something else, Dad ... If you ever want to
go skating with me and Gwen, that would be great. Anytime. I
mean it.

*They leave. NORA is sitting at the table. TOM joins her.*

**NORA:**  They're all different. They grew up to be different
people. They never really agree about anything. That's just
the way it is ... You look a little sad. And confused. Look on
the bright side ... You're still here. There's still a possibility
that you could stay here, and make something positive out of
the experience ... Excuse me.

*She goes out to the back porch. Shouts.*

Attention! Attention fanatics! You can stop watching now. Nobody in this house is going to prison. The problems in this house are being resolved … I'll keep you posted!

*She comes back in.*

**TOM:** I'm going to get a job.

**NORA:** Don't do anything rash.

**TOM:** I want to make some money. Help out.

**NORA:** We get by. And money isn't very important around here anymore. Compared to … other things, I mean. But if it's something you need to do .. . Well, all right. But … (*sits across from him*) Here's some advice about that. Here's what I have to tell you about that idea. You shouldn't take a job with a lot of tension. Take a job that makes you happy. Even if it only pays a little.

*Lights start to fade.*

We can't have you working at something that makes you tense, and angry, and resentful. We can't afford the chance that you'll bring tension, anger and resentment home. Maybe you could get a job making things. Little things that are useful. And pleasant to look at. Or a job taking care of things. Or fixing things. Fixing things is useful and rewarding. Filled with satisfaction. Or a job outdoors. Outdoors is the best environment. A job outdoors fixing and taking care of things would be the best. Maybe you could get one of those jobs taking care of a golf course. That could be very nice. Of course that's seasonal work. But maybe seasonal work is good. You wouldn't be overdoing it that way. You wouldn't get too tense. You'd have over half a year to recover. (*TOM is nodding. Lights are fading*) What do you think. I think we should investigate the golf course idea. It's up to you though. There can't be pressure. These are only ideas … Suggestions. You know … hints.

*Blackout.*


*End.*